British History
General Editor

PUBLISHE

History of Ireland

History of Scotland

History of Wales

Please see overleaf for forthcoming titles

FORTHCOMING TITLES

Peter Catterall *The Labour Party, 1918–1940*
Eveline Cruickshanks *The Glorious Revolution*
John Davis *British Politics, 1885–1931*
David Dean *Parliament and Politics in Elizabethan and
Jacobean England, 1558–1614*
Susan Doran *English Foreign Policy in the Sixteenth Century*
David Eastwood *England, 1750–1850: Government and Community
in the Provinces*
Colin Eldridge *The Victorians Overseas*
Brian Golding *The Normans in England 1066–1100:
Conquest and Colonisation*
Steven Gunn *Early Tudor Government, 1485–1558*
Richard Harding *The Navy, 1504–1815*
Angus Hawkins *British Party Politics, 1852–1886*
H. S. Jones *Political Thought in Nineteenth-Century Britain*
Anthony Milton *Church and Religion in England, 1603–1642*
R. C. Nash *English Foreign Trade and the World Economy, 1600–1800*
W. M. Ormrod *Political Life in England, 1300–1450*
Richard Ovendale *Anglo-American Relations in the Twentieth Century*
David Powell *The Edwardian Crisis: Britain, 1901–1914*
Brian Quintrell *Government and Politics in Early Stuart England*
Alan Sykes *The Radical Right in Britain*
Ann Williams *Kingship and Government in Pre-Conquest England*
John W. Young *Britain and Western European Unity since 1945*
Michael Young *Charles I*

History of Ireland

Sean Duffy *Ireland in the Middle Ages*
Hiram Morgan *Ireland in the Early Modern Periphery, 1534–1690*
Toby Barnard *The Kingdom of Ireland, 1641–1740*
Alan Heesom *The Anglo-Irish Union, 1800–1922*

History of Scotland

Bruce Webster *Scotland in the Middle Ages*
Roger Mason *Kingship and Tyranny? Scotland 1513–1603*
John Shaw *The Political History of Eighteenth Century Scotland*
John McCaffrey *Scotland in the Nineteenth Century*
I. G. C. Hutchison *Scottish Politics in the Twentieth Century*

History of Wales

A. D. Carr *Medieval Wales*
Gareth Jones *Wales, 1700–1980: Crisis of Identity*

Please also note that a sister series, *Social History in Perspective*, is now available, covering the key topics in social, cultural and religious history.

EARLY MODERN WALES, c.1525–1640

J. GWYNFOR JONES

St. Martin's Press

First published in Great Britain 1994 by
THE MACMILLAN PRESS LTD
Houndmills, Basingstoke, Hampshire RG21 2XS
and London
Companies and representatives
throughout the world

A catalogue record for this book is available
from the British Library.

ISBN 0–333–55259–8 hardcover
ISBN 0–333–55260–1 paperback

Printed in Hong Kong

First published in the United States of America 1994 by
Scholarly and Reference Division,
ST. MARTIN'S PRESS, INC.,
175 Fifth Avenue,
New York, N.Y. 10010

ISBN 0–312–10362–X

Library of Congress Cataloging-in-Publication Data
Jones, J. Gwynfor, 1936–
Early modern Wales, 1525–1640 / J. Gwynfor Jones.
p.   cm.
Includes bibliographical references and index.
ISBN 0–312–10362–X
1. Wales—History—1536–1700.   2. Wales—History—1284–1536.
I. Title.
DA715.J635   1994
942.905—dc20   93–26870
                                                                CIP

For Eryl, Gareth and Eleri

CONTENTS

Contents

PREFACE

This study examines current thinking on some significant developments in Welsh society in the period between the Tudor settlement of Wales, 1536–43, and the Civil Wars. It also offers a personal view of these developments. I have taken the year 1525 as a starting date because it was in that year that the Council in the Marches was revived. It was from then on also that events occurred which led to anxious views being increasingly expressed concerning the condition of law and order in the Principality and the Marches and, in due course, to various measures being taken by the government to settle the political problems of those regions. The so-called Acts of Union (1536–43) are convenient pegs on which to hang virtually all developments and trends in Wales for the remainder of the period covered in this volume. In this context the Tudor settlement and its consequences can, in some respects, be deceptively easy to interpret. However, attitudes and forces existed that make such a historically conventional approach questionable. This study raises certain issues concerning the character of the governing classes and the society in which they lived: their stability and, at times, their insecurity, their power, their susceptibilities and weaknesses, their public spirit and their private enterprise. It would be misleading to adopt a narrow view of individuals and families who had prospered and had allegedly abandoned the restrictive pattern of communal life for more rewarding experiences elsewhere in the centres of power – whether they were in the countryside or, more usually, in the urban areas. Those who were drawn to participate in government, who enhanced their landed power, who were socially mobile and who dabbled in legal, political and cultural matters were deeply influenced by a diversity of forces, both native and alien, thus revealing complexities that require unravelling by the political and economic historian, and the sociologist as well as the literary expert.

Use has been made of original sources (adapted into modern English) chiefly to highlight the way contemporaries gave expression to their opinions and feelings in an often challenging and perplexing age. I am indebted to Mr Brian Ll. James, formerly Keeper of the Salisbury Library at University of Wales College of Cardiff, and Dr Medwin Hughes of the Department of Welsh at the same college, for reading the work and making suggestions from which I have benefited greatly. However, I alone am responsible for the material and interpretations contained therein. Thanks are also due to the staffs of various libraries, especially at the University of Wales College of Cardiff and the South Glamorgan County Library at Cardiff as well as at the National Library of Wales, Aberystwyth. Dr Jeremy Black has given expert guidance and I wish to thank him, Ms Vanessa Graham, my publishing editor, and Mr Keith Povey, Editorial Services Consultant, for their courtesy and assistance at all times. I also wish to record my debt of gratitude to Dr Trevor Herbert of the Open University in Wales who, as Director of the Welsh History and its Sources Project, permitted me to use two maps drawn by Mr Guy Lewis of University College, Swansea. It is appropriate that I acknowledge the work of several historians of the Welsh Tudor and early Stuart periods who, over the last fifty years, have contributed significantly to our understanding of this formative century in the history of Wales. Lastly, I would like to thank my wife for her encouragement and forbearance – not once over the last two years did she complain that this project kept me in the study for far longer than I had anticipated.

J. GWYNFOR JONES

GLOSSARY

arddel   A once laudable custom that was illegally used by
              marcher lords to employ criminals and outlaws in
              their private armies.

bonheddig   The qualities and virtues of gentility that were
              featured in the mode of behaviour adopted by the
              sixteenth-century gentry.

brëyr   A chieftain or nobleman, representing the highest
              ranking freeman in the medieval Welsh native clan
              community.

commote   A subdivision of the *cantref* (hundred) and the
              most convenient unit used for administrative and
              jurisdictional purposes.

cyfran   The division of clanlands between all sons accord-
              ing to the medieval Welsh laws of inheritance.

cymortha   A means of dispensing communal aid in rural
              communities that was illegally exploited by marcher
              lords who used it as a means to impose forced
              exactions on tenants.

eisteddfod An assembly of professional bards to formulate and
              modify rules of the poetic craft maintained by the
              traditional bardic schools.

gafael   A holding of heritable land forming part of the *gwely* (see below) under the native clan system varying in size and dispersed in scattered parcels.

gwely   Clanland held in joint-ownership by coparceners or joint-occupiers claiming descent from a common ancestor who was the first permanent settler on the land.

plasty   The hall or mansion of a noble or gentle family regarded as the focal point of regional leadership.

priodawr   The individual free clansman characterised by his descent from a common ancestor, military prowess and eventually his landed proprietorship.

uchelwr   A person of high birth claiming free clan status and the forerunner of the sixteenth-century Welsh squire-gentleman.

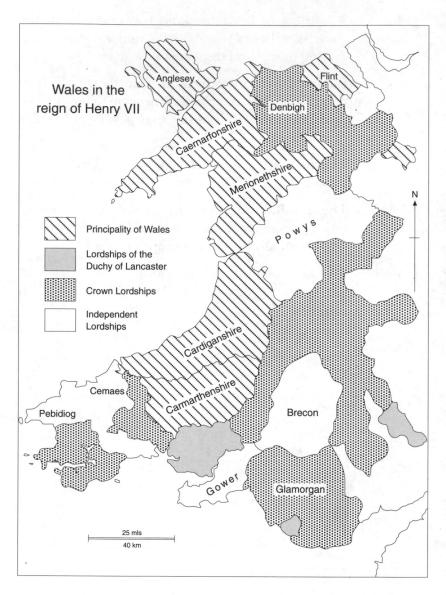

Reproduced with the permission of Dr Trevor Herbert, Director of the Welsh History and its Sources Project.

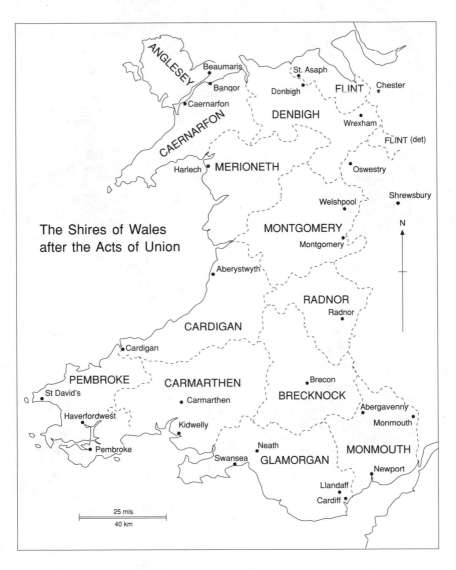

The Shires of Wales after the Acts of Union

Reproduced with the permission of Dr Trevor Herbert, Director of the Welsh History and its Sources Project.

INTRODUCTION

King Henry the Seventh, knowing and pitying their thraldom and injuries, took order to reform the same and granted unto them a charter of liberties whereby they were released of that oppression wherewith they were afflicted by laws more heathenish than Christian.

Thus did Dr David Powel, vicar of Rhiwabon and well-known antiquary, set about extolling the virtues of Henry Tudor after his accession. He was referring specifically to the Charters of Enfranchisement that Henry granted to communities in north-east Wales and to the Principality of North Wales in the years 1504–8, which released them from the laws of Henry IV and granted them other liberties. Powel was not the only Tudor commentator to admire Henry's beneficence, and the subsequent legislation – better known as the Act of Union – that assimilated Wales judicially and administratively to England in his son's reign in 1536, because in the same context Rice Merrick (Rhys Meurig) of Cotrel in Glamorgan, Humphrey Llwyd of Denbigh, and George Owen of Henllys in Pembrokeshire, among others, described in glowing terms these enlightened policies in Wales. Henry Tudor had much to commend him, not least his illustrious Welsh pedigree extending back through his forebears in Anglesey to Ednyfed Fychan, seneschal of Llywelyn the Great, Prince of Gwynedd, in the thirteenth century. Such inspired writers wrote principally to applaud what Owen considered to be 'a joyful metamorphosis' in the social and economic life of Wales. Powel describes Henry Tudor as a messianic leader installed in

1

office to redeem his nation and to restore the liberties of which their worthy British ancestors had been deprived by the Saxons. He wrote in a distinctly prophetic manner that was popular at the time, and interpreted Henry's role as that of the liberator come to emancipate his people. The charters were interpreted mainly as symbolic grants of freedom conferred by the 'son of prophecy'. Old cherished rights and privileges were restored, oppression lifted, and whole communities were liberated from the 'Saxon yoke'. The picture, of course, is far from realistic; whether Henry had the time or inclination to fulfill the demands of contemporary poets is doubtful, but he did display an interest in his Welsh pedigree and, at a time when the Arthurian traditions were revived, named his son and heir after the legendary sixth-century British hero. Of greater importance, however, is the fact that in the last years of his reign Henry felt himself secure enough to grant the most progressive sections of Welsh society in the early sixteenth century opportunities by which they might achieve their ambitions, and his actions served to maintain and consolidate the unity and loyalties of the gentry. He strengthened the alliance between the Crown and the gentry, thus laying the basis of the policy pursued by his son and Thomas Cromwell in the 1530s. Unknowingly, Henry VII made the Tudor settlement possible.

Historians have referred to the legislation of 1536–43 as a significant milestone in the history of Wales at a time when the national sovereign state, as it emerged in England in the 1530s, absorbed the Principality and marcher lordships. This Welsh legislation is often viewed as the avenue along which the favoured classes progressed with relative ease, consolidating their political hold over their localities, extending their commercial and family interests, and publicly serving the Tudor state. That was certainly the way in which sixteenth-century commentators (especially in the latter decades) viewed the situation, for they, like their contemporaries, had prospered immensely through the acquisition of land and office, the bases of regional power and authority. New dynamic forces were released that facilitated the growth of a virile, if economically restricted, class of landed proprietors, who manipulated what resources lay at their disposal for their own benefit and who enjoyed regional domination.

The century that spanned the period from the Tudor settlement in 1536–43 to the eve of the Civil Wars in Wales has been justifiably labelled the 'age of the gentry'. That, however, does require some qualification because several periods in the history of Wales might well merit a similar description from the mid-fourteenth century down to the eighteenth century. The label, in this instance, perhaps more accurately describes the 'coming of age' of the gentry in an era, after the new Tudor dispensation, when they flourished and imposed their authority and leadership – often on a backward and conservative society. The Tudor and early Stuart centuries, in this context, can be interpreted as the crucial 'middle' period in the development of that class of landed proprietors, the *bonheddig* or *brehyrion* (high-born freemen), most of them descendants of warrior-clansmen who settled permanently in *gwelyau* or kindred patrimonies in the twelfth and thirteenth centuries. Their forebears were the aristocracy of Wales whose nobility rested not on conquest but on lineage, and they commanded deep-seated loyalties in their communities as bardic evidence and pedigrees amply prove. Thus the equality of status that characterised membership of the *gwely* (clan patrimony) gradually decayed. Simultaneously, the medieval economy disintegrated and in its place emerged a new system by which men owned and worked the land. The basic principle was individual ownership of land and a desire to be rid of encumbrances that savoured of the old way of life in order to taste the fruits of social authority and economic advantage. It was a process that survived the dynastic upheaval in the 1460s and 1470s by the prompt repair of material damage and the acquired skills of the gentry to ride the shifts and disasters of factious manoeuvrings so as to appear eventually on the winning side. It was during the sixteenth century that they established themselves as governors *de jure* when they shouldered the responsibilities of keeping the peace and good order in the localities.

The last two centuries of the Middle Ages, which saw the disintegration of the kindred structure and traditional modes of landholding, were chiefly characterised by the ruthless determination to prosper of up-and-coming individuals. Most of them were *priodorion* – free owners of clan properties – who had survived the crumbling native system and who, in diverse ways, had sidetracked the legal constraints imposed on their freedom of action and that stifled individual enterprise. The use of a Welsh 'mortgage' system, known as *prid*, became increasingly popular among emergent native gentry in the fourteenth and fifteenth centuries whereby the prohibition imposed on the alienation of Kindred lands was lifted. It was a cumbersome legal devise but many *prid* deeds have survived indicating that lawyers skilfully provided a loophole enabling the most tenacious landed proprietors gradually to augment their clan properties by purchasing others and establishing estates on a capitalistic basis. A small group of favoured Welshmen, striving to overcome the penalties imposed by the anti-Welsh legislation of Henry IV (1401–2), obtained 'letters of denisation' from the Crown granting them equality of status with the English and liberating them from the stigma of racial inferiority.

The gradual effects of war, plague and revolt, together with the declining features of economic life, also heralded a new period of landownership and tenurial relations and served to loosen further old bonds that tied men to kindred and communal methods of landholding. In the early sixteenth century, however, clan proprietors were still closely linked with their respective clans despite the disintegrating social order. The tenurial structure and rights associated with it continued to function, and the *gafael* – individual inland units of clan properties – as a holding associated with kindred groupings was still recognised as territory coveted by eager proprietors. The practice of partible inheritance had seriously afflicted the Welsh economy, with its most devastating effects being felt mainly in lowland areas where the agrarian structure was more advanced. The strains imposed on the old landholding structure appeared in the emergence of tenacious clansmen and alien urban settlers, who grasped every available opportunity to advance their own interests and avoid the time-honoured restrictive practices that membership of the free clan imposed upon them.

The gentry fulfilled two prime functions in the post-1536 period, namely to establish stability as regional administrators in the Tudor state and to promote their own family interests by acquiring properties and enhancing their fortunes based on their landed estates. These features were often linked together, but were at times at variance with one another. It was not an easy task for the most eligible *uchelwyr* (privileged native freemen) in rural society to attend to both these functions with equal assiduity, yet records show that they did so remarkably well regardless of the intrusion of private ambition into public office. The grandees among the gentry rose to power by diverse means, principally by the flexible use of their material resources and shrewd political insight, the more modest among them – decidedly conservative in their outlook but out for the main chance – managed to keep pace with current developments. The steady growth and status of the broad spectrum of gentry revealed common features such as their basis in land, office-holding, education and the adoption of a social code of conduct characteristic of the English Renaissance gentlemen of the period. Alongside, and complementary to, the advances in landownership made by the new gentry, religious changes served to promote further their reputations as the dominant order. Vested interests ensured that the majority increasingly attached themselves to the tenets of the New Faith, despite the reluctance of many to declare their loyalties in the crucial middle years of the century and the firm adherence of some influential families to Roman Catholicism.

The origins of the gentry served to bind them firmly together in politics and helped to broaden their horizons and extend family interests within Wales and beyond Offa's Dyke. They displayed an avid enthusiasm for pedigrees and kept a vigilant eye on their material welfare. By the eve of the Civil Wars they had achieved the ascendancy in government and politics in the localities as well as a degree of maturity in their appreciation of broader constitutional affairs. It was clear by the early decades of the seventeenth century, however, that the common bond established between the Crown, Parliament, the law and the Anglican Church had become the cornerstone of political activity among the majority of actively engaged gentry in the government of Wales. The Stuarts were well received principally because they were considered to be ancestrally the natural successors to the Tudors and because their policies were designed to preserve the established order.

1

SOCIAL AND ECONOMIC FOUNDATIONS

It would not be inappropriate to describe the period between the Tudor legislation of 1536–43 and the outbreak of the Civil Wars as the assertive age in the history of the Welsh gentry. A. H. Dodd, in his classic *Studies in Stuart Wales* (1952), ventured to label the history of Wales in the seventeenth century 'in the main, the history of a class'. To a degree that observation can be justified since most written sources have a direct or indirect bearing on families who claimed gentility and on aspects of gentle life, and reveal features of social ranks that had gradually formed following the decline of the medieval clan and feudal systems in the Welshries and Englishries respectively. Given the nature of the social structure of England and Wales in that period, this background is not difficult to explain. The large group of families who prided themselves on illustrious ancestry and who were often subject to economic pressures that compelled them to seek or defend status, considered that their main asset – besides a slender stake in property – was a claim to impeccable ancestry.[1]

Sir Francis Bacon aptly described the quality of prime gentry in England in one of his most famous essays. 'It is a respectable thing,' he maintained, 'to see an ancient castle or building which is not ruinous.' 'How much more,' he continued, 'is it to see a primitive aristocratic family which has stood against the waves and long times because nobility is the work of power but primitive nobility is the work of time.'[2] Doubtless, this is a fitting reminder of how contemporaries described the essence of nobility as viewed in a conventional and by then almost obsolete context. It is in similar terms also that the principal features of Welsh gentility in the sixteenth century were viewed. Emphasis was placed on the claim to noble ancestry derived from medieval founders. A proven line of descent was not the only factor, but evidently established links between the family and its antecedents upon which claims to inheritance in land were based. The status and prestige enjoyed by an increasing number of gentry families enabled them to achieve regional ascendancy. Parading a good ancestry implied two things, establishing connections between a Welsh brand of nobility and ancient kindred stocks and developing a regional identity, hence the emphasis on the values of inheritance and heritage that were overtly displayed by emergent landed families in the mid-fifteenth and early sixteenth centuries.

Land, Wealth and Status

The population of Wales – scattered over remote rural communities and towns – increased from approximately 226,000 in the mid-sixteenth century to approximately 342,000 in 1670. A marked increase occurred in north Wales, particularly in the north-east, where immigration had led to further social and economic advances. The county that showed the greatest rise in population, however, was Glamorgan with a 66 per cent increase – from 29,000 to 49,000 – where immigrant families again developed the agricultural and industrial resources. Of the five most populous counties in the mid-sixteenth century, four were in south Wales, namely Pembroke, Carmarthen, Glamorgan and Brecknock, and between them they accounted for almost half of the population of Wales (46.6 per cent). Among the towns Carmarthen had 2,150 inhabitants by mid-century, but the average population was about 900 because, of the 87 towns in Wales, a large proportion were declining (such as Hay-on-Wye and Kidwelly). It has been estimated that approximately 9 per cent of the population of Wales lived in urban communities. They were centres of commercial activity and, with the increase in social mobility, in periods of economic stress migratory patterns were deeply influenced.[3]

Social and economic changes in the communal landowning structure in Wales and the Marches led to the decline of the old agrarian order and created a new order based on the acquisition and development of freehold properties as independent units. During the course of the sixteenth century the new freehold estate became a more common feature: population increased, urban centres developed, and a greater concentration on stock rearing and arable farming created a recognisably new order by mid-century. The more agriculturally developed regions of north-east and south Wales as well as coastal areas in the north and south were relatively prosperous, and even in remoter and conservative hinterland areas progressive steps forward had been taken in agricultural improvement.[4] Although Thomas Churchyard's romantic view of Wales and its gentry in *The Worthines of Wales* was restricted mainly to eastern regions, it drew attention to clearing woodlands and creating arable land.[5] Further intrusions were made on common land and trespassers often challenged the rights of freeholders which led to prolonged and expensive lawsuits in the central Chancery and Exchequer courts. 'In these areas,' it was said on behalf of Montgomery and Radnorshire freeholders in 1572, '[there are] diverse persons within these counties, preferring their private lucre and gain before the welfare of their country.' Not only had they encroached on open grazing lands, but they had also moved their stock and the hired animals of others on those lands during the summer months.[6]

The increasing amount of church property that came on the market following the dissolution of the religious houses sharpened the wits of the gentry in their efforts to augment their possessions. Threatening the rights of common freeholders was not the only factor, as the Court of Augmentations records amply demonstrate, and the intensity of disputes increased as more land became available on the market. The gentry pursued their interests as well by encroaching on vacant bond vills, particularly in royal lands, devastated by the impact of plague, rebellion and economic recession. The bond population had declined substantially by the close of the fifteenth century, and many holdings lay waste and were unprofitable for the Crown. The gradual erosion of bondage gave shrewd proprietors the opportunity to further their stake in property and strengthen their alliance with the Crown. That was the objective, for example, of the forward-looking Maredudd ab Ieuan ap Robert of Y Gesailgyfarch in Eifionydd, the founder of the powerful Gwydir family and estate in north Wales, who moved from the commote of Is Gwyrfai and settled with his motley band of followers in the remote and strife-torn southern areas of the hundred of Nanconwy near the marcher frontier where, it was stated, he might 'find elbow room in that waste country among the bondmen' and 'fight with outlaws and thieves than with his own blood and kindred'. That was the view put forward by his descendant, the redoubtable Sir John Wynn, but it appears that Maredudd's knowledge and cautious handling of his affairs in areas of Gwynedd, once populated by bond families, was more evident than any desire on his part to avoid the threats of recalcitrant kindred.[7]

On an increasing level landed estates emerged, usually on a rent or leaseholding basis, thus the *rentier* class, whose wealth was derived from rents or investments, enjoyed the income and capital invested by them in properties. In Wales generally, however, the majority of landowners were modestly placed freeholders.[8] Although a small group of families had prospered – some to a point beyond expectation – by the end of the sixteenth century, the situation, as George Owen of Henllys described it in 1594, should not be exaggerated. The most powerful suitably established themselves in coastal areas and agriculturally richer regions in the borderlands, such as the Bulkeleys of Anglesey and Caernarfonshire, Mostyns of

Flintshire and Caernarfonshire, Perrotts of Haroldston, Pembrokeshire, Mansels of Margam and Oxwich, Morgans of Tredegar, Monmouthshire, and Glamorgan, Vaughans of Golden Grove, Carmarthenshire, Herberts of Chirbury and Cardiff, and Salusburys of Lleweni in western Denbighshire. Others, equally opulent, such as the Wynns of Gwydir, and lesser families like Plas Iolyn, Nannau and Llwydiarth, were situated in inhospitable inland regions but were no less ambitious. The most eligible among these families normally provided the country squires (*armigeri*) who held sway as governors in their respective counties. Not all gentry could boast the same income, even though they claimed the same ancestral status. Arbitrary gradations did exist which distinguished the more affluent from their inferiors, and at the lowest point of the gentry scale yeomen and 40-shilling freeholders would parade their pedigrees as flamboyantly as their superiors.

A large proportion of the Welsh gentry were poorly endowed materially in the early sixteenth century. According to the Subsidy Rolls of 1543 and 1546, only a select number of gentry families had achieved county status. In Caernarfonshire, for example, it was considered that a freeholder valued at £10 in goods or £5 in land a year was worthy of holding office: others valued at £20 or more a year owned 18 per cent of the total wealth which was distributed equitably between freeholders.[9] Their condition in Wales generally was not as impoverished as historians in the past have been led to believe, and although Rowland Lee, in one of his most famous letters to Thomas Cromwell, declared on the eve of the Tudor legislation in 1536 that the majority of Welsh freeholders north of Brecknock were materially inferior and not yielding an income higher than £10 a year, there was an increasing number well above that sum that he appears to have ignored. Regardless of severe economic constraints, the gentry displayed sufficient energy and initiative to advance their own prospects and support heads of cadet families. However, they were hit by the dire effects of financial inflation which reached a high rate by the close of Elizabeth's reign. The process of letting land increased and rent values rose above the level of inflation. This affected tenants who were increasingly subjected to the designs of unscrupulous landowners. 'For now,' George Owen commented, 'the poor tenant, who lived well in that golden world, has been taught to sing his lord a new song...and so much does he fear his greedy neighbour he is forced, two or three years before the lease ends, to beg his lord for a new lease and to save over many years to accumulate money.'[10] Increased pressure on tenants in the Principality and marcher areas often caused friction between them and proprietors, and accounted for the proliferation of suits in the courts concerning unjust seizure of land and oppression. Although retaliation of this kind did, in part, curb the vicious activities of greedy landed gentry, generally it served chiefly to consolidate the powers that they already enjoyed. The expense involved in bringing such cases before the courts caused hardship, particularly to poorer tenants who found it an uphill task to maintain their opposition to substantial gentry who had sufficient material and legal resources to protect their interests in the law courts.

Besides their skills in estate management, the Welsh gentry were steeped in a knowledge of their origins and history of their own nation. They placed much emphasis on the study of history and its interpretation, as they viewed it. That interpretation was often largely confined to antiquity and the use of historical material designed to promote family reputation. A variety of sources illustrate the prime features of their gentility, namely noble descent, inheritance, the social graces, consanguinity and communal identity. Their birthright, considered to have divine approval, gave them the grace and favour that characterised men of quality. It was a feature that appeared in the large corpus of bardic tributes and in the testimony of Tudor gentry as revealed, for example, in Sir John Wynn's *History of the Gwydir Family* (*c.* 1600):

> Nevertheless, by the goodness of God we are and continue in the reputation of gentlemen from time to time since unto this day... God has shown mercy to our kind that, ever since the time of Rhodri, the son of Owain Gwynedd, lord of Anglesey, our common ancestor, there lived in the commonwealth in eminent sort

one or other of our name and many together at times. I have in my mind, in the perusal of the whole course of the history of our name and kindred, compared or likened God's work in that to a man striking fire into a tinder box for, by the beating of the flint upon the steel, there are a number of sparkles of fire raised. Whereof but one or two takes fire the rest vanishing away.[11]

Any appreciation of the content of this section needs to take into account Wynn's motives when compiling his *History*. The higher a gentleman ranked in society the more ambitious – and indeed anxious – he became to superimpose his authority which he claimed to have stemmed essentially from his noble lineage. Wynn and his contemporaries were well aware of the key contributions of genealogy and 'descent', as he called it, in the process of establishing ancestral pre-eminence.[12]

The years *c.* 1450–1600 have been regarded as the formative era in genealogical studies, particularly after the Acts of Union and the increase in public service in Wales, the promotion of some families into the ranks of the aristocracy and the far-reaching effects of economic growth. In the highly reputed bardic school of Gruffudd Hiraethog in the mid-sixteenth century, for example, some of the most notable among Welsh bardic expositors rose to prominence as genealogical experts, social commentators, herald poets and guardians of gentry values. In the latter half of the sixteenth century they emphasised the principal features which displayed honourable descent, such as regional leadership, the holding of office, the possession of land, and eventually the adoption of the Protestant faith. To enhance their prestige the services offered by the newly established College of Arms also encouraged them to seek further visual means of demonstrating their superiority. In Wiliam Cynwal's manuscript, containing family arms, the five reasons given for preserving genealogy and armorial bearings were: to resolve matrimonial disputes, to settle inheritances, to facilitate legal inquiries, to establish kindred affinities, and to confirm merit for public office.[13]

Although the imposition of English law lessened the importance of pedigree in affairs relating to property inherit-ance according to old Welsh legal procedures, the preservation of pedigrees continued to thrive, again primarily for legal purposes, in the courts of Great Sessions and they are contained in plea rolls, gaol files and protonotary records. In days when increasing emphasis was placed on legitimacy in claiming land and when litigation became more common, genealogical data became increasingly meaningful. Professional poets, such as Simwnt Fychan, Wiliam Llŷn and Wiliam Cynwal, who were prime representatives of their milieu in Wales, constituted the last generation of herald poets in a period when the social and economic climate threatened the itinerant bardic system and when granting false pedigrees to seemingly unworthy gentry was becoming a more common feature. Attempts were made, usually for financial reasons, to attribute to individual members of nouveaux riches families – 'gent of the first head', as they were called – the status that had traditionally been preserved for well-established Welsh gentry families. Siôn Tudur and Edmwnd Prys were perceptive commentators on the ills of the late Elizabethan age in Wales and were among the chief critics of the new order and the manner in which it had been applauded by some poets. They accused upstarts for demanding status and for being prepared to bribe poets for that purpose, and also severely censured their fellow poets for allowing this disreputable practice to become so widespread.[14]

Such intrusions into an altogether traditional social structure symbolised a significant transition in communal patterns of activity in the sixteenth century when the hierarchical and patrilineal features were becoming less marked. Social mobility and the utilisation of status to achieve public office and commercial prosperity revealed the rigid adherence to rank and the established social order. Although the emphasis continued to be on recognised status in the regional context, attributes of Welsh gentility were being increasingly accorded to others – usually of English descent. Descendants of Welsh families, which had been elevated to the ranks of the aristocracy, were still considered worthy of approbation by the very nature of their inheritances, and among them Sir William Herbert, first earl of Pembroke, ranked highest. He was considered by Richard Price, a younger son of Sir John Price of Brecon, legal administrator and humanist scholar, to be 'ennobled on account of his splendid descent, his extensive authority and his material prosperity'.[15] Likewise, but this time representing the *advenae*, Sir Edward Stradling of St Donat's was equally commended for his interest in and extensive knowledge of Welsh antiquities. He compiled *The Winning of Glamorgan* (*c.* 1561–71) which traced his ancestry allegedly to the Norman lords who settled in that lordship in the late eleventh century. He pursued that recreation aided by Sir William Cecil, who claimed to be descended from the allegedly Welsh family (later known as Seisyllt) established at Allt-yr-ynys in Herefordshire and who sought Stradling's assistance to trace his own stock.[16]

Friction and Strife

Compiling pedigrees and genealogical tables was very much the order of the day. Despite the modest status enjoyed by the majority of Welsh gentry, they used what means lay at their disposal to achieve their aims. Welsh property law was finally abolished in the statute of 1543, and its impact at the time, despite paucity of evidence, might well have caused rifts between members of forward-looking families keen to identify themselves with the prosperity that landowning offered effi-cient and ambitious operators. A kindred-based society was also subject to dissension, and the law was often used to pro-mote the interests of dissatisfied kinsmen. The clearest example of that view is best found in Bishop Richard Davies's censure of rapacious officials and landowners. 'For what is an office in Wales today,' he asked, 'but a hook for a man to draw to himself the wool and the crops of a neighbour?' He then proceeded to describe the majority of the gentry as main-tainers of evil and their halls as 'a refuge for thieves'.[17] An exaggerated view maybe, but Rhys ap Meurig, the modest gentleman and antiquary of Cotrel in Glamorgan, declared that the purport of the legislation in 1536–43 was to ensure

15

that 'what was then justifiable by might, although not by right, is now to receive condign punishment by law'.[18] It was not easy to justify such a statement in view of the rivalries that occurred, even in his own county, between prominent gentry over private and public affairs. Prolonged family vendettas often upset the political balance as, for example, in the case of the Salusburys of Rug in Merioneth and their satellites who opposed Plas Iolyn, Rhiwlas and Llwyn, and the animosities generated between Sir John Salusbury of Lleweni and his kinsmen of Rug and Sir Richard Trefor of Trefalun and his supporters.[19] Rhys ap Meurig's comments, however, are more meaningful when applied to the changes that had formally occurred in the political and legal structure of the Marches and the policy to extend the sphere of English law into them.

Family and kindred feuds were as severe in Wales after the Act of Union as they had been before. Kinship, in fact, had a dual effect on community life at that time, depending on the circumstances: it could strengthen bonds of affinity within the family, but could also incite violence and hatred. For example, Sir John Salusbury, a younger son, suffered when he came to his inheritance after the execution of his brother, the traitor Thomas Salusbury, who was implicated in the Babington Plot (1586). It took over a decade for family fortunes to revive. Although he was appointed squire of the body in 1595 and elevated to a knighthood in 1601, he was accused by his enemies of discreditable behaviour in his conduct of public business and other matters. Indeed, such was the force of the opposition that he was denied the deputy-lieutenancy and a commission of the peace in his county in 1597. 'Many eyes are cast upon you,' Henry Stanley, earl of Derby informed him in 1590, 'and sundry there be that thirst after your fall.' 'Their malice still increaseth more venomous than adders,' he further stated, 'if they can pluck you down they will...they will smile and cut throats.'[20] Disreputable behaviour that affected relations between gentry families was not viewed with undue alarm in those days, and there is little evidence to prove that onslaughts of this kind created any long-term upheaval. Of greater importance was the impact of such intense competition on stability within the realm. Edward, Lord Zouch, lord president of the Council in the Marches, on coming to office in 1604 referred disparagingly to the strife caused by blood relatives. It was harmful to peace and security, he maintained, for a public servant to cling too firmly to kindred loyalties rather than attending to the affairs of the realm. At the time the new lord president was concerned about the sad effects of bitter feuds on regional security in relation to a specific case of gross misgovernment involving Sir John Wynn of Gwydir who, at the time, was the most powerful man in his region. He was sorry to learn that men's affections had hindered the cause of justice: 'Where blood calleth for vengeance,' he declared, 'the commonwealth will suffer.'[21] Zouch was confronted by a number of problems demanding instant attention, not least the opposition to his position as lord president of the Council and the potential Catholic threat on James I's accession. His predecessor, Henry Herbert, second earl of Pembroke, likewise aware of the need to maintain stability in a period of tension, had been deeply disturbed by the contest between Sir Edward Stradling and his kinsman Thomas Carne of Ewenni. In an attempt to calm the situation he was prepared to visit St Donat's personally to try to resolve the differences between them. 'Both sides,' he intimated to Stradling, 'have partisans which causes sadness to your friends and rejoicing to your enemies.'[22] So much emphasis was placed on a man's 'credit' or reputation that it was difficult for him to reassert his pre-eminence if he had been publicly censured.[23] William Salusbury of Rug, for example, was regarded as a man of 'many good parts' who kept his promises as a steadfast friend in his property dealings with his neighbours and – wily though he was and out for the main chance – was considered to be a person of integrity in his locality.[24]

The Rise of Families

Renaissance influences had drawn attention to the importance of integration and social harmony in maintaining the well-

17

being of the commonwealth, a factor that featured prominently in contemporary commentaries. In the Welsh context, during the period 1540–1640, the gentleman's residence was regarded as a mark of regional precedence. Landed property and the country mansion were the two prime visible features of power. In the *Itinerary in Wales* (*c.* 1536–43), John Leland, the first royal antiquary and librarian, and a 'pioneer in the method of direct enquiry and first-hand observation', on his perambulations briefly noted several Welsh castles, most of them in ruinous condition.[25] Churchyard also made similar comments and remarked that they had been replaced by attractive country mansions.[26] George Owen echoed their thoughts: 'Now we see the old castles of Wales,' he declared, 'from whence in old time issued out daily our destroyers and disinheritors, all in ruin and decay, and on the contrary the houses of the gentlemen and people to flourish and increase.'[27] Evidence shows that a number of these houses in Tudor and Stuart Wales were rebuilt or renovated, an indication of the importance of these focal points and resident proprietors even in the early seventeenth century.

The concept of the county community became a recognised feature as governmental institutions became increasingly centred on the shire-towns and commanded the loyalties of those involved in administering local affairs. When considering the counties and regions of Wales, as in England and on the continent, diversity, singularity and continuity were the prime characteristics.[28] The increase in social mobility was more evident in some communities than others, especially in progressive anglicised areas. In communities often afflicted by economic difficulties social changes occurred over a much longer period. The most conspicuous among them – and the first category of landowners – were the traditional families that sprang over many generations from well-founded kindred stock. One such example is the Nannau family in the parish of Llanfachreth in Merioneth whose gradual acquisition of properties from the mid-fourteenth century onwards enabled it to maintain its hold over an area extending from Penrhyndeudraeth in the north of the county to Llwyngwril in the coastal area of the south-west. By the mid-Tudor period it had attained the ascendancy in the county community, and successive heads of the family exploited the limited resources at their disposal to offset the challenge of rivals.[29] Another family of considerable repute that also stemmed from native roots was that established at Clenennau in the commote of Eifionydd. It grew steadily from the latter years of the thirteenth century onwards and achieved prominence in the mid-fifteenth century with its consolidated estate in the townships of Penmorfa, Trefan and Pennant. The nucleus of the estate lay in Clenennau, and its shrewdest owner was Morus ab Elisa, the father of the redoubtable Sir William Maurice, a prominent figure in Welsh political life in James I's reign.[30] Of similar calibre were the Pryses of Gogerddan, Lloyds of Bodidris, Vaughans of Golden Grove, Trefors of Bryncunallt and Trefalun, the Bodeon, Prysaeddfed, Plas Coch and Gwredog families, among others, of Anglesey, and Mostyns of Flintshire and Caernarfonshire, all of which produced a succession of male heirs well endowed to administer public and private affairs.[31]

In the second category there appeared those families whose ancestors had been granted land by the thirteenth-century princes of Gwynedd in return for public services, notably in administrative, diplomatic and military capacities. Without doubt, the most powerful among them were the antecedents of the 'Tudor' family of Penmynydd, Anglesey, and the Gruffudd family of Penrhyn which sprang from the stock of Ednyfed Fychan, chief counsellor to Llywelyn ab Iorwerth (the Great). Three successive heads, all named William, of the Penrhyn family, in the period c. 1431–1531, became closely involved at a high level in the administration in north Wales. The first William Gruffudd served as deputy chamberlain and his son and grandson acquired the chamberlainship. Similarly, the founder of the Mostyn family of Gloddaith obtained land from Llywelyn ab Iorwerth, and it was eventually the union of the Five Courts of Mostyn, Pengwern, Trecastell, Tregarnedd and Gloddaith that brought the family to the forefront of social and political life in north Wales in the latter half of the sixteenth century.[32] Tudur Goch, the founder of the Glyn family of Glynllifon in Caernarfonshire, benefited when Edward III gave him lands in Nantlle following his distinguished military service in France. By the sixteenth century such families had acquired a social cachet all of their own, enjoying privileges derived from the dual source of honourable descent and public service to native Welsh princes.[33]

The third and most interesting group of landowners represented the *advenae*, the immigrant urban population, many of whom had settled among Welsh communities since the twelfth century. They were located usually in two distinct areas, the towns of the Principality and the urban districts of the Marches to the east. They boasted Anglo-Norman lineage and had either migrated with the early settlers or had been induced, in return for grants of lands and privileges, to come to Wales in the fourteenth and fifteenth centuries to colonise the towns and strengthen the economy. Through inter-marriage and public office, their power extended into all parts of Wales, in urban and rural areas, and by the early sixteenth century they were recognised for what they were: namely, gentry of alien stock who had firmly entrenched themselves in the Welsh countryside. Henry Lacy, earl of Lincoln and lord of Denbigh, pursued a policy of strengthening the English hold over lands east of the Conwy river after 1284 by adopting an exchange system and moving whole native kindreds to less hospitable regions in the western part of the lordship and by allowing incoming families to enjoy English privileges in the borough of Denbigh and surrounding townships.[34]

Besides, the castellated boroughs of the Principality towns in Wales were small and geared to marketing Welsh produce. After a period of decline, especially among the modestly sized urban centres dependent largely upon military and adminis-trative activities, a revival occurred by the end of the sixteenth century and small but thriving market towns emerged. In north-east Wales the most powerful family of Norman extraction was Salusbury, which had its senior branch at Lleweni near Denbigh. It established its connections far and wide in areas east of the Conwy river, at Bachymbyd and at

Rug in Merioneth. Sir John Salusbury (*d.* 1578) became chamberlain of North Wales and manipulated other public offices that enhanced family prestige throughout the province.[35] Equally powerful were the Bulkeleys of Anglesey – originally a Cheshire family that settled at Beaumaris. An early marriage into the Penrhyn family established its reputation even further and similar ties with the Boldes of Conwy extended its sphere of interest in eastern Caernarfonshire.[36] Others of the same milieu used what means lay at their disposal to fortify their position, such as the Pulestons of Emral, Mansels of Oxwich, Penrice and Margam, Bassetts of Beaupre, Breretons of Borras and others of equal status. Their imposing pedigrees and the bardic tributes composed in their honour reveal how well integrated into Welsh society and culture they had all become by the mid-sixteenth century.[37]

The fourth category of landed families were those founders skilfully moved into new territories where lands were exchanged and encroached upon on a large scale. This adventurous spirit characterised men like Maredudd ab Ieuan (previously cited), the founder of the Gwydir estate, who settled at Dolwyddelan Castle and then Penamnen in Nanconwy before moving north into the upper Conwy valley.[38] There were others like him, but he achieves prominence because his exploits were related in the narrative *History* of the family which traced the events leading to his settlement in that remote area. Lineal succession and organisational talents enabled successive heads of the Wynn family to achieve pre-eminence in the affairs of north Wales down to the third decade of the seventeenth century. Maredudd's fame was based essentially on his acquisition of bond vills and prudent use of retaining to establish peace and good order rather than perpetuate the disorder that prevailed in the uplands of Hiraethog and Nanconwy.

Means and Resources

Within these four categories economic factors dictated that some families rose more rapidly than others in social rank.

21

They all benefited from the acquisition of church lands as well. From the mid-fourteenth century onwards the Church had seen an increasing number of its properties gradually slipping away from its grasp into the hands of aggressive lay proprietors. Some acquired offices as superintendents of monastic lands and were thus in a position to exert pressure when they considered it necessary. Maredudd ap Tudur of Plas Iolyn in Hiraethog, for example, became steward of Aberconwy abbey lands and those of the Knights Hospitaller in Ysbyty Ifan and the adjacent area.[39] His grandson, Robert ap Rhys, Henry VIII's chaplain and Thomas Wolsey's servant, obtained some lands, including tithes, appertaining to Ystrad Marchell abbey and the Hospitallers. Cadwaladr Price of Rhiwlas in Merioneth obtained other lands belonging to that abbey in Penllyn, Basingwerk abbey lands in Flintshire became part of the Pennant of Downing inheritance, and Sir Rhys Mansel of Oxwich and Penrice acquired Margam abbey.[40] In Monmouth-shire, Llantarnam was appropriated by a branch of the Morgans of Pencoed, and the earl of Worcester obtained Tintern for services rendered and to compensate for loss of privileges as a marcher lord.[41] In the Llŷn peninsula, the Bodfel family grasped Bardsey Island and the Owens of Plas Du – notorious later as a recusant family – were given the rectory of Aberdaron.[42]

Such families varied in their potential but, within their respective ranks, growth and prosperity depended almost entirely on engrossing secular and ecclesiastical properties. Their value in society was calculated largely on the amount of property they could accumulate and on how much income they derived from it. Added sources of income came from the exploitation of lead, iron, coal and other minerals. The Nannau family experimented with iron at Ganllwyd, the Mostyn family – particularly during Sir Roger Mostyn's period – dug for coal at Whitford in Flintshire, and Sir John Wynn began to exploit – not altogether successfully – the lead deposits in the uplands above his residence, and elsewhere.

All in all, the Tudor social and cultural patterns had been well and truly established among gentle families by mid-century.

Cohesive features among them often led to the closing of the ranks, chiefly to protect their own interests. In property disputes, for example, they acted as arbitrators because of their knowledge of the background histories of the contestants, and would maintain political solidarity by reinforcing the network of family relations. The landed estate and the *plasty* (mansion house) were central features of their acquired superiority. The process of competition for leases continued as eagerly as ever, and they were renewed, wherever possible, on favourable terms. The grammarian Dr John Davies (Siôn Dafydd Rhys) purposely acclaimed the fortified house built by Sir Edward Stradling at St Donat's.[43] The poet Morus Dwyfach sang ecstatically to his patron John Wyn ap Maredudd of Gwydir in his new mansion which he favourably compared to Windsor and St Paul's.[44] Sir Richard Clough, employed as Sir Thomas Gresham's commercial agent at Antwerp, built two new houses decorated with tiles at Bachegraig and Plas Clough,[45] and in remote Merioneth, Glan-y-llyn, the new residence of Hywel Fychan, was described by Wiliam Llŷn in glowing terms.[46] Sir William Herbert's house in Cardiff was regarded as a wonder for all men to see,[47] and Plas Mawr, Conwy, built by Robert Wynn, a scion of the house of Gwydir, in 1576, represented what was best in late Tudor Renaissance architecture. The plaster-work, armorial bearings, expensive curtains, panelled walls, refined furniture and other embellishments gave that house and many others a reputation to be envied.[48]

Once they had consolidated their positions in the rural areas, a sizeable minority, typified by Sir William Herbert at Cardiff and Robert Wynn at Conwy, gradually settled in urban centres, particularly shire-towns, and began to build for themselves prestigious houses. The essence of good housekeeping was the quality of the charity and patronage provided by the resident gentleman in the town or the country. Indeed, householdership featured significantly in the traditional order of gentle living in Wales and was highly valued in the bardic grammars that established the criteria of poetic eulogy. Such a display of liberality, where it survived, was a common denominator in sixteenth-century Wales, although in its latter period it was also seriously challenged by the increasing estrangement of the gentry from their native environment.

Lavish hospitality, according to status and means, was still very much the order of the day as several poets testified of their most noteworthy patrons. What is difficult to estimate, however, is the nature and extent of decline in the numbers of practising patrons in rural and urban areas by the eve of the Civil Wars. Rare glimpses are also caught of the aristocracy at leisure as, for example, the record of a feast held in honour of Henry Herbert at Cardiff in 1574.[49] Together with his wife and Lord Talbot, his brother-in-law, he was honourably welcomed by most Glamorgan and Monmouthshire gentry on his visit to Cardiff Castle where, in his own citadel, he was lavishly entertained; 'where, keeping a very honourable and sumptuous house to all comers, they [i.e. he and his companions] continued, for the space of...days, riding abroad and visiting their friends and viewing the country'. In Anglesey, the reputation of Sir Richard Bulkeley III (*d.* 1621), who built Baron Hill near Beaumaris, was greatly admired. *The History of the Bulkeley Family* – a seventeenth-century compilation – graphically drew attention to his qualities. 'Of very good memory and understanding,' it was said of him, 'in matters belonging to housekeeping, husbandry, maritime affairs...he was a great housekeeper and entertainer of noblemen...and strangers, especially such as passed to or from Ireland.'[50]

In addition to the appearance of new and renovated buildings in the Welsh countryside, surnames had by then also become common among the most opulent who abandoned the customary patronymic style. It was a sign of the times that new features of gentility should attract those who wished to realise their ambitions. The practice of primogeniture highlighted tendencies that had been continuing over a long period among progressive families. Alongside the customary features of a hierarchical, patriarchal and patrilineal system, it also had a role in designing the social make-up of landed gentlemen. They adopted the *grazia* (gracious demeanour) which was a prominent feature among their compeers in

England and attached themselves, wherever possible, to a code of conduct compatible with that of the aristocracy, vestiges of which were found at Raglan, Cardiff and Lamphey (the old Bishops' Palace), which eventually became the principal Devereux seat in south-west Wales.[51]

The Character and Education of the Gentry

The principles expounded by Sir Thomas Elyot and other commentators on the nature and function of gentility were adopted by typical Welsh careerists who considered that broadening horizons enabled them to participate fully in the public and private activities of the English gentleman. The medieval free clansman (*priodawr*) had progressed to become the typical Tudor Renaissance gentleman. Features of gravitas (sobriety of conduct) appealed to them, and intellectual dimensions were added. 'Alas, yow will he ungentle gentle,' Stefano Guazzo declared, 'if you be no scholars', and, in that context, education played a vital role in fulfilling the needs of ambitious gentlemen.[52] The purpose of education fundamentally was to enable young gentry to assume responsibilities in the state. 'I understand your good diligence and careful considerations of my causes which also be your own.' Morus Wynn of Gwydir informed his son in London, 'in the continuance thereof you shall not only profit yourself in time to come but also win and procure all men to think and speak well of you which is to the comfort of me and rest of your friends, and namely to hear that you take pain in your study which, above all things (besides the service of God), shall be to you most commodious.'[53] Family prestige obviously counted for much to him, and the heir was expected to conduct himself in such a manner that would uphold the family's status. In a more aggressive way Sir William Herbert of St Julian's in Monmouthshire defended his position in a letter in which he deplored the claims made to equal status by one of the influential Morgan family in that county. If he wished to prove his superiority, he explained, then he had to be a male successor to an earl, a descendant of ten earls, and prove that he had royal blood flowing in his veins. This was because of the fact, Herbert added, that through his grandmother, who sprang from the Devereux family, his ancestry could be traced legitimately to Edward IV. Rather disingenuous perhaps, but very much in line with the practice of the age to defend – even bolster – worthy lineage.[54]

The traditional aristocracy were unable to maintain their old power and prestige. They were undermined by the Tudors and a new mobility arose to prominence in government characterised by skill, perspicacity and an abiding loyalty to the state. In a period when educated laymen attained greater importance in public affairs, the emphasis on practical skills became paramount. Although they continued to follow military careers in their younger days, they later applied their discipline as well as their organisational and administrative talents as officials at a time when the Tudors required the services of men proficient in the art of government and diplomacy.[55] In Wales, the educating process had a threefold effect on the Welsh gentry who had become conscious of the impact of new attitudes and pressures upon them: since Wales had never enjoyed an aristocratic order similar to that in England, the status of the highest ranking families was increased so that they enjoyed positions equal to those held by the upper English gentry. Secondly, they were given the opportunity to compete with one another for primacy, and thirdly, a two-tier system was created in the landed structure of Wales. Those higher up the social ladder – with incomes of £500 upwards – had the resources to pursue their ambitions while the more modest but equally alert gentry, broadly within the £10 to £500 range and extending from the middle ranks of landed proprietors down to modest freeholders, despite economic hardship grasped what opportunity they could to strengthen their families for the future (see pp. 39–42). Dr David Powel of Ruabon, in his letter-dedicatory to Sir Philip Sidney, to whom he presented his edition of Gerald of Wales's *Itinerarium Cambriae*, emphasised these specific points. 'Furthermore,' he maintained, 'what more suitable service can a man give other than he presents himself entirely in the interests of the state.' He continued: 'Those who have been endowed and adorned with these virtues are to be considered, not only as good men, but also true gentlemen.'[56] The educating dimension involved far more than merely imparting knowledge, for it contributed substantially to create the image of the just governor as interpreted in contemporary social commentaries. 'Gentlemen and the people of Wales have increased tremendously in learning and grace,' George Owen declared, 'because now large numbers of youths are maintained at the universities of Oxford and Cambridge and in other good schools in England where they prove themselves to be learned men and good members of the commonwealth of England and Wales.'[57] The same view was expressed by Humphrey Llwyd. In his opinion there was no man so poor that he could not afford to send his children to school.[58] An exaggerated comment, perhaps, in view of the lack of resources in the less well-endowed areas, but his observation referred principally to those families established in the most conservative parts of Wales who did send their sons to the universities and inns of court, and to the new grammar schools that began to appear in Wales to 'contribute virtuous and godly education'.

The universities adapted themselves to the new circumstances created by the Reformation, and new colleges were established, such as Jesus College, Oxford (1571), by Dr Hugh Price of Brecon, a doctor of canon law and prebendary of Rochester cathedral. It was the first Protestant institution of its kind at Oxford and Price left property valued at £60 a year to the college. It is estimated that about 2,000 Welsh students entered Oxford and Cambridge between 1570 and 1642. Most of them went to Oxford, where the highest entries from Wales were recorded between 1570 and 1642, although Queens', Magdalene and St John's colleges at Cambridge attracted north Wales students because of the benefactions offered there. The inns of court also attracted the sons of gentry and professional men, and about seven hundred entered from Wales in the period 1545–1642. A smattering of legal knowledge enabled them to practise law, administer their estates, supervise the conduct of their legal disputes, and function as justices of the quorum in courts of Quarter Sessions. The inns, like the universities, instructed young gentry in Renaissance values associated with polite and courteous society and introduced into the mansions of rural Wales a new and more progressive outlook and lifestyle.

Tudor and early Stuart grammar schools, which were established in the urban and rural parts of Wales, catered for members of the wealthier sections of the community and those of lesser means for whom endowments were often provided. They taught the classics and, after the Elizabethan religious settlement, the tenets of the Protestant faith, the instruction of which established the principles of public order and political and religious conformity. They also offered young gentry opportunities designed to enrich their experiences and serve in Church and state. Gentry households were also centres of learning where the sons and daughters of prime gentry, as well as able sons of tenants (such as William Morgan, translator of the scriptures into Welsh, who was instructed at Gwydir), were taught the rudiments of the classics and reared in the accustomed polite manner. The endowment of Henry Rowlands, bishop of Bangor in c. 1609, led to the opening of Botwnnog school – a 'petty school in Llŷn'[59] as it was once called – and Geoffrey Glyn, a scholar and Catholic deeply influenced by a humanising zeal, founded Friars school in Bangor in 1557. Cowbridge school in Glamorgan was established by Sir John Stradling who inherited his uncle Sir Edward Stradling's estate in 1609. Robert Wynn of Conwy had intended establishing a school in the town, but when that proposed venture failed he arranged that his eldest son was placed under guardianship and reared 'in the fear of God, nurture and knowledge', and educated at 'one of the universities or Inns of Court or other similar place of learning'.[60]

Good education at all levels provided major benefits: acquiring classical learning and legal and administrative training, fostering intellectual stimulation and broadening social horizons and, most importantly, nourishing the ideal of the proper Tudor gentleman. Sir John Wynn, in a letter to his eldest son at Lincoln's Inn in 1605, seeking his advancement as the next lineal successor to the estate, made the point clear: 'I prefer your well-doing and good education,' he said, 'so much as I make no difficulty to bestow what I do give you though it might serve well to supply of my other wants.' 'The director of all good thoughts guide your heart and mind to his service above all,' he continued, 'and next to commendable course of life in the commonweal whereof the greatest comfort and joy shall rebound to yourself.' His comments echo the sentiments of equally ambitious fathers who considered that their sons' academic achievements contributed significantly to enhancing their own personal reputation. Education was provided for the sons of gentry of all ranks and was valued primarily for its contribution in promoting public service and defining the role of the family in community life.[61]

The 'Grand Tour' also became a practical means of elevating family status as an extension to a classically based education. The most eligible young gentlemen enjoyed the privilege of travelling to acquaint themselves with the social graces in an European context, to maintain family reputation, and obtain knowledge designed to enable them to assume public responsibilities. 'For hard sure it is to know England,' Sir Philip Sidney remarked, 'without you know it by comparing it with some other country': 'no more than a man can know the swiftness of his horse,' he added, 'without seeing him well matched'.[62] The prime purpose was to obtain experience of lands and states and broaden knowledge of Renaissance culture. Attempts were also made to assess and measure the material and moral prosperity of those lands and evaluate their political institutions – their laws, administration, offices and government. They appraised the whole state and identified differences between regions in each so that they became proficient in statecraft. 'If, therefore, you will be a profitable traveller and come home a better man than you went out,' Sir John Stradling remarked in *Direction for Traveilers* (1592), 'you must seek to be enriched with three things...they are wisdom of policy, knowledge or learning, manners or behaviour'.[63] An Elizabethan governor was often measured by these standards. Early in the century, Italy, the cradle of Renaissance culture, was the most fashionable destination for European visitors; later it was Germany because of Protestant influences and, in the latter years, France attracted young gentry. Those who travelled from Wales were also involved in foreign trade and business. Sir Thomas Stradling travelled to Germany and France in 1548–9 and from there to Italy accompanied by Sir Thomas Hoby who translated Castiglione's *Il Cortegiano* into English in 1561. By virtue of their positions as ambassadors, Sir John Herbert visited Denmark, Poland, Holland and France, and Sir Edward Carne of Ewenni went to Boulogne, France, the Netherlands, Rome and Flanders.[64] Sir Edward Stradling was attracted to Italy, and Dr John Davies maintained that the consequence of this was that 'experience had produced in him learning and learning so many virtues'. Siôn Trefor III, who rebuilt Trefalun in 1567, and was patronised by the Sackvilles, travelled to Rome in 1563.[65] That was also the ambition of Sir John Wynn Junior of Gwydir in 1614, and his travels took him to France and Italy. His long sojourn abroad, however, was not looked upon favourably by his father and brother-in-law, Sir Roger Mostyn, nor by contemporary poets who begged his return.[66] When Sir Thomas Salusbury considered travelling to France he was aware of the expressed opinion that he should stay at home because he was the only fit heir to the estate. He, unlike the young scion of Gwydir, took the view that he should acquaint himself with his own country and be known to his friends and kindred as well as study the people among whom he was to reside. Although the Court was an honourable calling, he maintained that for him to return to the country would mean settling in a new world. 'Our countrymen,' he observed, '...are a crafty kind of people, and...bear an internal hate to such as make themselves strangers unto them.'[67] The words offer an insight into the character of a society marked by conservatism and a pride in resident leadership. In an age when the nouveaux riches struck it lucky in commercial and business circles, representatives of the 'old order' became increasingly aware of the need to maintain their precedence by means of foreign travel, albeit for intellectual reasons.

Marriage, Culture and the Family

Cultural visits abroad were not the only means of broadening the gentry's interests. Increasing matrimonial relations bound families together on both sides of Offa's Dyke. Emphasis here was again placed on law, convention and family welfare. The prime motive of marriage was to produce a legitimate male heir to continue the succession and increase family possessions and contacts. Marriage was also a device to create further integration between families of repute in the realm, thereby enhancing national solidarity. The best examples of prudent marriages in Wales doubtless are the remarkable four successive unions that attached Katherine of Berain with some of the best families in north Wales of her day – the Salusburys of Lleweni, the Wynns of Gwydir and Thelwalls of Ruthin, her second marriage being to the successful merchant and factor, Sir Richard Clough of Bachegraig. These marriages served to create a powerful network in the years c. 1550–90.[68] Marriages also strengthened public relations and established a Welsh family's position in London and the provinces. Needless to say they were all arranged on a contractual basis: 'the best marriage', it was said, 'lies in the highest portion', and Sir Richard Wynn of Gwydir resented his father's intention to marry him off to the highest bidder. Great care was taken to ensure that the best match was obtained, but it was with some reluctance that London-based families sought brides in the remoter parts of Wales.[69] Often marriages occurred between local or regional houses leading to the emergence of powerful cadet families. The dynastic motive was paramount and served to consolidate family and landed interests in the community. To marry beneath one's rank was frowned upon and often deplored. In 1619, for example, Mary Bulkeley, a member of the cadet family of that name which had settled at Dronwy in

Anglesey, without her mother's consent, decided to marry 'a loose beggerly fellow not worth a groat in all the world', a situation that caused some trepidation to her kindred. Consequently, her brother, Robert Bulkeley, who served in the household of Dr Theophilus Field, bishop of Llandaff, was advised to write to her 'a letter in Welsh to dissuade her from such idle courses and to be more discreet and better advised in her proceedings'. Moreover, John Thomas Bassett of Llantriddyd bequeathed lands in Bonvilston to his daughter Elizabeth on condition that she married Thomas Bassett, the son of his kinsman William Bassett of Beaupre. Matters of inheritance tended to weld families of the same rank together; to avoid a series of *mésalliances* the gentry stood firm to preserve ancestral dignity. The 'centre of gravity' for all families was the reputation they established based on successful matrimonial relations designed to increase material resources. It was often tied to cultural identities that shared common features.[70]

Nevertheless, there were forces at work that were gradually undermining those lineaments among an increasing number of landed gentry and that eventually were to sever them from family tradition. This view, however, should not be pressed too far. Although opinions and attitudes changed, the reorientation of the Welsh gentry in cultural matters was not unavoidable and, it appears, not immediately catastrophic. Certainly, there were clear signs of the withdrawal of literary patronage, but the extent to which this was merely a sixteenth-century phenomenon is questionable since it can be traced much earlier in some cases and later in others. However, as early as 1547 William Salesbury – the most eminent Welsh Protestant humanist of his day – seemed to be aware of an impending crisis[71] and, twenty years later, Gruffydd Robert, the Roman Catholic scholar who fled to Rome and later Milan after Mary I's death, in his preface to his *Gramadeg Cymraeg* in 1567, satirised the Welsh gentry who, upon seeing the steeples of Shrewsbury and the River Severn, forgot their Welsh and spoke poor English.[72] In his work *Lloegr Drigiant ddifyrrwch Brytanaidd Gymro*, which Gruffudd Hiraethog presented to

Richard Mostyn, who spent part of his time in England, his intention was to provide Welshman in London with learning and information. The work included proverbs, miscellaneous extracts from medieval Welsh prose and poetry, the 24 feats, a list of graduates in poetry and song, a copy of the 'statute' of Gruffudd ap Cynan (rules governing the bardic order) and an explanation of the Welsh mutation and intricate bardic systems. All these details served to remind Richard Mostyn of the heritage that was in danger of being forsaken. Gruffudd appealed to a scion of a prominent family that had supported Welsh bardic culture to cherish his mother tongue. He was aware of the plight of those who were forced to abandon their communities to seek what fortune they could elsewhere,[73] and referred to the treacherous practices of those who had deliberately abandoned their traditional lifestyle. While he aimed his criticism chiefly at those 'who tarry a little away from home and hate and forget their mother tongue', Henry Perri, priest and scholar and a native of Flintshire near the English border, took it upon himself to rebuke even the homekeeping gentry for not attending sufficiently to the needs of the Welsh language.[74] Since they, he said, did not appreciate its value then the language could do them no service. In that respect he voiced the opinions of a small band of scholars who, at the time, were eagerly awaiting the opportunity to elevate the Welsh language and its literature to a status equal to the classics. With regard to the gentry they were confronted by two major problems – namely, intermarriage with English-based families that established households where Welsh was often discarded, and the increasing involvement in law and administration, usually through office-holding, which sadly affected allegiances to native cultural affairs. Paradoxically, the poets as the chief exponents of this culture, while voicing their grievances, applauded and enjoyed the benefits of Tudor policy as it affected the public lives of their patrons. They extolled the virtues of individuals who were regarded, in a Welsh context, as the epitomy of the Tudor governor, and their role in the central and regional departments of government was highly commended. Their grievance, however, stemmed from a serious abuse of that authority in that it became a means by which the gentry gradually and voluntarily withdrew their patronage.

Morus Kyffin harshly commented on those who discarded native culture because they considered that clinging to it was damaging to their reputations.[75] He was one of the few exceptions who had served abroad – in his case in military campaigns in Ireland and on the Continent – but who was still eager to foster cultural interests, presumably because of the deep influence that Wiliam Llŷn had had upon him in earlier days. Nevertheless, he was in a position to view the attitudes of others in similar circumstances and to note that increasing involvement elsewhere, by its very nature, caused them to become estranged and that their inability to read Welsh, let alone appreciate its literature, signified the emergence of a new breed of gentry. Simwnt Fychan, at the turn of the century, referred disparagingly to the 'young men in towns who despised works in our tongue', the type of comment that was becoming more common in the early decades of the seventeenth century.[76] At that time individual scholars attempted to pursuade country gentry not to follow the trends established by their more opulent peers. In 1630, Rowland Vaughan of Cae'r Gai in Merioneth deplored 'anglicised Welshmen' – in other words, those among the privileged families who despised their language and promoted the exclusive use of English. Robert Holland, translator of James I's *Basilicon Doron* in 1604, hoped that Henry, Prince of Wales, might learn the native language and live among his people. Moreover, Sir John Wynn of Gwydir expected that his daughter-in-law would master enough Welsh to converse with tenants in Llanfrothen, Merioneth, and the poet Meurig Dafydd and Siôn Dafydd Rhys praised Sir Edward Stradling for mastering the language. Again in Glamorgan, the Kemeys family employed a Welsh tutor for their heir, as did the Lewis family of Y Fan. These may well be isolated examples, but in view of the large corpus of conventional bardic material and other evidence that has survived in the decades before the Civil Wars, the role of the Welsh language among gentle families, and attitudes towards it, among gentle families need to be reconsidered.

Social and Economic Hardship: Attitudes and Pressures

The long period of high prices was harmful to all sections of the community, and there was a distinct awareness of the effects of economic depression following bad harvests and extortive practices. The plight of the poor was thrown into high relief in attempts made by a succession of Poor Law statutes, and the commission of the 1567 *eisteddfod* held at Caerwys in Flintshire to curb the persistent wanderings of unruly beggars and vagabonds in north Wales. The 'vagrant and idle persons naming themselves minstrels, rithmers and bards', it was declared, had 'lately grown into such an intolerable multitude' that their movements had not only caused disquiet among gentry but also had sorely affected the itineraries of licensed poets.[77] That, however, was only part of the problem because social deprivation was severe in Wales at that time.

Poverty and destitution, as surviving legal records show, caused real hardship, and in time of crisis mobility became an increasing feature in urban and rural areas in England and Wales. Much of it was caused by the impact of poor agricultural conditions and natural disasters. John Penry partly blamed economic recession for the poor spiritual condition of the nation. The 'unseasonable' harvest of 1585, he maintained, yielded little corn, and the following winter destroyed the cattle. The 'very sinew of their maintenance is gone,' he added, and many 'that lived well and thriftily are fain to give over both house and home and to go abegging'.[78] Regardless of Penry's motives, he drew attention to a serious social problem at the time. William Vaughan of Tor-y-coed, Carmarthenshire, who established a colony called 'Cambriol' in Newfoundland hoping to escape from economic hardship in Wales, denounced the destitute condition of Welsh agrarian life in late Tudor days. The country, he said, was 'not half

35

stocked' and cornfields were 'so bare of corne that a stranger could think that the earth produced such grain naturally wild'. In the third part of Vaughan's treatise he attributed poverty in Wales to bad physical conditions whereby 'thousands do perish for want of relief'.[79] In 1623 Sir John Wynn was himself in dire straits following the bad harvest that had seriously depleted his income. Between February and midsummer of that year his expenses and debts had amounted appreciably. In all, he was £3,000 in debt and despairingly declared that his living consisted of large tenements and tracts where no corn had grown over the previous two years. The price of cattle, wool, sheep, butter, cheese and other commodities was very low, which accounted for the £1,000 shortage in rent income compared to the previous year: 'my tenants have not where-with to pay,' he declared, 'the bread-corn is that exceeding rate that a number do die in the country for hunger…the rest have the impression of hunger in their faces exceeding the memory of any man living'.[80] Equally penetrating were the caustic remarks made by the Denbighshire poet, Edward ap Raff, who severely reprimanded sharp operators who profited from the ills of others when the price of corn was high in 1597.[81]

There were some sharp practices also among gentry who wished to maintain their status and regional predominance and who, by fair means or foul, provided for their families. Attempting to maintain sumptuous households involved a significant increase in expenditure. The value of landed incomes was falling, particularly where landlords depended almost entirely on rents. The price of goods doubled by the end of the Elizabethan era and some proprietors were non-resident, not necessarily because of the attractions of the metropolis but owing to financial impoverishment. 'Your heir,' one poet remarked of a patron, 'will not abide by his lands and will rather stake his reputation on a spotted dice.'[82] It was doubtless considered that depression at home might be compensated by the acquisition of favours and opportunities elsewhere. Under such circumstances it is hardly surprising that poets extolled the virtues of the remaining faithful heads of households up to the outbreak of Civil Wars, urging them to cling firmly to what vestiges remained of their traditional culture. Having said that, it is not an easy task to estimate how many of those families survived. Times were more fluid, it is true, but judging by bardic output it appears that a substantial core of dependent poets and others who were self-maintaining remained. Patronage and the itinerancies may well have been less frequent, but they did survive. In this context it is debatable to what extent another feature of bardic decline, namely its medieval organisation and conservatism, had by the mid-seventeenth century caused its demise and had rendered it irrelevant in a new social environment. What is clear, however, is that Siôn Cain, who succeeded his father Rhys Cain as a household poet and whose last poems cannot be dated later than 1648, was considered to be the last of his profession.

Bardic criticism was levelled primarily against those heads of families and other influential gentry who, in view of the benefits they derived from office-holding, chose not to heed warnings. Siôn Tudur and Edmwnd Prys and others, while commenting bitterly on the ills of their age, particularly the oppression and cupidity of ruthless businessmen, usurers, administrators and those who tarried for far too long from their native land, were themselves aware that it was material prosperity that ruined cultural standards if it was not applied to the needs of the community. They were fully aware that a flourishing society was essential if the quality of regional life was to be maintained, but they were dismayed because the gains and benefits of the gentry were used for other purposes. Persistent absenteeism was deplored and several poets echoed the sentiments expressed by Sir Roger Mostyn in 1614 when he considered that the heir to the Gwydir estate – who was at the time in Italy on the 'Grand Tour' – should return to reside among his tenants in Llanfrothen and attend to urgent family and local government business. 'His absence,' Mostyn declared to his father, 'must needs be a discomfort to you and to all his friends, especially to those that desire the raising of your house', a comment that emphasises the basic feature of honourable householdership.[83]

Not all sons of the gentry forged strong links with native culture. The effects of financial strain placed severe constraints on an increasing number of those who would normally have patronised Welsh poetry, but also a number of younger sons hardly established any contact with traditional cultural practices through no fault of their own. Since their material prospects were poor combined with the fact that not all of them married into local families, it is likely that they moved out of their father's household at the earliest opportunity to seek their fortunes elsewhere. In their case the impact of social reorientation was stronger. Although a sizeable proportion did return to establish cadet families, thus augmenting the numbers of gentry families, only a minority patronised Welsh literature. Among them, the most prominent were the Wynns, Salusburys and Prices in the north and the Vaughans in Carmarthenshire and Cardiganshire, the prime reason being that they resided in areas which, although they were subject to mainstream English cultural influences, maintained strong connections with native affairs. In this context it is debatable whether the poets were dependent solely on the munificence of eldest sons in charge of senior branches of prominent families. Heads of junior branches were also highly esteemed for their bounty and applauded as warmly as any senior *paterfamilias* in the early decades of the seventeenth century. That, of course, is only part of the story, and the plight of younger sons in Wales is a theme worthy of further investigation regarding the extent to which social reorientation occurred, among whom and for what specific reasons.[84]

The problem was acute in England as well. The broadening of gentry interests together with the threat of economic impoverishment involved them in heavy expenditure that led, among all ranks of privileged society, to a marked reduction in hospitality. An increasing number lost prestige in their native regions, especially in the north of England, because they had moved to London where they settled over long periods and sought advancement – the 'younger sort' it was said *c.* 1578, 'to see and show vanity and the elder to save the cost and charge of hospitality'.[85] It was a far cry from the ideals expounded by

Elyot by the turn of the seventeenth century when notions of honour and status were becoming subject to commercialisation, principally through the sale of titles under the Stuarts. It is, therefore, not surprising that the Crown sought to induce gentry to stay for longer periods at home to maintain their residences and lands, supervise their tenants, and govern the countryside.

The problem, though closely related to cultural affairs, was not exclusively a matter of dwindling patronage. Bardic sources, yearning for the dawn of a more auspicious age, refer to the 'bold and fearless ones' as representing all that was undesirable in community life, and it is difficult to identify such alleged 'oppressors' other than to generalise about unscrupulous administrators and the like. Doubtless, among them ranked some social climbers, usually the nouveaux riches determined at all costs to gain at the expense of others in commerce and trade and land acquisition. Lawyers and administrators, reaping a rich harvest from conditions of hardship, were also deplored. In some sources lawyers were subject to ridicule. In William Vaughan's opinion, they were 'two-legged asses' who impoverished their clients. The *Golden Fleece* (1626) provides a section deploring the multiplicity of lawsuits in the Wales of his day which caused hardship among impoverished tenants.[86] In 1618 James Howell, while encouraging his father to end a suit against an adversary (who happened to be a lawyer), gave him timely advice. Since his opponent 'is one of the shrewdest solicitors...being so habituated to lawsuits and wrangling' and the court of Westminster Hall far from his home, he was advised to withdraw from further involvement because 'law is a shrewd pick-purse and the lawyer...is like a Christmas box which is sure to get whosoever loses'.[87] Legal chicanery was viewed as a serious problem in relations between landlords and their tenants and cut deeper into men's purses.

The correspondence, estate records and legal activity of the gentry revealed their alacrity when dealing with property matters. This, in part, testified to a degree of increased wealth. In 1594 George Owen believed that this increased prosperity had raised incomes in Pembrokeshire and in Wales generally, in some instances, to £500 a year 'so that now there is no shire in Wales but is able to yield sufficient number of gentlemen that may dispend £100 a year good land.'[88] Despite heavy debts, the Salusburys of Lleweni were valued at around £1,500 on Sir John Salusbury's death in 1612.[89] Some were placed higher up the scale, such as Sir Richard Bulkeley III. According to the history of the family, his estate in Anglesey was valued at £2,500 a year, in Caernarfonshire £800 and in Cheshire £100, and he had 'always a great stock of ready money lying in his chest'.[90] The Mostyn and Gwydir families in the early seventeenth century were valued at £3,000 and, in other parts of Wales, some estates were valued at between £1,000 and £3,000 and others between £500 and £700.

The biting effects of inflation and the constant financial demands of the Stuarts placed increasing burdens and caused further hardship since the gentry were largely dependent on borrowed money and the greed of the usurer. 'If you will never pay your debts so long as you can find patches to purchase,' one London-based Welsh administrator warned his rash brother, 'I will never expect to see you free: for my own part I could wish you to regard your credit as much as your lands and leave that unquenchable thirst of purchasing more...until you be a clear board with all the world...when a man shall purchase money to purchase land withal it is little for his credit and less for his profit.'[91] Acquiring loans at heavy interest rates incurred heavy debts that affected other aspects of social and economic life generally within the family. Sir John Salusbury, even when his estate appeared to be financially at its strongest, in 1607 negotiated with Sir Thomas Myddelton for a loan of £1,000 to pay his debts.[92] The fortunes of the collateral family at Bachymbyd, however, flourished. John Salusbury had followed the earl of Essex in 1601, and since he had lived beyond his means was forced to sell part of his land. He mortgaged Bachymbyd to John Williams, a wealthy London goldsmith and native of Hafod Lwyfog near Beddgelert, for £3,000. His brother, William Salusbury ('Blue Stockings', as he was called), was a shrewd businessman. He inherited in 1611, reacquired the alienated lands, and added substantially to them.[93]

Efforts were made – some of them reasonably successful – to supplement income by exploiting mineral resources on estates and increasing commercial activities, particularly on the coastlands. The trade-routes from south, west and north Wales to Ireland and along the Bristol Channel were very active and the cattle and wool trades, the mainstay of the rural economy, flourished.[94] The dependence on the drovers for ready cash to defray expenses and maintain the household supplemented the fluctuating income largely accruing from fixed rents. The squeeze on landed gentry in periods of acute economic hardship and taxation demands restricted their movements and, in certain circumstances, led to further extortive practices. *Cymortha* (illegal exaction) had always caused some anxiety to the government and, despite legislation banning it in 1534, it was still widely practised in the early seventeenth century. Henry Herbert, second earl of Pembroke, in 1596 rebuked two of the north Wales deputy-lieutenants for not attending as diligently as they might to their duties, reminding them that since they 'have ever been forward in *comorthas* for your own private gains' they should be 'much more forward in this *cymortha* for the public good of the whole state'.[95] It was still considered to be normal practice to collect tributes on landed estates – not that all landed gentry were as unscrupulous as John Games of Aberbrân who, in a suit filed against him in Star Chamber, was reputed to have extorted money in the fairs and markets of Brecknockshire accompanied by armed retainers.[96] Nevertheless, the problem could and did seriously affect relations between landlord and tenant, and *cymortha*, although it was used on occasions as a fund-raising activity, was primarily a forced exaction.

Another practice that was on the increase was land enclosure, the acquisition of wastes and commons that deprived tenants of rights of pasturage. The most notable case was the on-going dispute, begun in 1564, between Roger Williams of Llangybi and his tenants over the manor of Tregrug in Monmouthshire, a contest conducted in the

Council in the Marches and the leet court of the manor until 1623 when his grandson, Sir Charles Williams, provoked his tenants into taking action to hinder his attempts to enclose lands with fencing for hunting purposes. There were many other factors that caused ill-will between landlords and tenants and between rival landlords.[97] Although its extent and effects should not be exaggerated, armed retaining continued to be a constant threat in the early seventeenth century. Past instincts died hard and irrepressible gentry often took matters into their own hands, relying on the retinue to enforce the lord's will. Courts of law at regional and county level, however, were active in keeping law and order and attempts were made, with a measure of success, to maintain order and stability (a theme discussed more fully in Chapter 3, pp. 111–27).

Trends and Transitions

All these economic tendencies created new conditions and new attitudes in Welsh society. In a broader more political context, significant shifts occurred that strengthened the concept of 'British' unity, a theme contained in some bardic acclamations but increasingly flaunted in correspondence and public declarations by gentry who desired to associate them-selves with their newly acquired citizenship. The traditional allegiance to the Tudors, based on ancestral and political grounds, eased the transference of loyalties to the Stuarts. The 'British' context was interpreted essentially in two interrelated ways. In the first instance the gentry regarded themselves as 'Cambrians' who, under the Tudor dispensation, had been granted equality of status and allowed to govern their own nation after a long gruelling period of oppression.[98] This view was demonstrated in the most overt fashion in the writings of George Owen and other contemporary commentators. It was that past legacy, clad in prophetic terms, that was memorable and appealed to them. The second strand to this 'British' theme embraced ancient traditions whereby the gentry claimed, by virtue of their descent from illustrious British or early Welsh forebears, the right to participate in government, and this claim became more potent after the union of the two Crowns of England and Scotland in 1603. This historic perspective of the British past was converted by contemporary antiquaries into reality in the arguments advanced for Welsh recognition in British politics in the early Stuart period. The political implications of this theme will be considered on another occasion, but its social aspects are significant in view of the Tudor interpretation of history. Natural leaders of Welsh society considered themselves worthy inheritors of and successors to the British *imperium* which revived the largely defunct vaticinatory tradition. The Shropshire poet Arthur Kelton in 'A Commendacion of Welshmen' (1546) realised the significance of the 'British' interpretation of history when recounting the benefits that the Welsh nation had obtained from Henry VII and Henry VIII.[99] Furthermore, Sir William Maurice's long and tedious speeches in the Commons encapsulated what was implied in such a tradition. More pointed and relevant, however, was the comment made by William Vaughan who was elated by the harmony established between the two nations, a typical response to the success of the Tudor settlement. 'I rejoice that the memorial of Offa's Ditch is estinguished with love and charity,' he maintained, 'that our green leeks, sometimes offensive to your dainty nostrils, are now tempered with your fragrant roses...God give us grace to dwell together without enmity, without detraction.'[100] His words echoed past sentiments, but essentially represent what was regarded as central in Welsh political thought at the time and crucial to the well-being of Welsh gentry.

The Tudor century created a new vitality among the Welsh gentry and laid the basis for active participation under the Stuarts. They were so closely bound to their roots that English writers in this period had no difficulty in identifying the aspiring Welshman who had settled in the border towns or who was making his way to London. Whatever his pretensions, he was still much regarded as one who could expertly rattle off his pedigree as Humphrey Llwyd remarked in *The Breuiary of*

Britayne (1573), when referring to the Welsh 'overmuch boasting of the nobility of their stock...somewhat high-minded and in extreme poverty acknowledging the nobility of their family.'[101] In the broader political context the gentry ethos was tied to the spirit of the age in all spheres of activity. They were concerned to safeguard privilege and fulfil obligation in line with their hierarchical concept of society. These features were cherished mostly among the gentry who remained at home and, despite economic disabilities, country squires displayed a buoyancy hardly surpassed by their equals elsewhere. The social structure of Wales by the eve of the Civil Wars continued to be dominated by concepts of hierarchy and patrilinealism despite the spread of egalitarian tendencies. In public and private affairs the political settlement had, by the accession of James I, become the cornerstone of activity among the gentry. It was the imposition of English property law that gave them further initiative to build on what had already been achieved by their forebears.[102] While partible inheritance survived, particularly in parts of the Duchy of Lancaster and isolated Welshries, in the Welsh shires the new order had been stabilised. Although tenants were largely subject to their landlords, they filed suits against the most unscrupulous and took the initiative, often at great expense, to prevent landowners from undermining their rights. Some landed gentry, particularly the most eligible among them, used their resources to pursue their interests as freely as economic conditions allowed, thus enabling them to enjoy a powerful dynastic hegemony in their regions.

Three major features assume prominence in any examination of the social features in this century:

(i) The Tudor settlement provided the structure of community life and was the foundation that gave the Welsh gentry the immense power that they exercised. It provided them with the authority that they claimed had sprung from inalienable birthright. They were granted *de jure* what their predecessors had exercised *de facto*. It gave the Welsh equality of status, created a new concept of British citizenship, and established a firm bond between the governing classes, the Crown and the

newly established Protestant state. A cohesiveness emerged in
that the national heritage was preserved under the aegis of the
Tudor state. National sovereignty was the basis of authority
which safeguarded the welfare of community life, a concrete
manifestation of the manner in which the gentry aspired to
acquire offices and positions and parade territorial aggran
disement. Their advancement should not be interpreted too
narrowly in terms of economic expansion by means of which
they endeavoured to achieve political power commensurate
with economic strength. It is also a fact that some families
were on the downturn. It appears that the increase in wealth
among the most prominent among them – again partly in view
of the lack of aristocratic (= peerage) domination in south-east
Wales – accounted for their ability to wield public authority.
The Tudor settlement had been primarily instrumental in
establishing that situation.

(ii) The power exerted by the gentry was normally revealed
in a provincial context and signified regional solidarity. The
concept of the county community had emerged and families
enjoyed precedence based on their entrenched position in the
soil. This implied that regions varied and were insular where
loyal loyalties persisted, establishing close bonds of affinity
between kinsmen. Added to this phenomenon was the
continuity – indeed conservatism – that characterised the
gentry, even among those who had experienced foreign travel
and instruction. Continuity was a more potent factor in
certain regions than in others, but Welsh gentry – in view of
their social distinctiveness – remained strongly patriotic and
were regarded as such beyond Offa's Dyke. They were
tenacious but, despite mobility and the threats to the
established order, they absorbed the nouveaux riches within
their ranks and the hallmarks of traditional Welsh nobility
survived. By the mid-seventeenth century an organic growth
as well as strong bonds of allegiance had emerged among the
landed order tied to hundred, commote and parish. It
was this in-built source of strength that enabled the
Stuarts to acquire so much support in the Principality in the
1640s.

(iii) The varied nature of gentry life symbolised the development of new concepts of order and gentility which were generally accepted among all families claiming a degree of superiority. Conservative though the majority of these families might be, in terms of local loyalties and family ties they were attracted by the most enriching features of privileged English society, its manners and attitudes. Although Renaissance influences were gradually felt in the mansions of the Welsh countryside the gentry themselves reached out even further to acquire a distinct code of conduct in educational establishments and by means of matrimonial connections or offices. It was an essential part of their vocation to acquire the social creed current at the time. To be recognized and accepted implied earning respect. 'This journey [to London],' as one ambitious squire remarked in 1612, 'has made me known to the great ones and, I hope, respected.'[103] Above all else, the Welsh gentry desired recognition for what they were in their native environment and for what they purported to be in a broader circle of acquaintances. Thus their virtues were extolled by contemporary poets who accorded to them standards revealing the curious blend of medieval and Renaissance ideals. Their attitudes reflected their eagerness to convert their gentility into a pattern of life acceptable to and in conformity with recognised conventions in polite society. Regardless of the gradual reorientation and changes in attitudes, leading to broader and more influential spheres of activity, it is undeniable that Welsh gentility, with all its attendant features, survived well into the seventeenth century.

2

THE TUDOR SETTLEMENT, 1534–43

In 1532 Thomas Cromwell, King Henry VIII's Chief Secretary, noted in his private memoranda that he intended to examine the political problems of Wales. At that time, political circumstances in England were in the process of changing rapidly when the Reformation Parliament curtailed papal power and eventually abolished it. The 1530s represented one of the most crucial periods in the history of England when Henry VIII, from a position of strength, aided by Cromwell's statesmanlike qualities and parliamentary support, established the national sovereign state. The Reformation Parliament was a key institution to enforce the king's will and to put into operation the plans designed to destroy the power of Rome in England. Thomas Wolsey died in 1530, having failed in his efforts to secure the annulment of the king's marriage to Catherine of Aragon, widow of his brother Arthur. Parliament was summoned in November 1529 with the intention, among other matters, of attacking the Church's abuses. It was not envisaged at the time that an irrevocable breach might occur between the Church of Rome and the Church in England. Indeed, Henry was a conservative monarch, and no revolutionary doctrinal declarations were issued. It was considered necessary to demonstrate to the papacy the king's strength to force it into submission on the matter of the annulment. In 1532, steps were taken to curb the curia's authority by prohibiting the payment of episcopal taxes to Rome and to restrict benefit of clergy and the power of the ecclesiastical courts. The climax came with the submission of the clergy to the Crown when Convocation appealed to Henry to approve canon law and decided not to legislate further without royal permission. In November of the same year the papacy prohibited Henry from leaving Catherine and taking Anne Boleyn, the daughter of Sir Thomas Boleyn, one of his ministers, as his wife. He had known her since 1526. In the following year, action was taken to annul the marriage with Catherine.[1]

The year 1533 was crucial. In January, Anne Boleyn became pregnant and married Henry secretly. Soon afterwards Thomas Cranmer, the newly installed Archbishop of Canterbury, declared that Pope Julius II's licence, granted in 1509 to allow Henry to marry Catherine, was not valid and that they had never been legitimately man and wife. In June, Anne Boleyn was crowned Queen in Westminster Abbey, and in September Elizabeth was born. The Pope refused to accept the situation but Henry, with Thomas Cromwell's assistance and, backed by his Parliament, proceeded to deal with the situation by threatening papal power in England. In the same year, the Act in Restraint of Appeals prohibited appeals to Rome, and in the preamble to that Act the king's new constitutional authority was defined. It was declared formally that England was a free sovereign state with the king as Supreme Head. There were no strong historical precedents to claim such rights, but it was Cromwell's intention to sever England as an independent state from Rome's authority. In that context England was declared to be an 'empire' free from all external political power.[2] During his travels abroad Cromwell had familiarised himself with such a concept in Roman law; he was also knowledgeable in the political theories of Marsiglio of Padua who defended the authority of the Holy Roman Empire when it was threatened by the papacy intent on assuming full jurisdiction within Christendom.

Henry VIII adopted the full lay authority – the *imperium* – purported to have been divinely granted to him. That creed was contained in the preamble to the Act of Appeals, the realm governed solely by the king. Beneath him, within their respective spheres in Church and state, religious and secular authorities exercised their jurisdiction, and in the following year the Act of Supremacy sanctioned the imposition of royal power on the Church: the king was granted *potestas jurisdictionis,* the right to govern the Church and exercise his legal authority within it. Thus was established the basis of national sovereignty claimed and possessed by Henry VIII and legalised in the House of Commons in 1533–4 by statute. This implied that the king had by then established his full jurisdiction in the realm through Parliament and had thus created a firm alliance between Crown and people.

Instability and Turbulence

The result of these momentous constitutional changes was the further decision to abolish surviving political franchises and lordships. No monarchy, fully possessed of its new-found strength, would tolerate the continuation of independent lordships in which medieval forms of government were practised. In order that these autonomous feudal franchises might be dissolved, Thomas Cromwell proceeded by Act of Parliament in 1536 to complete what Henry VII had begun by establishing strong links with the Welsh gentry.[3] In the preamble there is a specific reference to that intention, and the Act itself contained clauses that refer generally to England and Wales, especially with regard to criminal matters. It declared that the king was the only source of law in the state, and 'shall have the whole and sole Power and Authority, thereof united and knit to the Imperial Crown of this realm as of good Right and Equity'. This was a step in the direction that king and Parliament took in due course with regard to Wales and the Marches. The situation in the Principality and independent lordships in the west had caused the government growing concern years before 1536. The old Norman lordships were unstable and largely obsolete, and the administration of the

Principality was not as efficient as it might be. In the northern Principality based at Caernarfon, the Gruffudd family of Penrhyn – descendants of Ednyfed Fychan – were in the ascendant. Sir William Gruffudd II had occupied the office of chamberlain from 1483 to 1490, thereby establishing several influential family connections. The same was true of his son, Sir William Gruffudd III, the second chamberlain in the family, who served in that office between 1508 (except for a short period in 1509) and his death in 1531. Through marriage he was related to the Stradling family of St Donat's in Glamorgan and was also a kinsman of Sir Rhys ap Thomas of Dinefwr, knight of the garter, chamberlain of Cardiganshire and Carmarthenshire and constable and steward of the lordship of Brecknock. Sir William Gruffudd served in military campaigns in France in 1513 under Charles Brandon, duke of Suffolk, was present at the siege of Thérouanne, and in the same year was knighted in Tournai.[4] His contemporary in the southern Principality based at Carmarthen was Sir Rhys ap Gruffudd, a staunch Catholic, the representative of the powerful Dinefwr family and successor to the inheritance of his grandfather, Sir Rhys ap Thomas, who had helped Henry Tudor to seize the throne in 1485 and who virtually ruled south Wales until his death in 1525. Although Sir Rhys ap Gruffudd did not acquire the same political authority as his grandfather, particularly the offices of chamberlain and chief justice of South Wales, he wielded tremendous power and was highly respected with influential contacts in the seats of government outside Wales.[5]

Sir Rhys ap Gruffudd's wife was Catherine Howard, the daughter of the second duke of Norfolk who was probably responsible for intensifying the rivalry between her husband and Walter Devereux, Lord Ferrers, steward of Princess Mary's household and a prominent member of the Council in the Marches revived in 1525 and established at Ludlow. Devereux obtained the office of chief justice of South Wales and chamberlain of Cardiganshire and Carmarthenshire and, owing to his promotion, Sir Rhys ap Gruffudd could hardly conceal his jealousy. In June 1529 the first clash occurred between them regarding the maintenance of Sir Rhys's retinue at Carmarthen during the assizes, and he was imprisoned. He was freed on bail and, following an appearance in Star Chamber, the two men were ordered to come to peaceful terms. However, the spirited lord of Dinefwr, conscious of his lineage and rights, was dissatisfied with the situation that continued to threaten his position and, together with his uncle James ap Gruffudd, he was accused in the following year of treasonable activities, having allegedly plotted with James V of Scotland to depose Henry VIII. The evidence for Sir Rhys ap Gruffudd's involvement was slim, but he was found guilty and executed on 4 December 1531. It is not easy to understand why he was condemned to death. According to Eustace Chapuys, the imperial ambassador, it appears that he made an enemy of Anne Boleyn who became marquess of Pembroke in September 1532. In a critical period in the history of England it is considered that Sir Rhys ap Gruffudd, the most powerful among the gentry of his day in south-west Wales, said to have owned lands and a personal fortune amounting to about £2,000 a year, posed a serious threat to the survival of effective government in south-west Wales. According to Elis Gruffydd, soldier and historian of Calais, it was divine judgement on Sir Rhys ap Gruffudd for the illegal practices of his predecessors, especially his grandfather, that accounted for the final outcome of the proceedings against him. One thing was certain: the Crown could not tolerate a strong Catholic power entrenched in the far west near to unsettled Ireland at a time when final decisions were being taken to combat papal power in the realm.[6]

The execution of Edward Stafford, duke of Buckingham and lord of Newport, Brecknock, Hay, Huntingdon and Caus, ten years earlier was yet another example of a monarch eager to impose his authority and unwilling to tolerate a powerful and unscrupulous baron whose ancestral claims seriously threatened his throne. Buckingham was intent on reviving his family's authority and attempted to do so by oppressing his tenants and exacting heavy penalties, which was largely responsible for his downfall in 1521. In addition, he attempted to revive his claim to the English throne because he was descended, on his grandfather's side, from Anne, daughter of Thomas of Woodstock, fifth son of Edward III and, on his mother's side, from John Beaufort, son of John of Gaunt. His father had supported Richard III and his power increased tremendously through accumulation of property and offices during his short reign. Their friendship, however, did not last long because of Richard's delay in granting him more lands and offices, and he decided to plot against him and support Henry Tudor. His rebellion, however, failed and he paid the price on the scaffold.

Edward Stafford was a powerful figure in the south-eastern Marches and his execution removed one of the most threatening lords.[7] Henry VIII was sensitive to the dynastic situation in England and was aware of Buckingham's potential claim. Armed with loyal support among his tenants and retainers, the arrogant marcher lord posed a serious threat. He and Thomas Wolsey, the king's chancellor, were inveterate enemies, and in that context it is not surprising that Sir Rhys ap Gruffudd's power a decade later should have posed a similar threat to Henry. It was feared that the Spanish fleet, with Irish assistance, might land off the coasts of west Wales intent on deposing Henry and restoring papal power. That was not the first time that continental powers had threatened England via the western coasts – as shown by Henry Tudor's own experience – and it would not have been a difficult task to land forces in Anglesey, Pembrokeshire and the Llŷn peninsula.

It was evident, therefore, that the situation in Wales caused Henry VIII and Cromwell much concern in the early 1530s. Cromwell was a layman, a lawyer and ambitious royal minister. He was the son of a Putney blacksmith and had served in Wolsey's household. He was shrewd and cunning, and once he came to serve in the royal household he gained favour with the king himself. Indeed, his rise was very rapid: he travelled in Italy and served as a soldier in the French army and the Low Countries; he also became a moneylender and, in 1523, was elected Member of Parliament. Soon after Wolsey's death he was elevated further: for in 1530 he was appointed a member of the King's Council and, in the following year, became one of the king's closest advisers. In 1534 he was made the King's Chief Secretary. Cromwell was anti-clerical, and in 1535 was promoted to the office of vicar-general with powers to exercise the king's powers in religious affairs. He became influential and contributed significantly to the constitutional development of the realm in the 1530s. Because of his shrewd understanding of the political situation, it was not surprising that he paid increasing attention to Wales in 1533. His political beliefs convinced him that the problem of Wales was serious enough to merit parliamentary legislation in 1534, two years before the final step was taken to assimilate the country with England. Attempts had been made before 1536 to resolve the problem in Wales and the Marches. When a strong monarch ruled, it appeared that the marcher lordships might become directly subject to the Crown.

Although the Crown did not fully realize its potential in those areas it became royal policy to exert its prerogative power in the Marches. By the close of the fifteenth century Henry VII possessed most of the lordships, but the power of the duke of Buckingham and the earl of Worcester prevented him from fully extending his authority. The Worcester family was particularly strong because, as a result of his marriage to Elizabeth, daughter of William Herbert, second earl of Pembroke, Charles Somerset obtained the lordships of Gower, Kilvey, Crickhowell and Tretŵr, Chepstow and Raglan among others. The Crown was aware of the lack of good government in the Marches generally and of the need to reform the multiple jurisdictions that existed there. In 1528 and 1535, by means of ordinances, it was decided to reform financial administration in the lordship of Brecknock. Royal officials from then on were to appoint deputies there if Worcester did not supervise his own officers and ensure that they conducted their affairs justly.[8]

Welsh matters were considered in the King's Council in December 1533, one item on the Council's agenda being 'reforming the administration of Wales to maintain peace and justice'. As far as is known, no more was done at the time to follow Edward IV's policy for he, in 1473, had held a conference with marcher lords at Shrewsbury when agreement was reached on matters regarding the reform of government; however, no final decisions were reached. Sometime in 1533 or 1534 a detailed survey was compiled of the main weaknesses in Wales that hindered peace and good order, and references were made in it to corrupt juries, livery and maintenance, the collection of *cymortha* and cattle-stealing. It was written by Thomas Holte, the king's attorney, and some specific proposals were made – namely, that offenders were not to be fined for committing murder but, if that were the case, then the fine would go to the king. It was proposed that primogeniture should be practised and partible inheritance (*cyfran*) abolished, that Wales should be divided into shires, justices installed in office, and English law universally imposed.[9] It is clear that Cromwell, who approved these proposals, was eager to introduce concrete reforms designed to abolish the political and administrative order that was in decay. He considered a measure to provide justices in Welsh shires and, in line with Henry IV's penal legislation (1401–2), conceived a policy that would have prevented Welshmen from holding office in Wales. He did not proceed further along those lines, however, since he feared that such a policy might fail to achieve anything positive. 'The condition of Wales', among other matters, was in Cromwell's mind early in 1534 and, in the same year, he noted that there was need to reform officialdom and the general state of disorder in Wales, and that gentry freeholders and yeomen should be appointed to arrest papists.

The redemption of Great Sessions in eyre in the Marches, which had become common practice in the most powerful lordships in the fifteenth century, brought short-term financial benefits to the lord and the tenants. However, it did cause resentment in communities which contributed to the redemption fine and were anxious to see law and order established. Henry VII had taken steps to see that marcher lords placed their men under bonds to guarantee good conduct. Forced agreements to redeem sessions could cause disruption, as was the case among the Buckingham tenants in the lordship of

Hay in 1518. Matters were not resolved, although the Crown attempted to stabilise the situation dominated by aristocratic influence in the southern and eastern Marches. Offices were farmed leading to corruption, embezzlement, extortion and a general misuse of power – as occurred allegedly in the case of Sir Richard Herbert of Montgomery, the earl of Worcester's deputy. Financial administration was also inefficient as the ordinances issued in 1528 and 1535 reveal regarding the lordship of Brecknock. The general malaise in the marcher lordships – whether in royal or seignorial possession – accentuated the king's urgent need to restore order and establish his authority on a permanent basis.[10]

In 1531 proposals were put forward by Dr James Denton – who at the time was chancellor to the Council in the Marches – for the conversion of the lordships into shires. However, the king, although agreeable to the plan, did not act upon it.[11] Shortly after Henry Somerset, earl of Worcester, John Salusbury, steward of the lordship of Denbigh, and John Salter were concerned with the damaging effects of perjury and other illegal activities.[12] Thomas Phillips, in May 1532, complained in a petition to Cromwell of the poor condition of law and order in Wales,[13] and he was not the only one to voice an opinion on the matter at that time. John Parker denounced *cymortha*,[14] and on 3 June 1534 a report was prepared by the government emphasizing three examples of the misuse of law in Wales – namely, irresponsible juries, *arddel* and *cymortha*. These abuses were not new features in the Principality and the Marches. Juries had frequently been intimidated in order that verdicts favourable to serious offenders might be returned to save them from the full penalties of the law; by misusing *arddel*, private armies were formed in the Marches to assist lords in maintaining their power, and illegal taxation was collected through the abuse of the old and once laudable custom of *cymortha*. It is probable that this incisive document had spurred the government on in 1534–5 to propose firm legislation to redress the chronic situation in Wales. Cromwell was eager to strengthen royal power through the Council in the Marches and, in April 1533, noted the need to 'establish a council in the marches of Wales'.[15] At the time the lord president was John Veysey, bishop of Exeter, but his leadership was weak and left much to be desired.

The creation of the Council in the Marches in 1471 was one example of the manner in which Edward IV tackled the tense political situation, in a period of civil war between the rival houses of York and Lancaster. It was established primarily to administer the court and possessions of the Prince of Wales, but grew in its influence and obtained royal commissions early on to deal with legal and military matters in Wales and the Marches. It appears that the Council caused some misgivings among the lords because it was a royal instrument operating within their territories, threatening their sovereign rights. The Council could not exercise its powers as extensively as it desired because it relied on prerogative authority only and not on the power of statute. Its early history was intermittent and the evidence for its activities scanty before 1525, when it was revived by Thomas Wolsey at the same time as the duke of Richmond's Council at York. It may have been restored as a response to Henry VIII's attempt to intrude his friend Charles Brandon into north-east Wales; what is certain, though, is that it formed part of a plan to employ a conciliar system to strengthen government in unstable regions. Although it administered Princess Mary's lands, its authority had grown. From c. 1489–90 onwards, and especially in 1501, Henry VII had provided it with greater powers, and it was used as a prerogative Council to reinforce royal power in the Marches with the authority to enforce lords to maintain government and good order in their lordships. The Council was re-established by him as a body to control aggressive gentry who pursued their ambitions, even in opposition to royal officials and marcher lords. One of these was Edward Stafford, duke of Buckingham, and in 1504 Henry VII reached an agreement with him that obliged him to operate the law more harshly and to hand over criminals to the shire authorities or lordship officials where they had perpetrated their crimes.[16] Thereby, Henry attempted to get to grips with the situation in the

Marches; but, as a conservative king, medieval in mind and spirit, he failed to grasp the essential problem – namely, the very existence of the Marches and the need to eliminate them with the aim of creating a unified realm. Henry was determined to maintain the political order as it existed and that was the situation in 1536 when the axe finally fell on the lordships as independent units. In 1534–5 Rowland Lee, exercising his authority under the old order, attempted to seek legislation to supplement his punitive measures, and concentrated on the issues most adverse to the cause of peace, order and efficient government.

The Council, in Lee's period, possessed governmental power in Wales and the Marches. Instead of dealing only with the private affairs of the Prince of Wales in those regions, its authority had been extended through commissions of *oyer* and *terminer* (to hear and determine) as well as another commission which empowered the Council to administer law and order in private matters. Armed with this authority, members of the commission travelled the Marches and English border counties and attended courts of Quarter Sessions, and they were also granted power, by means of formal agreement, to bind marcher lords to administer law effectively. Paucity of evidence, however, precludes a detailed examination of some specific problems that beleaguered the government regarding the Marches at that time. Also, since Veysey was unable to attend to his responsibilities as effectively as the government may have desired, it did not appear that the marcher problems were given the attention that they required at the time. Thomas Phillips complained in his petition that no effort had been made to reduce cattle-stealing or punish corrupt officials in the Marches. His criticism was echoed by Sir Edward Croft of Croft Castle in Herefordshire. The condition of Oswestry and Powys, in his opinion, was very serious. In a letter to Cromwell and Sir William Paulet, comptroller of the royal household, he referred to Veysey's absenteeism and the fact that only four officials were present at Ludlow to deal with matters relating to law and order.[17] In his opinion Wales was badly governed and criminal offenders were not being punished with sufficient severity. He attributed that to the fact that lord presidents of the Council, since its origin, had invariably been bishops who, by virtue of their status and office, could not impose the death penalty. If a more energetic lord president was not appointed, he declared, then it would be impossible to restore law and order to Wales. Similar strictures were made by Thomas Croft, son of Sir Edward Croft, some months later. He complained that a hundred people had been killed in the Marches since Veysey came to office and that no one had been punished for those crimes.[18] On that basis he believed that the Marches constituted the most unruly area within the realm. It is hardly surprising, therefore, that Cromwell assiduously set about dealing with the problem.

Rowland Lee: Repression and Legislation

In the 1530s the Council in the Marches became more prominent as a key institution in Cromwell's plans for Wales. It does not appear that absorbing Wales into England was part of those plans in 1534 when a new lord president was appointed to replace Veysey. He was the redoubtable Rowland Lee, who came to office in March of that year. He was a native of Morpeth, Northumberland, and had been educated at Cambridge where he graduated in law. After ordination he was appointed prebendary of the collegiate church of Norton by William Smyth, bishop of Lincoln, and he received other livings. Cromwell's son Gregory was placed in his custody, and Lee became royal chaplain and a master of chancery. From 1531 to 1534 he was consistently in royal service: he was involved in the legal affairs surrounding the annulment of Henry VIII's marriage to Catherine of Aragon and secured the formal allegiance of the archbishopric of York to the king's newly established power. He was one of those appointed to administer the oath of allegiance to Anne Boleyn and to terminate the convocation of York by declaring that the Pope no longer had any legal authority in England. He acquired the temporal possessions of the diocese of Coventry and Lichfield in 1533 and was elevated to the see in January the following year. Lee and two others were the first bishops to take the oath acknowledging the king as the supreme power over the Church. He was not the only bishop of Coventry and Lichfield to become lord president of the Council in the Marches because Geoffrey Blythe had assumed the office in 1512, and William Smyth before him in 1493. Rowland Lee came naturally into the episcopal succession by virtue of office because each of his predecessors had been bishops in English dioceses. The first to be appointed was John Alcock, bishop of Rochester in 1473, and Lee was fifth in succession and certainly the most remarkable among them. He had been ordained a priest by William Smyth and, together with Cromwell and others, he functioned as Wolsey's deputy in the dissolution of religious houses. He was extremely loyal to Wolsey and served the Crown after his fall, especially in matters regarding the king's marriage. There is a striking similarity between the public services of Cromwell and Lee, with one obtaining the most influential position in the realm and the other the most powerful office in Wales and the border counties. Both of them had similar motives and intentions: they had discussed state matters, had kept a vigilant eye on their own preferments, and had agreed on fundamental political principles. Sir Edward Croft opposed the appointment of bishops as lord presidents because of the constraints placed on their powers in secular affairs, and believed that there was need for a strong administrator who could wield the 'sword of justice' to achieve his aims. It is therefore surprising that Lee was appointed to his position in the Marches. On the other hand, Cromwell knew him well and was fully aware of his energy and unyielding determination to effect governmental policies, and consequently he was granted official dispensation to impose the death penalty. John Vaughan, Thomas Cromwell's servant, knew him well, and in November 1537 warned his master what type of man he had appointed to that bishopric. 'You have recently,' he said, 'helped a worldly creature, a mole and enemy of all godly learning to the office of his damnation –

papist, idolator and fleshly priest – a bishop of Chester [Coventry and Lichfield].' By that time, however, he had certainly made his mark as an unscrupulous governor in the Marches.[19]

Lee had very few members of the Council to aid him with his enormous task, and although he seemed loath to complain about that in his early days at Ludlow he did inform Cromwell in 1535 that he alone administered the law in the Marches. In view of Cromwell's continued anxiety about the condition of Wales, it is surprising that he did not apply the remedy immediately. However, the King's Chief Secretary knew full well that Lee possessed the extraordinary skills to deal with the situation in the Marches, and he allowed him to carry out his duties since there was uncertainty as to what the Council's fate would be. According to Elis Gruffydd, the Welsh soldier serving in Calais, Lee accomplished remarkable feats such as hanging 5,000 malefactors in six years, some of them royal officials. His testimony was doubtless exaggerated, but Gruffydd was correct in his statement that illegal sanctuaries of thieves and murderers in the Marches were causes of grave concern, as also was the decision to destroy by legislation all independent franchises in the realm.[20]

Like his predecessor, Rowland Lee was a worldly character and, like Cromwell, a lawyer who had been in Wolsey's service. In office he travelled extensively and tirelessly in the Marches and border counties, and exhaustively set about reducing his area of jurisdiction to a state of order. The liveliest and most authentic description of him appears in Sir William Gerard's second *Discourse on Government in Wales* in 1576 where he is described as being 'stout of nature, ready witted, rough in speech, not affable to any of the Welshry' and a relentless oppressor of hardened criminals. This famous view of him was written by a public figure, justice of the Brecknock circuit of great sessions and deputy lord president of the Council in the Marches, who was educated at Gray's Inn in the year of Lee's death and who doubtless knew of him.[21]

When Cromwell appointed Lee he considered that he had found the right man to accomplish the task at hand at a time when he himself was still garnering information and gradually forming a constructive policy for Wales. It is certain that Cromwell was aware of the need for a stronger presence in the Marches so that criminals might be punished more severely to combat the increase in offences committed in that region, and that more efficient government might, in due course, strengthen royal control in the area. He desired to see established in the Marches a Council that would force lethargic and oppressive officials to fear the consequences of their misdoings.

The activities of the Council in the Marches before 1534 seemed not to have increased royal power substantially in the Marches. Although it had originally been intended as a prerogative institution of government, it had gradually developed to become more intrusive in matters regarding the state; and by the time Lee came to office it had been reasonably well-established, although little has survived concerning its conduct of affairs. In the last resort it was the force of Lee's own personality and the assistance that he received from Cromwell and his fellow-counsellors that was chiefly responsible for the Council's belligerent policy during the two key years before the assimilation of Wales to England. One of these counsellors was Sir Thomas Englefield, judge of Common Pleas and, according to Sir William Gerard, a man 'for learning and discreet modest behaviour comparable with any in the realm'. Lee thought highly of him, and both served – albeit in different ways – to further the interests of the state and to establish law and order. Another person for whom Lee had a high regard because of his support in the Marches was Sir Richard Herbert of Montgomery, a powerful squire, and Lee, in his tribute to him on his death in 1539, regarded him as 'the best I know of that name'. 'I miss him so much,' he continued further, 'as if I would have lost one of my arms, governing these regions in Powys, Ceri, Cydewain and the land of Clun.'[22]

Rowland Lee realised that it was not possible to achieve his aim in the Marches simply by punishing criminals and considered that legislation was needed to consolidate what he had already accomplished. He was aware that castles had to be renovated and rebuilt in the borderlands to keep prisoners and as stations where his agents might be posted or given hospitality on their travels, and he corresponded with Cromwell on that matter. In December 1534 he wrote earnestly to him referring to the need to repair Radnor Castle. 'Eight thieves have escaped from it this year,' he explained, and he despondently added: 'What is the purpose of catching thieves without a place to keep them?'[23] He was also firm in his view that he and his colleagues were accomplishing what they could 'to administer justice'. He travelled often and, from Worcester in July 1535, he reported to Cromwell that he had moved at that time to Gloucester and had intended to visit Bewdley and Shrewsbury.[24] He could then be closer to Wales because, as he explained, 'although they have been reformed well that time without causing fear in them they will certainly return to their unhappy behaviour'. He placed much emphasis on creating fear and suspicion of one another among the people: he acted quickly and mercilessly, and all his letters to Cromwell declare how confident he was, if he received continual support, that he could reduce the Marches to order. Much, however, depended on Cromwell's support. 'Your comforting letters,' he maintained on one occasion after a bout of ill health, 'has made me strong and healthy and able to return to serve the king.'[25] He devoted himself entirely to his task: 'I am a stranger at home,' he wrote from Ludlow in April 1536, 'because of my business here.' He also added: 'in these regions there is found very good control'.[26] He accomplished his tasks by means of a variety of methods, not least by employing spies to discover offenders and pardoning those who assisted in betraying others. 'It is better to liberate one who can say the truth,' he said, 'and punish six or more.'[27] He described the success of his oppressive policy and was delighted with the increasing numbers of offenders who had submitted to his authority. He referred on one occasion to the large numbers of outlaws who had surrendered voluntarily, even without a guarantee of safe-conduct. Although he probably exaggerated the situation, there is no doubt that his crude policy was bearing fruit. In his opinion the higher a convicted criminal ranked in society the more necessary it was to hang him. 'Because the said Lloyd [i.e. Richard Lloyd of Welshpool, a notorious cattle-stealer] is a gentleman and a thief and a receiver of thieves,' he explained in January 1536, 'to hang one of that kind would cause forty to fear for their lives.'[28] In an official survey of government in Ireland in a period of uprising in 1601–3 and of the effects of military occupation among tribal chieftains, a reference was made to this ruthless method adopted by Lee to overcome the problems in Wales. So terrified had malefactors become, it was reported, that Wales was pacified under his rule in no time. The commentator drew attention to the significance of Lee's policy in public legal affairs in the Marches – namely, his shrewd ability to deal with practical problems in the most effective way. That sums up his contribution – no more, no less.[29]

Lee knew the nature of Welsh society well because, within a short time, he had learnt how potent a factor blood relations were in Wales. A kindred society that allowed a corrupt jury system to operate, together with poor economic conditions, created almost insuperable problems for law officers in the Principality and the Marches. He made constant references to the deficiencies in the social order although he made very little effort to reform the situation. He found no effective way of coming to terms with conditions in the Marches other than to punish criminals harshly. Little evidence survives to reveal that he intervened in Principality affairs, and the main reason for that was that the Council in the Marches had centred its activity and authority in the borderlands and also because the administrative machinery of the Principality, albeit not completely efficient, was at least operating within a well-established pattern.

One of the main problems confronted by Rowland Lee in the Marches was the obsolete methods used to acquire and inherit property as well as the legal customs in the Marches. Henry VII attempted to create conditions that would ensure that the structure was being operated consistently throughout

the lordships, but it did not seem that such a policy succeeded. Lee himself, regardless of his energy and drive, did
not create more favourable conditions that might break new
ground in the manner in which law was administered. From
that standpoint he found himself completely fettered. His only
course of action was to destroy with his own power what he
considered to be the main causes of lawlessness, and his vision
was narrow. He took delight in his success in punishing
criminals, and in his letters to Cromwell he would at times give
a graphic description of exploits – some of them on the eve
of the assimilation of Wales with England. 'Although the
thieves...have hanged me in their imaginations,' he retorted,
'I am confident that I shall be equal to them soon in all acts.'[30]
He considered that he had 'civilised' Wales and caused 'the
white sheep to care for the black ones'. He also endeavoured
to protect the constitutional rights of the Crown, and firmly
declared his opposition to 'the oppressive authority of the
bishop of Rome' to the extent that he was prepared to preach
in his diocese despite the fact, on his own admission, he had
never been in a pulpit.[31] So eager was he that he intervened in
the long-standing rivalry between the Cholmondeley and
Mainwaring families in Cheshire (which stood at that time
within his jurisdiction), and he assured himself that there were
in that county more murders committed than in Wales in the
years 1534–6. He also established his authority in the border
shires and proceeded to repair castles and suppress uprisings
as much as he could in Shropshire, Herefordshire, Worcester-
shire and Gloucestershire. He undertook the task of pacifying
those communities in as diligent a manner as he did in Wales.
In July 1535, John Bedow and two others from Hereford were
punished publicly for misusing royal letters. Thus Lee set out
to suppress criminals and establish the Council's authority as
an instrument of the king's power in areas where royal
institutions were operating.[32]

In this connection the significance of Rowland Lee's career
as lord president of the Council in the Marches needs to be
clarified. He functioned as a reliable royal servant and was
conservative in his nature and outlook, and wholly dependent

on the support of his master Cromwell. He represented the government's view of central affairs regarding the safety of the realm and rose to prominence by virtue of his loyal service to the Crown. In addition, he used conventional methods of controlling the situation in Wales and the Marches. He used his Council to enable him to function in the most practical manner possible, and he discharged his duties in a severe and informal way. 'What shall we state further,' he stated in 1536 when referring to one of his hanging sessions at Ludlow, 'all the thieves in Wales quake for fear.'[33] Although he operated more harshly than his predecessors, he is not to be regarded as a shrewd observer of current political trends. He was effective only in so far as he operated within the narrow constraints of his vision. He was unable to deal with purely constitutional affairs because such matters were, it seems, beyond his capabilities. His activities can be interpreted as being the simplest way of destroying lawlessness. He refused any assistance from Wales except when he welcomed criminals as spies and informers to betray others of their own kind. He failed to grapple with the fundamental problem in the Marches and, to that extent, he misinterpreted the situation there.

The tribute paid to Rowland Lee by Sir William Gerard in 1576 revealed his approval of Lee's strong administration and aim to ensure that Welsh loyalties to the Crown were maintained. Similar was the testimony offered by Dr David Lewis in his critical survey of the legal condition of Wales at about the same time. In his opinion Rowland Lee was a worthy example of an official who used his power and authority in order that he might execute his tasks efficiently. 'Joseph is recommended as a wise and prudent governor,' he explained, 'because he governed the Egyptians harshly and in my country it has been attempted to administer the medicine in the time of Bishop Rowland and Mr Englefield and since the short time when Sir Hugh Powlet [a Gloucestershire lawyer] was there, and by seeing that experience is proven to be the best mistress, in my opinion, she should be followed.'[34] Despite Lee's emphasis on direct intervention, he realised that legislation was necessary to consolidate his efforts in the Marches.

The preamble to the third of five statutes passed in 1534–5, in a rather prolix manner attempted to justify the legislation and referred to three different aspects of the condition of government in Wales and the Marches at that time. First, it is acknowledged that various legal customs that existed in Wales and the Marches had been abused and were not considered effective enough. Secondly, so serious were the weaknesses of the government and officials employed to administer it, that it was no longer possible to keep the peace without introducing a new corpus of legislation to transform the situation. Thirdly, it was evident that grave disorder was continually harmful to the state's stability.[35]

The chief weakness in the administrative framework in Wales was the division between Principality and the Marches. By the early decades of the sixteenth century the Marches had more than four centuries of history behind them, their customs extending back to the Norman invasions. The Principality was established in 1284 by Edward I, although its origins are found in the days of the princes of Gwynedd who introduced legal reforms and innovations with a view to creating a native feudal Principality in the thirteenth century. In 1267, when Llywelyn ap Gruffudd acquired the title Prince of Wales, his new constitutional status laid the cornerstone of the Principality.[36] The marcher lordships possessed privileges inherited after the old Welsh kingdoms were conquered. They were essentially royal prerogatives, and the most damaging was the right to despoil and levy war. Gradually the 'custom of the march' emerged, a body of diverse legal practices from early Norman times, when the Crown allowed military commanders to conquer Welsh lands and to possess them. Although the king maintained his power as feudal overlord, receiving homage and fealty, he did not usually interfere in the internal affairs of lordships except in special circumstances – for example, in matters involving forfeiture, when a lord rebelled, or escheat, when there were no inheritors. Regardless of feudal overlordship it appears that successive kings did not choose, for various reasons, to involve themselves in the private affairs of the lordships, and the result was the growing supposition that it had abandoned the right or authority to exercise its power in this way. That was the basis of the insertion often found in legal documents relating to the Marches – '*Brevis domini regis non currit in Wallia*' ('The Lord King's writ does not run in Wales' [i.e. the Marches]). That assertion was based on the independence and privileges claimed and enjoyed by marcher lords within their jurisdictional franchises but, when circumstances allowed, attempts were made to reinforce royal prerogative power. There are examples of some powerful kings, such as Edward I and Edward IV, acting from positions of strength, attempting to intrude more effectively in marcher affairs. There is no doubt, however, that the Marches were a thorn in the side of successive English monarchs although an increasing number of lordships, for various reasons, had become royal possessions by the end of the fifteenth century.

Some significant questions arise concerning this legislation. Could the full power of English law be operated in the Marches before the lordships formed a constitutional part of the realm? It appears that the Crown exercised its legislative powers in this instance on the basis of prerogative power, using its position as feudal overlord regardless of the 'custom of the March'.[37] Moreover, to what extent were the Marches a source of complete lawlessness? Judging by Rowland Lee's evidence they were areas about to become law-abiding. To what extent were the Welsh Marches more unstable than other parts of the realm such as the northern parts of England? A comparative study is needed of these two border areas before a judgement can be reached as to the extent of the lawlessness that existed in Wales on Lee's appointment. One thing is certain – that circumstances in those border areas made it easier for lawlessness to prevail and for protection to be granted to malefactors. Maladministration and lack of uniformity were intensified by the relative ease with which criminals could move from English shires and the Principality into the Marches and between lordships in that terrain.

What was the situation in the Principality? How effective was the legal machinery there? Its authority was based on the

Statute of Wales (1284) and English criminal law was practised alongside a mixture of English and Welsh civil law. Despite the tensions between the Welsh and the English communities that had settled in the Principality, its structure survived racial animosities, and the bad effects of social and economic disintegration in the later Middle Ages as well as the Glyndŵr Rebellion; although administrative control declined during a period of civil war, the Principality continued as a self-contained and functioning unit of government. Regardless of Sir John Wynn's harsh verdict in the *History of the Gwydir Family* on the condition of law and order in parts of north Wales, it appears that government was in some semblance of working order. Wynn's interpretation of circumstances was not exactly correct. As a privileged squire who had gained much from Tudor government in the latter years of the century, it is hardly surprising that he deplored a political order that caused so much unease. However, he did concede that the administrative institutions of the Principality were efficiently controlled and that there were signs of economic advancement. He commented on the prosperity and civility of the three major castellated boroughs – namely, Caernarfon, Conwy and Beaumaris – 'whereby civility and learning flourished in that town [i.e. Caernarfon]: so as they were called the lawyers of Caernarfon, the merchants of Beaumaris and the gentlemen of Conwy'.[38] Wynn's commentary described conflicting interests in mid-fifteenth-century north Wales which revealed a declining kindred system besieged by new social and cultural forces.

In fifteenth-century Wales significant economic developments occurred that heralded the emergence of a new society. The Glyndŵr Rebellion did not affect all parts of Wales to the same degree, and in the southernmost parts commercial life continued to flourish. The impact of the revolt on the towns of Wales varied, the most serious damage being caused to those in the north and west. Nevertheless, the castellated boroughs continued to develop their economic resources. Furthermore, a sharp-eyed and spirited group of gentry, some of them associated with the towns, rose in the social order and thrived by the acquisition of land and office (see Chapter 1, pp. 9–21). Among these up-and-coming families, Rowland Lee, on his own admission, found many of the most persistent offenders in Wales and the Marches. They used whatever means possible to further their interests, and one notable example on the eve of the Tudor settlement was Philip Herbert, steward of the lordship of Magor in Monmouthshire. According to Lee's evidence he employed many liveried retainers on his lands to his own profit, and was another example of the ruthless marcher lord with strong local connections, intending to create an 'independent' domain for himself.[39]

From this historical reality emerged the unstable features of political life in Wales in the early 1530s. The broad division between the Principality and the Marches was but one factor. There existed also divisions, based on race and privilege, between the prosperous boroughs and impoverished rural communities and between native inhabitants and the *advenae*. In both sectors in the Principality special features appeared that caused constant tension between the Welsh and the English. However, although cultural division continued to cause much unease, as reflected in bardic evidence, social integration was far advanced when Henry VII came to the throne.

It was the intricate legal system in the Marches that caused problems, and it is in this context that the significance of the legislation of 1534–5 should be interpreted. Most of the statutes – six in all – applied to the Principality and the Marches. References are made to 'Wales and the Marches'; however, on reading the content, it is clear that Lee and the government were most concerned about the troublesome borderlands. The statutes were aimed principally at alleviating the situation in lordships that had a mixture of legal and administrative customs. It was the legal entity that gave these regions their unique standing. In the Marches the lord and his *jura regalia* were unified within the territorial *dominium*. The connection was inseparable. There was no land without its lord and that lord functioned according to the legal customs he had acquired or inherited. Consequently, Rowland Lee proceeded to destroy that power by applying the Crown's prerogative powers and adapting them in an attempt to solve the complex situation.

Legislative Measures

In the 1534–5 statutes the preambles declared the general intent and the reason for the legislation. They emphasised the need to protect the lord's subjects inside and outside courts of law, thus signifying the essential features of good lordship. In Cromwell's mind the only secure way of accomplishing this was by installing royal power in the Marches, albeit on a prerogative basis. While Lee performed on stage, Cromwell waited in the wings for the opportunity to present his constructive and ambitious programme of reform shortly after the Crown had been declared Supreme Head. Although Henry VIII's new position in Church and state did not empower Cromwell to act politically in the Marches, it gave him the added incentive to attempt a final solution to the problem.

The series of statutes represents the climax of the Crown's attempts to extend its natural royal powers into the Marches and to consolidate the authority recently achieved in Church and state. In 1534 legislation enforced the practice of equity law in the courts. The first statute – which reveals that motive clearly – is aimed at improving the quality of the jury system by punishing acts of perjury, an old problem that was particularly prevalent in a kindred society.[40] Offenders transgressed 'equity and justice', the basic principles of common law. Perjury destroyed good administration of the law. 'This is an immoral offence which is common in Wales,' Lee declared when referring to the acquittal of criminals for murder in 1536, 'and it needs to be reformed...and therefore, through maintaining and secret action, the parties were found not guilty...My Lord, if this is not reformed farewell to all good control.'[41] In the preamble, 'followers, friends and kindred' are to be punished as well for their illegal activities. An officer was to be appointed to prevent corruption of juries, but if a juror did commit perjury he was to be summoned before the Council in the Marches or the judge of the court that had wrongly acquitted a felon. The statute displays the spirit of the legislation at this time, the prime motive being to strengthen loyalties to the state that the Crown endeavoured to accomplish by exercising its prerogative powers in the Marches. The basis for that was establishing law and order. Law was not regarded merely as preventative or punitive, but also as a means of defending and maintaining a peaceable community – hence the emphasis on the establishment of a common legal system. Success in government entailed reassuring the people of the defensive powers of the law. Legal processes should not be tampered with since they constituted an offence against the state. This is the principle expounded in this statute and, in order that common law might be strengthened, equity law was exercised. Common law cannot be changed but can be supplemented.

Corrupt juries were considered an evil, and common law was insufficient to deal with the problem in the Marches. It was no easy task to impose any external power in these areas, and in this matter the dual nature of society created animosities that exacerbated the situation. The government was expected to protect the law, but the Crown first had to claim its prerogatives in the Marches before it attempted to exercise them. This statute and the authority given to the Council in the Marches served to further this aim.

The same motive is found in the second statute, which placed responsibilities on ferrykeepers on the River Severn to prevent felons in Somerset and Gloucestershire from escaping to south Wales and the Forest of Dean to avoid due processes of law. That usually occurred at night, and in the Marches these felons enjoyed 'diverse privileges' in the lordships.[42] The practice of maintenance made it difficult to track them down and bring them to justice. Illegal trading in cattle made the various ferries, particularly Aust and Portishead, popular venues for exporting stolen animals into the Marches and from there into adjacent English counties. The lack of a uniform legal system again largely accounted for this offence, and the clash of jurisdictions complicated the situation. To rectify the anomaly it was decided that justices of the peace in Gloucestershire and Somerset were authorised to summon ferrykeepers before them to bind them by law not to convey illegal people and goods across the river to Wales. That was another attempt to extend royal power since responsibility was placed on ferrykeepers and justices to ensure respect for the law. English legal officers were now employed to safeguard the interest of the king's subjects in these unstable border areas.

The next statute also dealt, but at greater length, with similar problems, and steps were again taken to ensure that the agencies of government in English shires enquired into the prevalence of illegal practices and, in many cases, to punish felons for performing criminal acts in the Marches.[43] The preamble relates at length the nature of the disorder prevalent in Wales and the Marches. Courts of law were to be respected and kept in an orderly fashion, and compensation was to be paid to individuals subjected to unlawful exactions – principally in the Marches. It was no easy task to control marcher officials of gentle stock accustomed to exerting their power without restraint. The Crown interfered in the relationship between lord and subject, and steps were taken to prevent the carrying of arms within 2 miles of a town, church, fair or other public places. The Crown was prepared to go to any lengths to minimise the possibility of disturbances, even to the point of placing restrictions on the use of arms which, in days when there was no standing army and when so much depended on local militias, might jeopardise defence preparations.

In addition, some abuses – such as *cymortha* and *arddel* – were abolished by law in the Principality and Marches. Both customs in the past had been perfectly laudable and practised chiefly in rural areas. There were various meanings to the practice of *cymortha*, but it was normally considered to be aid or assistance given to neighbours or kindred who had fallen on bad times.[44] In that respect it constituted a charitable act in a close-knit community. By the fifteenth century, however, it had become an exaction demanded by the lord of his tenants to meet his 'expenses'. It was yet another method adopted by unscrupulous lords and their deputies to maintain their income by oppressing others. Similarly, with *arddel*, another laudable custom whereby in the early Middle Ages a lord would be legally bound to supervise the movements of his subjects. The situation in this context, however, was essentially different in that notorious criminals could be hired by lords to serve in their private retinues by the payment of an advowry fine. Consequently, *arddel* payments could be made in different lordships, and by moving from one lordship to another felons could deny being under the protection of a lord in the lordship where the crime was perpetrated by claiming that he served another – thus avoiding the penalty that might be imposed upon him. 'The same Lords Marcher,' it was declared, 'have and do pretend a Custom and privilege, that none of the King's Ministers or Subjects may enter, to pursue, apprehend and attach any such Offender ... by reason whereof the same Offenders went unpunished.'[45] The situation was intolerable and created two problems: namely, the freedom allowed criminals, and their employment in the private retinues of lords. They were the 'very precious jewels' that also operated among the feudal families in the Scottish Marches. It was not a new situation: Henry VII had attempted to legislate against retained liveries in 1487, but to little effect because of aristocratic domination and turbulence.

The feudal aristocracy, especially in the north of England, continued to keep retainers, and in the Welsh Marches the effects of revolt, plague and unstable political conditions eased the movement of undesirable elements – unemployed soldiers, outlaws and criminals – into service. Payments were made to free convicted felons. This 'damnable custom', as it was called, was practised in the Marches, particularly in the small lordship of Mawddwy, before 1536. In the eastern marcher areas bands of brigands terrorised the countryside and were particularly active in the Hiraethog mountains of Denbighshire where there existed the notorious 'wasp's nest', according to Sir John Wynn, on the site of the sanctuary of the

Order of St John at Ysbyty Ifan. Long after the Tudor legislation (1536–43), this practice operated in the lordship of Mawddwy where the famous 'red brigands' were active, and in the Pumlumon mountains (as recorded by George Owen), and the border areas of south-east Wales. 'The great disorders in Wales,' Dr David Lewis maintained in 1576, 'especially in south Wales have grown much of late by retainers of gentlemen whom they must after the manner of the country bear out in all actions be they never so bad.'[46] Both he and Richard Price of Brecon were equally critical of the practice of *cymortha* among gentry respected in their localities as men of reputation. The activities of Philip Herbert in Magor (previously cited) were deplorable and Rowland Lee questioned the wisdom of granting George Mathew of Radyr in eastern Glamorgan a *placarde* to enable him to collect *cymorth*. 'Truly it [his privilege] is right large,' he maintained, '...for he is so befriended that it shall run through all Wales to his advantage.' Maintaining private armies also served to exacerbate an already tense situation since it fragmented authority and strengthened seignorial *jura regalia* which was damaging to the execution of royal policy.

Although the task of extending royal power was not easy, a serious attempt had been made in this statute to combat an ever-growing problem. More power was given to assize judges and justices of the peace in English shires to intervene more effectively in the legal affairs of the Marches which represented a serious intrusion into feudal privilege. The intention was to co-ordinate the administration of justice as efficiently as possible with a view to undermining the extra-judicial powers of lords and their deputies.[47] Another measure dealt with the forays made by Welshmen into the border English shires and their attacks on inhabitants, and judges of assize were authorized to imprison offenders for a year. The Forest Laws in the Marches were also reformed to prevent extortive officials from profiteering at the expense of tenants and other forest users. Since the king was the greatest of the marcher lords at that time, this type of legislation was designed to suppress maladministration and high-handed behaviour on his estates – a timely reminder of the king's urgent need to attend to the deficiencies in his own territory.[48]

An overview of this legislation reveals the determination of the Crown to establish its authority in the Marches. Although legislation cut deep into the heart of marcher privilege there was no indication that total dissolution of the system was envisaged. Nor can it be said that the power of the lords was undermined: rather, they were expected to safeguard the interests of law and order more efficiently and to supervise their officials more diligently. Where possible, royal power was extended as a counterpoise to corrupt marcher practice, and the Council in the Marches was strengthened as an instrument to facilitate the Crown's intervention in the Marches. It is difficult to know to what extent this legislation succeeded since the final Tudor solution was provided so soon after, but it doubtless laid a foundation for further developments. These statutes, for which Rowland Lee and especially his deputy Sir Thomas Englefield were responsible, were designed specifically to deal with immediate problems. The aim was limited to establishing law and order in one of the most disorderly areas of the realm, but the statutes' significance lies in the fact that they represent the climax of royal policy to impose prerogative power under new circumstances and conditions.

A New Approach: The Assimilation of Wales and England

Clearly, Rowland Lee did not possess Cromwell's qualities and skill when dealing with government affairs in Wales at the time. He also lacked his tact and foresight and applied himself to little more than the specific problem as it appeared to him. While he exercised his authority in the borderland, Cromwell took advantage of the brief period when it seemed that the lord president's policy was achieving some success to give serious consideration to the circumstances in a broader context and to discuss with leading Welshmen who would eagerly counsel him on the ways in which the problems might be resolved. Among them were Sir Richard Bulkeley, William

Herbert, later earl of Pembroke, Sir Richard Herbert, Sir John Price of Brecon, William Owen of Henllys, Pembrokeshire, Sir Edward Carne of Ewenni, John Salusbury of Lleweni and his uncle and namesake, both of them prominent in the administration of Denbighshire from the 1530s onwards. It is said that Sir Richard Herbert (or possibly Sir John Price) sent a petition to the king about that time, requesting that Wales should be 'united' with England and Welsh law abolished. The authorship and authenticity of this petition are uncertain, but its contents are clear enough and typical of the views expressed elsewhere by Herbert and his fellow-officials in Wales. The petition was particularly critical of Welsh law, which was still operative in the Principality and the Welshries of the marcher lordships.[49] Although prominent landed proprietors had largely abandoned Welsh property laws, some vestiges of partible inheritance survived in the hinterland areas. Another petition was presented in 1534 by inhabitants of the Marches, demanding that primogeniture should be practised or that lands should be divided among heiresses, and that a Chancery should be established in Wales to process writs and other formal documents. It appears that prominent gentry in Wales and the Marches had co-operated to submit firm proposals for improvement in the administration of Wales.[50] Such counsellors, in various fields of activity, were experienced in administering law and were in close contact with the Royal Court and institutions of local and regional government. From among them Cromwell obtained the appropriate information needed to enable him to form his final policy. Nevertheless, Lee had stepped into the breach in a crucial period in the constitutional history of England and Wales. In an era of political tension Cromwell saw the necessity of installing a strong hand in the Marches to maintain peace in the last two years of the 'revolution in government'. He knew Lee well enough to realize that he would not create an upheaval nor damage the administrative structure of Wales except to the point that it helped to ease his policy. Consequently, together with Sir Thomas Englefield, who was his chief supporter, he felt strong enough to propose measures to Parliament in 1534, which served to erode further the historic power claimed and exercised in the marcher lordships.

Thomas Cromwell, however, had other more far-reaching plans. He had allowed Rowland Lee to pursue his tasks unimpeded, but his designs were more constructive. Although he agreed with the legislation in 1534–5, he regarded it merely as an interim measure. He probably realized that it would be difficult to impose more radical statutes in an area where particularism and diverse privileges continued to be strong. In his mind the only solution was to enforce English law fully in Wales. The first step in this direction was taken in February 1536 when the office of justice of the peace was introduced into Wales and Cheshire, thus adding a new and significant layer in the administration of local government to supplement the structure as it had existed in the Principality since 1284. The office had been well established in England since the mid-fourteenth century and had proved its worth. According to the statute, these officials (many of whom were justices of the quorum) and justices of gaol delivery were to be introduced into the eight existing counties – namely, the first counties of the Principality, Flintshire, and the lordships of Glamorgan and Pembroke where royal administration had long been established. Justices were to perform the same tasks as their counterparts in England and sheriffs and constables were to execute their commands and be subordinate to them. No reference was made to any property qualification which, in England, had been £20 since the mid-fifteenth century. Doubtless that was an indication that the Crown intended to employ Welsh gentry, many of whom, although they enjoyed regional power, were not as materially well-endowed as their equals in the richer areas of the borderlands and England.[51]

Rowland Lee doubted the wisdom of the plan to divide Wales into shires and strongly opposed the introduction of the office of justice of the peace. His famous letter to Cromwell in March 1536 is central to his thinking on the matter. 'And also for Justices of the Peace and of Gaol Delivery to be in Wales,' he declared, 'I think it not much expedient for there be very few Welshmen in Wales above Brecknock that may dispende ten pound land and, to say truth, their discretion less than their lands.'[52] In view of his attitude to crime in Wales it is hardly surprising that he held a low opinion of Welsh gentry at the time. He argued that justices of the peace and justices of gaol delivery in the border counties of England should continue to exercise their authority supported by the Council in the Marches. He had no confidence in the capabilities of the Welsh gentry to govern their own people on behalf of the Crown and considered that the recent more suppressive legislation was more appropriate. His attitude, however, does pose the question: in view of the fact that he spent his time in the borderlands how much did Lee know about the Principality of Wales? He ascribed the ineptitude of the Welsh gentry to lack of education and poverty, but it is not certain from where he derived his information. It appears that his relations with officials, especially in north Wales, were at best tenuous, but he was aware that partible inheritance was a serious drawback to economic advancement in the Welshries. The inferior status of many freeholders had accounted for the prominence of a handful of prime gentry usually associated with the plantation boroughs in regional government.

The statute creating the office of justice of the peace does not refer specifically to the appointment of Welsh gentry to the post, but it would have been impossible for Cromwell to find these officials elsewhere. Lee was not far off the mark when he referred to their relative impoverished state compared to their more prosperous peers in England (see Chapter 1, pp. 10–12). The majority were small-time freeholders who, although they and their predecessors had held modest offices in the Principality and the Marches, had not achieved prominent official status. That view was partly substantiated by George Owen when he referred to the illiteracy of the gentry whom the government was forced to accept as magistrates. The situation in Wales at that time, he declared, was similar to the position in England under Henry VI before the £20 property qualification was imposed on English justices.[53] The measure to establish quarter sessions courts was also opposed by Sir Richard Bulkeley of Beaumaris, who, like others of his class, feared for his own position in government and other objections were raised in north Wales, again possibly instigated by Bulkeley. In 1536 he replaced Sir William Norris as chamberlain, having acted as deputy for many years. He had served as sheriff of Caernarfonshire from 1527 to 1540 and remained active in local government, his name appearing first in the earliest surviving Quarter Sessions records. In view of his power it is hardly surprising that only gradually did the royal auditors and surveyors take charge of finances in the region.[54]

This raises a point regarding the nature of office-holding in Wales in the immediate post-Union period. Historians have emphasised the role of the Welsh gentry in public offices but, in view of the ambivalent nature of gentry status, it is not possible to calculate how many of those claiming gentility did in fact hold office. When the select group of upper gentry who obtained knighthoods in the Principality of South Wales are considered, however, evidence shows that the Devereux and Dinefwr interests were prominently represented. Likewise in Glamorgan, where opportunities to participate in local government were very limited, the Bassetts, Mansels and Mathews functioned as deputies, but prospects of holding office were confined to some families only.[55] Nevertheless, Cromwell's aim was to use what potential the Welsh freeholder class had to offer and, in the earliest commissions, prominence is given to a select group of modestly placed gentry eager to assume the privilege of office. The statute laid the foundation of a new approach to government based on uniformity, and soon after the 'Act for Laws and Justice to be Ministered in Wales' was passed in the last session of the Reformation Parliament.[56] The hallmarks of Cromwell's policy are again revealed in this Act as well as the new approach to establishing law and order in Wales: in view of changes in government he considered that the dual authority set up in Wales was unworkable and obsolete. He was equally aware of defence problems and the threats from abroad to the Welsh coasts and that Wales was not yielding in taxation all that it might be expected to contribute. He went to the heart of the matter and dealt at one stroke with the disease itself and not, as Lee had done, with the symptoms. Brittany had already, in 1525, been annexed to France, Ireland was seething with discontent, and Wales, regardless of the removal of Sir Rhys ap Gruffudd, the last overpowerful Welsh nobleman who might have caused an uprising in Wales, was in a vulnerable military position. In such a perilous situation Cromwell considered that Wales was ready to be assimilated into the realm of England. Whatever their material means, Cromwell also considered it essential to make the Welsh gentry part of the package in order to encourage their full participation within the governmental structure and to make them fully accountable for that government. His decision was not easy and he had considered reimposing Henry IV's penal enactments, particularly those debarring Welshmen from office. On the other hand, he was politic enough to realize that introducing such a policy would have been harmful and retrograde. Besides, to ignore Welsh freeholders would have caused frustration and discontent among leaders of repute. In short, Cromwell could not afford to ignore the potential that lay in the gentry: if he had, he would have been inept and shortsighted.

Immediately before the Act of Union a measure was carried confirming the king's rights in Wales and the Marches to hear criminal suits, to grant pardons and to appoint justices.[57] It was in the king's name only that writs could be issued from Chancery. The Act reinforced royal power yet further when dealing with the dual jurisdiction in Wales, and established the basis for a formal assimilation. The preamble to the Act of Union itself was partly unhistorical in that it declared that Wales had always been part of England, but that was merely legal convention. Although this preamble referred to Wales generally, its content applied mostly to the Principality that covered only half of the country. It was the old patrimony of the Princes of Gwynedd and other native rulers, and had been taken over as a going concern by Edward I in 1284. References in the preamble in 1536 to the laws and language of Wales serve to indicate further the differences between England and

Wales that had created 'distinction' and discord between the king's subjects in the realm. The aim was to 'extirp...the sinister usages and customs' that caused disparities between England and Wales and to create 'amicable concord and unity' between the two nations.[58] Some historians do not accept that the language was thought by drafters of the Act to be one of the 'sinister usages', but instead consider those to be the laws and customs in the Welshries and the Marches that had caused divergencies and disorder in the past. The preamble is vague on this point, but language is, after all, a usage and there would hardly have been any reason for referring to it at all if it had not been considered, as had the other customs, a hindrance to creating a common order. One thing is certain: though the fortunes of the language were to improve within three decades of this Act, when legislation provided for the translation of the scriptures into Welsh (1563), it was Cromwell's chief aim to impose the English legal and administrative structure on Wales. With a view to establishing unity and uniformity in public matters and bringing the Welsh people under 'the perfect order, notice and knowledge of his laws of this his realm', it was formally declared that the Welsh language should not be used in legal and administrative affairs and that no Welshman should hold any office unless he was familiar with English. Such a stipulation was in line with the ethos of current political thought and the doctrine of the imperium that was the foundation to Henry VIII's new-found authority.

Thomas Cromwell had studied the administrative features of the Principality very carefully and considered it appropriate that the new legislation should be based largely on its structure. Despite traces of inefficiency, it had stood the test of time and its government could conveniently be applied to other regions of Wales. The Acts of 1536 and 1543, therefore, were not innovatory: their aim was to extend the framework of administration into other newly created shires formed from the lordships of the Marches that were dissolved in 1536 as political units. That implied that Welsh land laws had to be abolished – which was finally accomplished in 1543. This created five new shires out of the lordships, establishing Monmouthshire on a separate legal footing, in line with Cromwell's thinking on integration in government; imposing English as the language of law and administration; setting up two exchequers and chanceries at Denbigh and Brecknock to correspond to those already well established at Caernarfon and Carmarthen, and introducing parliamentary representation. All writs and processes relating to Monmouthshire in actions of 40 shillings or above were to be sued by writs out of Chancery and suits tried by royal justices at Westminster by English assize judges. In addition to several other administrative changes, it was declared – significantly – that the Crown would retain the right to change or abolish any part of these provisions within a period of three years and that condition was later extended to six years.

In the second statute of 1543 the Council in the Marches was placed on a statutory basis, giving it more political power; the courts of Great Sessions were established in four distinct circuits, each containing three shires (excepting Monmouthshire); justices of the peace were appointed in each of the five new shires together with the *custos rotulorum*, sheriffs, coroners, escheators and high constables in each shire and hundred.[59] In this context the separate position given to Monmouthshire again shows that legislators treated Wales as conveniently as possible. It was attached to the western circuit of assize courts, not necessarily because they decided that it was an English county but, in view of the legal structure established in Wales, it was the most reasonable decision. Since one uniform law was now to be practised throughout the realm and because the county had not existed previously, any consideration of the 'Welsh' status of Monmouthshire was irrelevant. Moreover, precedent had been established in 1284 when Flintshire, for legal and administrative purposes, was placed under the jurisdiction of the justice of Chester while remaining a Welsh county.

The statute of 1543 is a lengthier, better-organized and more detailed measure than that of 1536. Cromwell had by then been executed and Welsh Members of Parliament, sitting in the House of Commons for the first time, participated in the formulation of this legislation. Despite its detail and attention to finer points of administration, this statute was not a natural progression from the first. Significant discussions had occurred in the period between the two statutes, and Dr Peter Roberts has shown that the years 1536–43 are crucial in any understanding of the ambivalent nature of Tudor policy in Wales at that time. Based on the power reserved for himself by Edward I in 1284, Henry VIII had established a unique relationship with Wales in 1536, and his ministers subsequently continued to deliberate regarding the form and content of the final settlement.[60] Two commissions had been established to investigate the boundaries of Wales and the laws of Wales respectively. The reports have not survived, but ambiguities did arise when their recommendations were followed. For example, the boundaries between shires had not been clearly drawn in 1538 since officers were ignorant of the powers they could exercise.[61] In December 1536 the sheriff of Herefordshire was uncertain as to what lordships were annexed to his shire.[62] Rowland Lee complained that he was uncertain of the relationship between him and existing marcher lords in criminal matters, and it was decided to send Justice William Sulyard to Wales to assist him in the task of shiring the country. As late as 1539 Sulyard sought further advice from Westminster on how to deal with these divisions.[63] It is possible that the commissioners appointed in 1536 were still continuing their investigations in 1540 and later, but there is no concrete evidence to prove that a survey of Welsh law was compiled. What is clear, however, is that opposition among landed proprietors continued to the operation of Welsh law, a further indication that their attitudes were firmly in favour of the imposition of a common legal system.

Such administrative ambiguities could of course be expected at those preliminary stages, but in 1541 new proposals were formulated regarding the government of the reformed administration. In that year recommendations that courts of Great Sessions and a Chancery should be established in Wales, and that the Council in the Marches should be abolished, were contained in a document entitled 'A Breviat of the Effectes Devised for Wales'. It was proposed to appoint five itinerant judges of whom the Justice of Chester would continue to exercise jurisdiction over Flintshire. Two of the remaining judges would preside over a circuit of six shires (in north Wales) and two over a circuit of five shires (in south Wales).[64] By then some significant changes had occurred in England, because in 1537 Henry VIII had a male heir by his third wife Jane Seymour, lady-in-waiting to her predecessors. According to the 'Breviat' it was intended to create a Principality specially designed for the new Prince Edward as Prince of Wales with a separate administration, a further indication of the close relationship established between the Crown and the Principality. Apart from setting up a Chancery the most remarkable feature in this document was this proposal to establish a new Principality for Edward who would enjoy 'the whole profits and the full authority of justice thereof and the gifts of all offices there'. This authority would be exercised under the King's overlordship and was considered to be the most efficient way of governing Wales at that time. Edward, however, was not created Prince of Wales and the newly conceived Principality did not materialise. The reason for that is not clear, but since Edward was very young and the king was eager to safeguard the succession, it appears that his plan could not be executed. It is evident, however, that he was seeking a way by which he could settle the problem of Wales, and the suspending clause in the Act of 1536 enabled him, over a period of three years at first, to 'repeal, revoke and abrogate' its provisions and to consider new proposals, a crucial clause that was also incorporated, with no time restriction, in 1543. It was a period of experiment, hesitancy and adaptation according to circumstances. The Act of 1543 was not like a typical Henrician statute but seemed to be a 'catalogue of legislative orders', which suggests that its provisions were formulated in the 'Breviat' of 1541 and had not been envisaged in 1536. They did not, therefore, follow on naturally from the first statute that assimilated Wales to England.

The Nature and Significance of the Tudor Settlement

The legislators in 1536–43 set about structuring the administration of Wales based on what had already been practised in the Principality. In 1267, in the Treaty of Montgomery, Llywelyn ap Gruffudd's constitutional status as Prince of Wales was officially recognized by Henry III. His authority extended into parts of the south-east Marches and from Cardigan in the south-west to the Dee estuary in the north-east. In 1284 Edward I, following his conquest of Wales, set about putting his newly acquired lands in order. By then the native Principality, after the war of 1277, had been drastically reduced to Gwynedd west of the Conwy. The lands were annexed to England, and in 1301 were vested in the heir apparent – Edward of Caernarvon – who was created Prince of Wales in that year. The native Principality had been incorporated within the realm of the English king with significant innovations, such as the creation of new shires and the imposition of English criminal law. Thus the Statute of Wales established a precedent in the constitutional history of Wales. The legislation of 1536–43 completed the process begun in native Wales in 1267 because, as Sir J. Goronwy Edwards declared, '"Wales" and the "Principality" of Wales had become co-extensive.' On the basis of the Principality the administrative and legal settlement created separate political unity in Wales and, despite the character of Tudor government at the time, gave to Wales a distinct jurisdiction and identity.[65]

What, therefore, were the constitutional features of the so-called Acts of Union and how appropriate is that title? Although Sir O. M. Edwards first used that description, it was A. F. Pollard who popularised it in 1902.[66] Generally, it is described as the legislation that united England and Wales politically, but that strictly is not correct. There were two 'unions' in 1536, namely the general union based on an unhistorical notion, and a particular union linking the Marches with shires in England or Wales or creating new shires. Only part of Wales was annexed to England in 1284, and by comparing statements in the preambles of the Statute of Wales and the Act of Union a striking resemblance can be seen.[67] It is clear that the Statute was taken as a model by the legislators in 1536, who established in Wales the shire system which had previously existed only in a part of Wales. The preamble to the Statute of Wales was a clear statement of the relationship between England and Wales, and because the Statute continued to be in force in 1536 it was used by legislators as a basis for the Tudor settlement. What it accomplished was the creation of unity based on the existing governmental structure. With that in view, together with the fact that Henry VIII retained for himself a personal relationship with Wales, it appears that the legislation in 1536 is paramount in any understanding of the constitutional framework of Wales over the previous two and a half centuries.

An assessment of the Tudor settlement reveals that in three respects only were innovations introduced that created administrative and legal unity between England and Wales – namely, granting equality of status to the Welsh people and imposing uniform law, the appointment of justices of the peace and parliamentary representation. In all other aspects, proposals continued the existing tendencies. The courts of Great Sessions were a natural progression from the chief courts of the Principality and the established officials of that Principality were continued, such as chamberlains, judges, escheators, coroners and sheriffs, and adapted to the new administration now imposed on the new shires and circuits created throughout Wales. In the 1536 Act it was declared that the new administration was modelled on the shires of north-west Wales. Consequently, the framework of the northern Principality was extended to cover the whole of Wales, including the new shires carved out of marcher lordships. Wales was united as a legal entity in itself, which remained until 1830 when the courts of Great Sessions were abolished. It is doubtful whether Cromwell, had he survived, would have agreed to such a policy and whether, in due course, he would have tolerated the use of the Welsh language at any level since that would have been contrary to his political beliefs. If there had been no political and economic upheavals in England in the 1540s and 1550s and if another minister of Cromwell's calibre had been in charge – or possibly a Prince of Wales who, as Henry VIII had envisaged, might have controlled government in the Principality – it is reasonable to assume that further deliberate steps might have been taken to suppress its use. An unlikely course of action, perhaps, because of the high proportion of monoglot Welsh people at that time, but not totally inconceivable in view of Cromwell's machiavellian designs.

What were the effects of this legislation and to what extent was it successful? Contemporaries were united in their acclamation for Henry VII and his son who, in their view, liberated the nation from its bondage. Social commentators were the exponents of the Tudor myth which maintained the tradition of the glorious British past and the inheritance that the Welsh people had repossessed and that gave meaning to their history. The most eloquent was doubtless George Owen in *The Dialogue of the Government of Wales*, a detailed and critical survey of governmental institutions in the Wales of his day: 'No country in England so flourished in one hundred years as Wales hath done sithence the government of Henry VII to this time,' he confidently observed, 'insomuch that if our fathers were now living they would think it some strange country...so altered is the country and countrymen, the people changed in heart within and the land altered in hue without, from evil to good and from bad to better.'[68] Owen's understanding of this success arises from his own interpretation of the relevance and effectiveness of the legislation in the Wales of the 1530s and his own day. He applauded the Tudors for providing for Wales a stable government and administration controlled by Welshmen of his own milieu. Rhys ap Meurig of Cotrel in Glamorgan, in the same context, drew the distinction that existed between Wales before and after the Tudor settlement. 'Now, since Wales was thus...enabled with the laws of England, and thereby united to the same...', he maintained in 1578, 'they are exempted from the dangers before remembered; for now life and death, lands and goods rest in this monarchy, and not in the pleasure of the subject.'[69] He referred to the establishment and functioning of a uniform system of law and institutions which gradually, during the following half-century, became a more potent force in Welsh public life. Similarly, the testimony of Dr David Powel, Humphrey Llwyd and Lord Herbert of Chirbury pointed to a positive declaration of favour on the part of the Tudors, acknowledging their lineal descent from Welsh *uchelwyr* and accomplishing their obligation to restore to the Welsh nation its inalienable birthright. In another more realistic context, the writings of the Welsh gentry and their attitudes to their new political and social environment also attest to their exuberant participation in constructive government.

The legislation of 1536–43 should not be interpreted merely as legislation that joined two countries together in a common bond of unity, but also as a means of integrating mutual interests and declaring the Tudor political creed relating to the nature and quality of the sovereign state. Thomas Starkey was eager to see established the 'common good' and Sir Thomas Elyot emphasised that the state, upholding equality of status, should incorporate the *res republica*, and accorded to the ideal governor his appropriate place in the common-wealth. The declaration in the Act of 1536 that the Welsh people were to enjoy all the rights and privileges of the English underlined this equality. Rowland Lee, in 1537, thought otherwise. Soon after the death of Sir Thomas Englefield, in view of the threatening situation in the Marches, he urgently requested that Cromwell should appoint someone in his place. Regardless of centralising tendencies and the policy to create new shires, Lee continued to show concern for the stability of a region whose government was about to be entrusted by Cromwell to those whom the lord president despised most.[70]

The Tudor settlement not only established the foundation of modern Wales, but also influenced various aspects of the nation's development. The most potent influence was found in the administrative structure and the uniform practice of English common law. The emphasis was placed on the constitutional authority of the monarchy and the extension of the king's law throughout the realm. Wales became a part of the 'body politic' within the English institutional system. It was English law that structured Wales within the central machinery, and although the country retained much that was separate and independent it was assimilated into England essentially on a jurisdictional basis. The most important feature of government in the sixteenth century was incorporating the English state under the authority of the king, Privy Council and Parliament, and the essential link between them was English common law.

Who exercised the political sovereignty in the king's name in the regions – the counties and hundreds – of Wales after 1536? The Acts of 1536–43 gave the Crown an opportunity to establish its corps of officials, who valued their positions. It promoted and exploited the interests and needs of a progressive group in society at the expense of the old aristocracy. They were educated as to how to appreciate and practise the new body of law and values attached to it. Within their respective areas they had been authorised to perform their tasks as part of their duties in the realm. Welsh governors derived their own authority from the same source, hence it is not surprising that emphasis was placed on interrelationship and interdependency between the Welsh gentry and the monarchy. From that standpoint the Acts of Union represented a significant development in the political thought of the gentry because, by means of statute law, they identified government essentially with the institution and role of the monarchy. Cromwell proceeded to solve the problem *quis custodiet ipsos custodes?* by placing the supreme authority in Crown and privy council. The agents in Wales interpreted the Tudor settlement as the raison d'être of their very existence as public administrators. This process had significant repercussions in a much wider field of activity including social, cultural and economic dimensions, and the total impact was contained in George Owen's reference to the 'joyful metamorphosis' that had occurred in Welsh society. The Tudor settlement may well have represented 'the climax of existing tendencies' that assisted the Welsh gentry further to progress in fields of activity other than politics and administration, but their importance lay in the future. The long-term consequences of the package were seen in the days when the Stuarts proceeded to test and exploit further the support and allegiance of the gentry. By then the inextricable bond of affinity between them and the Crown had been well established and appeared not to have threatened the relationship at the outbreak of the Civil Wars.

3

LAW, ORDER AND GOVERNMENT

In January 1576 Dr David Lewis, a prominent lawyer from Abergavenny and a baron of the Admiralty Court, complained bitterly to Sir Francis Walsingham, the Secretary of State, about the condition of parts of the old marcher lordships in central and south-east Wales, forty years after the passing of the Tudor legislation of 1536–43. He expressed anxiety about the situation because of the persistence of some practices that he considered to be damaging to good government in those lordships. His letter relates chiefly to such customs and, among other matters, he referred specifically to *arddel* and *cymortha*, and concluded that 'contempts and disorders must be severely punished and the better the man offender the greater the offence, and the punishment ought to be the more, which must be rather in body by imprisonment than in the purse'.[1] Lewis was obviously disillusioned and his observation echoed Rowland Lee's opinion on an earlier occasion. In his mind there were far too many deficiencies and incompetent officials allowed to exercise their authority. The Council in the Marches had lost its grasp of affairs. A year earlier the queen directed the Council to reform itself and to attend to the task of abolishing bad customs. Sir Henry Sidney was not able to attend to these matters immediately and Walsingham summoned Lewis and Sir William Gerard, chief justice of the Brecknock circuit, to advise him further in the matter. In response, Lewis's strictures were harsh and uncompromising and referred to specific deficiencies among prominent officers, particularly the sheriffs, justices of the peace, mayors and bailiffs, and drew attention to the inability or reluctance of officials to perform their services efficiently.

Dr David Lewis's comments are more important in view of his unfriendly relations with Sidney and the precarious political situation developing in England following the queen's excommunication. His letter reveals the poor social condition of the Marches and the failure to maintain law and order. Lewis doubtless was prejudiced but his strictures indicated that Tudor policy had not succeeded to the extent that, after almost half a century, the country was not well governed. This type of evidence does arouse suspicions as to the effectiveness of Tudor institutions in Wales, and it raises the issue as to what extent had the Welsh gentry, in view of the charges brought against them, succeeded in keeping a firm hold on the localities. Moreover, it may be asked how influential the gentry were as administrators and to what extent Thomas Cromwell's policies released to them the full power required to control the situation.

The Role of the Council in the Marches

There is evidence to show that, in the sixteenth century generally, the Council in the Marches was regarded as being an effective instrument of administration. In his office as deputy lord president, Gerard considered it sufficient to reduce the country to law and order and an institution well established on the foundations laid by Rowland Lee. George Owen also applauded the Council, and drew attention to its central role in government, its aim to 'civilise and pacify' the people, and its responsibility to maintain royal power and public administration in Wales. So essential had it become by the closing stages of the century, he observed, that its abolition would lead to anarchy: 'let that House or Council be dissolved but for a few years and no place erected to seek redress in adverse of those things, those that live now most quietly and think that Court unnecessary should first feel the smart and want thereof'.[2] That comment was written in 1594, and by then the Council had long since established itself and was recognised as the headquarters of government in Wales, and the lord presidents were, for the most part, well respected. The two most prominent were Sir Henry Sidney, who held the office from 1560 to 1586, and his son-in-law Henry Herbert, second earl of Pembroke, who succeeded him and remained in office until his death in 1601. They maintained closer connections with Wales, and evidence shows that they were not as impulsive as Lee had been. Although the rivalries between gentry continued, often on a large scale, it appears that the impact of the Tudor settlement was beginning to take effect and order established. Testimony was given to the untoward activities of individual lord presidents, but it is also evident that the relations of the Council with the localities were not as tenuous as one might suppose.

The duties of the Council in the Marches were broadly divided into two parts, legal and administrative. Since the totality of its records have not survived, it is not an easy task to assess fully the degree to which the institution was a success. By assessing the evidence that is available – especially administrative records from the period 1569–91 – it can be seen what type of governmental tasks were undertaken by the Council. Rowland Lee, Englefield and their contemporaries laid the foundation of the Council's activities at Ludlow. In his correspondence with Thomas Cromwell, Lee referred to his legal position and formulated legislation designed to alleviate the problem of lawlessness. He also restored castles in the Marches, chiefly to detain criminals awaiting trial.

In the Act of 1543 the Council was placed on a statutory basis, but the duties of the lord president and other commissioners were not fully defined. It was merely stated that the 'President and Council shall have power and authority to hear and determine by their wisdoms and discretions, such cases and matters as be or hereafter shall be assigned to them by the King's Majesty, as heretofore hath been accustomed and used.'[3] In other words, the Council was to continue as it had functioned before the Act, but the instructions unfortunately have not survived for the years between 1527 and 1553, and it was during that period that the institution grew to become a central feature in the administration of law and government in the countries of Wales and four border counties. George Owen particularised on the Council's equity jurisdiction 'to mitigate the vigour of law in diverse causes'.[4] According to the 1553 instructions, it heard civil and criminal actions brought by individuals who were too impoverished to take their suits to the central courts at Westminster.[5] It attended to all matters relating to misgovernment, such as the maintenance of private armies, false verdicts and other legal abuses. It had grown to become an organised court essentially different from how it had been when Mary Tudor moved with her household to the borderlands in 1525. The period of Rowland Lee's presidency is crucial in any assessment of the Council's responsibilities as a powerful royal agency. He was well aware of the need to reform the institution and often referred to that in his correspondence. It is also an interesting feature that the composition of the Council of the North established by Edward IV had changed by 1537 and that by then it had been an agent to administer the Crown's legal power rather than functioning as the king's personal Council in those regions, and it may be that the reform of the Council in the Marches had been chiefly responsible for that. In addition to its legal duties, the Council also assumed the responsibility of administering Wales although the information on that aspect is rather slight.

Among the Council's duties, executing the commands of the privy council in Wales was a priority. It also dealt with economic and defence matters, and had a police department and court where officials were appointed to administer Wales and the borders. The Council's chief duty was to supervise the activities of royal officials in the shires. The register of the Council for 1569–91 shows clearly that those aspects of the Council's jurisdiction were most important, but unfortunately the dearth of information on some other key aspects of its activities obscures any attempt at forming a full assessment of the Council's functions. Contemporary opinion, principally the observations of Sir William Gerard and George Owen, emphasises the legal side of the Council's activities, but it is evident that its administrative tasks, in view of the need to maintain law and order, and the increasing threats to the Welsh coastline throughout the century were largely responsible for the growth in its prestige. Occasionally, in Elizabeth's early years, the lord president was appointed lord lieutenant of Wales and the borders, especially in periods of crisis. From 1585 he was appointed to such a position on a regular basis when foreign relations were strained and after war with Spain had broken out. In that position he was responsible for supervising the castellated defences in co-operation with shire officials – the sheriffs and justices of the peace – but they, especially the sheriffs, enjoyed the greater power in such matters.

Regarding the membership of the Council it is apparent, from the evidence in Rowland Lee's correspondence, that there were only a few who assisted him in governing Wales. As noted above, in September 1537, after Englefield's death, Lee requested Thomas Cromwell to appoint someone in his place since he was overburdened with the task of pursuing felons, and he continued to remind his master of his exhausted state. He was aware of Englefield's qualities as a deputy, and he cynically remarked that 'Welshmen of the evil sort say one devil is gone, meaning Mr Englefield, and the writer is the other.'[6] He taunted criminals that they could never defeat him despite their hatred towards him. He could be very critical of the government at times; for example, he complained that he had insufficient resources to repair castles in the Marches. 'Wherefore,' he retorted when referring to the need to repair them, 'if the king's Highness will have this country reformed, which is nigh at a point, his grace may not stick to spend one hundred pounds more or less for the same.'[7] At the time he was at Presteigne 'among the thickest of thieves.' He feared that a quarrel might occur between the earl of Worcester and Walter Devereux, Lord Ferrers, respecting the stewardship of Arwystli and Cyfeiliog leading to uprisings that might endanger his authority. 'There was never more rioting in Wales than is now,' he observed, '...In Glamorganshire they ride daily; at Denbigh an assembly none like many years.'[8] His reference on that occasion was to Sir John Salusbury of Lleweni, a powerful figure who was ordered to keep the peace on fair day in May 1537 in the town of Denbigh. He had shown his opposition to the Council's decision to prohibit inhabitants of the town from bearing arms 'for he could rule them himself,' it was added, 'and drew his dagger at the messenger who rebuked him'. Salusbury was so influential that his behaviour, Lee maintained, was far more threatening than that of any other. So anxious was he at the time that he was forced to admit that the Council's authority was not being respected in Denbigh and its outlying regions, nor were its inhabitants and officials prepared to obey its commands. They complained of heavy taxation and oppression not in the spirit of the Tudor settlement of Wales. So much was the unsettled condition of mid-Wales and the Marches that Lee considered that only criminals inhabited Ceri, Cydewain, Arwystli and Cyfeiliog – 'Thieves I found them,' he disparagingly observed, 'and thieves I shall leave them.'[9]

In his last years as lord president, Lee was harsh in his response to lawbreaking. Four gentlemen of the 'best lineage' were executed in Shropshire in 1538, and he assured the king in the same year that his subjects in Wales were 'in good order'.[10] At the time he was more anxious over the situation in Cheshire since more murders and other offences had been committed there than in the whole of Wales over a period of two years. He was aware that these adjacent regions – and Cheshire at the time was within his jurisdiction – needed to be reformed to prevent any further lawbreaking in areas within the Council's authority. This Council exercised equity law to deal with awkward situations and suppressed illegal activity among Crown officials acting under the authority of unprincipled sheriffs who, because they held their office over long periods, were not easily removed. In such a situation Lee blamed the central government for being so complacent and ambiguous in its shiring of Wales. He could not administer

Wales efficiently, he remarked, because the commission, appointed in 1536 to investigate the boundaries of Welsh administrative units, had not reported its findings and he was not certain as to the extent of his jurisdiction. As noted in Chapter 2 (pp. 83–4), soon after the privy council despatched Chief Justice William Sulyard, a member of the Council, to Wales to assist Lee in accomplishing his tasks, and both of them wrote to Cromwell in March 1539 that the proposals for shiring territory to form Montgomeryshire were not acceptable to the inhabitants.[11] In April 1540 it was formally stated that the shiring of Denbighshire had been completed. Lee, however, was ignorant of the fact, and his only piece of information was that Sir Richard Herbert of Montgomery, one of Cromwell's chief advisers in Wales, when the proposals to shire Wales were first discussed had submitted a number of petitions from different parts of the Marches with the assistance of Humphrey Llwyd, Member of Parliament for Denbigh, for Cromwell's and Parliament's consideration.[12] That did not mean that Lee knew nothing of the intent to shire Wales, but rather that he had not been informed of the latest developments – which was not entirely unexpected in view of the fact that he had opposed the plan from the beginning. Lee was not the only one to express misgivings concerning the shiring of Wales. Sir John Salusbury of Lleweni, in letters to Cromwell, hoped that the creation of Denbighshire would not diminish his fees in the lordship, and complained that patents – exclusive rights – had been granted in the lordship and that one of the king's footmen had obtained by patent the 'common terms and farms' of the lordship.[13]

It appears that Lee was hardening his attitude towards the Welsh and the gentry of the borders. He clearly stated his opinion in 1539 that to hang one gentleman of status who committed a crime would save the lives of twenty and would be far more effective than hanging a 'hundred petty wretches'.[14] He believed that the Welsh had once more begun to thieve among themselves. However, his general view during his latter years was that Wales was far more peaceful, and he believed that he had successfully accomplished his task of pacifying the country. What does cause surprise is that he continued in office although he expressed some firm opposition to Cromwell's policies. Lee's death in January 1543 is a significant landmark in the development of government in Wales and the Marches since his career drew to a close a short period of dealing with the symptoms rather than with the root causes of the Welsh problem. He did not survive to see much of the implementation of the assimilating process excepting the shiring of the border areas, and it does not appear that he partook in discussions that resulted in the proposals entitled 'A Breviat of the Effectes Devised for Wales' in 1540–1 in an attempt to settle the final administrative framework. By the time the second item of legislation passed through Parliament as well as the measure that the Council was to be placed on a statutory basis, the hardy bishop had died. Consequently, but not directly as a result of that, further steps were taken to execute the new administrative order.

The Control of Local Government

Installing the courts of Great Sessions revealed that a separate legal structure was designed for Wales: one justice was to be appointed – increased to two in 1576 – to each circuit and the sessions were to exercise the authority of the courts of the King's Bench and Common Pleas. In due course it dealt increasingly with minor pleas of trespass, assault, perjury and debt. Old-established offices still survived, such as the chamberlainship and chancellorship in the Principality together with stewardships, bailiwicks, constableships, town-clerkships, mayoralties and the like, all of which were manned by local gentry who received the appropriate emoluments which supplemented their landed incomes. The sheriff's office – first established in the Principality in 1284 – was confined to one year to avoid keeping in office individuals who might misuse their authority over a long period.[15] This officer was the Crown's chief representative in the shire and, according to the Acts of Union, he was expected to serve the justices of the peace. Although he had been stripped of some of his authority he remained a powerful official, presiding over the county court, empanelling juries and executing writs, supervising lower courts among a multitude of other administrative tasks. He relied heavily on the deputy-sheriff who was usually an attorney and of lower status. George Owen had much respect for the officer as 'the chief man of substance in the shire...chief officer of trust and credit', who was in a position to influence the way in which government affairs were being conducted in his shire.[16] He was not above corruption, however, and there are numerous indictments against sheriffs who had allegedly abused their power for private gain. The office entailed considerable expense: prestige often had to be earned honestly or corruptly as circumstances allowed. Sheriffs were expected to offer hospitality to justices of assize and other governmental officials. George Barlow of Slebech, Pembrokeshire, complained about these burdens in 1617 when charged with several demeanours: 'whereby some sheriffs of the same county have been utterly undone and others greatly weakened in their estates and impoverished for...some have been put to £700, £600, others unto £300 charge, being men but of £300 freehold by the year or less'. Expensive though the office might be, it was also very influential. It was the constraints placed on the judicial powers of stewards and bailiffs in the lordships, the appointment (from 1543 onwards) of subsidy commissioners, and the limiting of the sheriff's term of office to one year that enabled eligible gentry, whose opportunities to wield authority in the past had been limited, to achieve prominence by allowing the shrievalty to rotate among them.

The most industrious officials, however, were the justices of the peace who held sessions of the peace quarterly, normally in the shire-towns and they obtained 4 shillings a day for their attendance. It was a key institution, and the local gentry eagerly sought commissions to boost their power and reputations. The commission also included ex officio members and professional lawyers or gentry with some legal knowledge designated justices of the quorum. Many of their tasks were performed outside the court, and usually two justices worked together. Gradually during the century closer connections were established – the 'clientage network' – with aristocratic factions in Wales and in London which enabled some magistrates to achieve positions of influence. George Owen, however, despite his adulation of the office, was aware of the danger that the prestige of magistrates might be impaired because socially inferior justices were commissioned.[17] When first appointed soon after 1536, the Crown had very little option – in view of the fact that Welsh freeholders were modestly placed in the social order – but to appoint magistrates who, because of their lowly positions, were despised by those whom they governed. By the 1590s the quality and abilities of landed proprietors were such that they were more highly respected and better-positioned to govern equitably and that should be reflected in the kind of magistrates appointed to the commissions of the peace. 'There is one chief feature to the office of Justice of the Peace,' George Owen observed, 'that a good man can do much goodness and an evil man much harm.'[18] One benefit Owen considered important was that the Tudors had placed Welsh gentry in charge of the government of their own regions, thus drawing on the vaticinatory themes so popular a century or so earlier.

The earliest evidence of the appointment of justices of the peace is in October 1541, although first lists of commissioners do not appear until March 1543. The earliest surviving indictment roll in Wales is that for Caernarfonshire in 1541–2 when it appeared that the local magistrates were fully occupied with their legal duties.[19] This office gave the gentry the opportunity to exercise regional power, which previously had been largely the preserve of a small exclusive group of fee'd officials appointed especially by the Crown in the Principality and in the marcher lordships. They were also expected to function on equal terms since all justices of the peace enjoyed the same measure of authority and performed the same duties. In the early years it appears that the majority participated in local government, but, with the gradual increase in the size of commissions, the burden of county administration eventually descended on a few key administrators. The new system was adaptable, and since there was no security of tenure there were hardly any attempts made to buy the office compared to the situation before 1536. The justices succeeded in maintaining law and order, in part because they had no deputies which, judging by past evidence, might be disreputable, thus lessening the possibilities of exploitation, and partly because they represented a system that prevented power from being concentrated in the hands of fee'd officials and that was subject to the jurisdiction of the Privy Council and the Council in the Marches. These features of English local government introduced into Wales also extended into the new counties the uniformity and flexibility that had been successful in the past. Regardless of the system's weaknesses, the newly commissioned justices acted under royal supervision and were subject to less criticism than fee'd officials had been, probably because they were anxious to establish standards of conduct in public affairs. The nature of the office illustrated the firm alliance and spirit of co-operation that had been established between the Tudor dynasty and the landed gentry in Henry VII's reign.

The Tudor settlement uncovered rather than concealed the fundamental weaknesses in its structure. Dr David Lewis wrote in a period of mounting tension and attacked Sir Henry Sidney's incompetence and leniency.[20] The Sidney–Leicester faction faced growing opposition at Ludlow in the latter years of Sidney's presidency when he lost the support of his closest friends. 'Your lordship had need to walk warily,' Walsingham warned him in 1581, 'for your doings are narrowly observed, and her Majesty is apt to give ear to any that shall ill you.' Moreover, Richard Davies, bishop of St David's, who was himself subject to the opposition of grasping gentry, in the previous year criticised inefficient and apathetic magistrates who failed to suppress recusancy in his diocese.[21] His comments reflected the unstable and changeable allegiances of Crown officials, and emphasised their negligence in performing urgent public duties. Indeed, the emphasis on order and discipline characterised Davies's comments, stressing the need to demonstrate loyalty, justice and safeguard royal prerogatives. Maintaining the body politic of the realm signified the strong alliance established between the Crown and the localities. Richard Price, in his letter to William Cecil in 1575, despaired of ever seeing order being restored to parts of the country although he considered that legislation might relieve the situation.[22] The economic situation in Wales reflected the deficiencies in local government that were caused by the survival of obsolete customs which the gentry themselves considered to be far too lucrative to abolish. Also, in conservative rural areas, kindred links and the position of the local lord were far too strong, and the dire economic conditions that often swelled the ranks of 'masterless' men who wandered around the countryside without employment and often became disaffected, the effects of primogeniture, and the plight of younger sons were causes of concern. Lewis was well aware of the symptoms of the malaise that characterised the years after the Tudor settlement, as was Henry Herbert, lord president of the Council in the Marches: 'For that which you shall now do,' he maintained in a letter to the deputy-lieutenants of Caernarfonshire in 1596, 'must be taken to proceed only from your good affections and dispositions to advance any action which shall be undertaken for the service of her Majesty and the safety of your country.'[23] Herbert, conscious of his responsibility to maintain defences, placed emphasis on preserving the integrity of the state. This implied the need to control passions and to exercise discipline in matters of public service. All these features appear to signify that the efficient government of Wales could not be taken for granted in the latter half of the sixteenth century. Certain elements of stability emerged in the legal and administrative structure, but the exercise of power was an entirely different matter. The duties of the local administrator were carefully supervised by commissioners of the Council in the Marches charged by the Privy Council to attend to such matters. Justices of the peace, sheriffs and other officials were highly rated in the localities as powerful landowners and experienced administrators and because they were regarded as essential links in the chain of command that bound government at the centre with administration in the provinces and because they represented – in a new social context – the surviving traditions of resident 'lordship'. It was this 'lordship' that Tudor government recognised when the lord president was appointed lord lieutenant over the whole of Wales, but that did not always succeed in reducing the country to some semblance of law and order. Sir Henry Sidney, before his return to Ludlow in March 1571, had spent some time in Ireland and had found difficulty in re-establishing his authority. The Privy Council anxiously observed the situation in Wales in 1570, and Henry Townshend – later appointed second justice of the Chester circuit – was despatched to Wales to decide the best way of reforming the country. He supplemented the queen's directions to the Council.[24] Sidney's presidency, as noted above, seemed not to be achieving anything positive, and a further period of absence between 1575 and 1578 did not help to improve the situation. His deputy, Sir Andrew Corbett, was inefficient, which obliged Sidney to defend his position by heartily testifying to what he firmly considered to have been a successful policy of equitable government. He was not at all times satisfied with the situation as he confessed in 1585, but in 1583 he had reassuringly informed Walsingham that he valued his 'great and high office in Wales' because 'a happy place of government it is, for a better people to govern or better subjects to their sovereign Europe holdeth not'.[25] That might well have been the case, but a mere show of allegiance does not at all times necessarily imply the practice of good government. Sidney showed complacency and reconciliation: Sir William Gerard, on the other hand, while being prepared to acknowledge the loyalty of the Welsh to the Crown, emphasised more that the Welsh had been subjected to the Crown through Lee's harsh policies.

Although local government was not strikingly efficient, county officials must not be considered to have been completely negligent. It is true that they did not form part of an efficient bureaucracy, but in critical times they were evidently aware of their duties and the consequences of neglecting them. High and petty constables in the hundreds and parishes respectively were often reluctant to pursue their tasks with any degree of urgency or efficiency. Moreover, lower (or 'base') courts in the hundreds and manors were poorly managed and subject to intolerable abuse, their officials exercising too much authority – thus undermining the county court which was considered by George Owen to have been undervalued.

In Wales, the most pressing items of business besides the routine affairs of administration were defence matters. Popish threats and activities abroad and plots at home caused much anxiety. In such circumstances emphasis was placed on improving and supervising the trained bands and levies. In November 1574, Sir Henry Sidney, in his absence, urged the Council to attend more consistently to their duties 'for the benefit of the country publicly so that we cannot be accused of negligence by assisting to promote good plans to keep order'.[26] At about the same time it was decided to investigate the possibility of reform in the Council.[27] Concern was expressed in 1576 about its condition, the year when Dr David Lewis presented his grievances, George Owen also hinted at criticism in the latter years of the century and was aware of the weaknesses that generally marred government efficiency. In view of the essential need for the Council, however, he strongly advocated reform rather than abolition.

An examination of the personnel of local government officialdom in the years 1536–1603 reveals that the majority came from well-established families. Office-holders were aware of two main duties: to serve the needs of the realm, and to maintain stability in their respective regions which implied promoting their own interests. In their official capacities they represented three major aspects of local administration, namely finance, defence, and law and order – essential features that secured for them royal favour. When pressed into action they pursued their tasks reasonably well and possessed the skills of organisation, discipline and loyalty characteristic of the lay governor in their generation. In his letters to the Caernarfonshire deputy-lieutenants in 1596–7, Henry

Herbert, earl of Pembroke, urged them to be more enthusiastic in performing their service to the state in a period of political crisis and war with Spain. He expressed his concern to preserve the 'public weal' and the need for public officers to safeguard their own 'credit'.[28] Political commentators in Elizabethan England, such as William Lambarde, placed greater emphasis on maintaining the organic unity of the Protestant state; it was interpreted in its broadest context and applied to the new authority established by Henry VIII. Old-established institutions and offices were adapted, others were introduced, and the political structure in Wales reflected the policy, as defined in the 1536 Act, to 'reduce them [the Welsh people] to the perfect order, notice and knowledge of his laws of this his realm...and to bring the said subjects of this his realm, and of his said Dominion of Wales, to an amicable concord and unity'.[29] The aim was to create Wales as an integrated province within the 'commonwealth' or nation-state. It was the realisation of that unity that explained, partly, why no uprising occurred in Wales and, partly, why there was no revolt against the government as in Ireland and parts of England.

The Imposition of Law and Order

The lack of strong and sustained aristocratic leadership, especially in the latter half of the century, was also partly responsible for the sense of calm in Wales. Of greater importance, however, was the extension and impact of gentry power in the localities. There were vestiges of lawlessness, but an assessment of the situation – as represented in the records of the court of Star Chamber – must not be taken at face value. Charges brought in that court were often malicious, as were those in the Council in the Marches. There was also an increase in suits from Wales in the reign of Elizabeth I, particularly from the border regions; this is evidence not only of unlawful behaviour, but, more significantly, of the fact that the gentry were prepared to defend their reputations by involving themselves in legal proceedings. Gentry were also severely punished in Star Chamber. Sir William Herbert of Swansea, for example, was fined 1,000 marks for conducting an affray in Cardiff in the 1590s in the course of a feud between him and the Mathew family of Llandaff. In many other suits prominent county officials were accused of mismanagement of public office, such as Sir Richard Pryse of Gogerddan and Morgan Lloyd, deputy-lieutenants of Cardiganshire, who were charged with obtaining £3,300 from the county's armour and exacting *cymortha*. Star Chamber records contain many suits accusing Welsh officials of extortionate practices, administrative inadequacies, misconduct, embezzlement, forgery, distraining on goods, oppressive behaviour and collusion with pirates. The indictments were often malicious and intended chiefly to tarnish the reputations of rival landowners. Despite the court's popularity, little evidence survives to reveal the outcome of many of these actions.[30]

In the latter half of the sixteenth century there was a brisk trade in a variety of courts including the Great Sessions and the Council in the Marches. The gentry also used the Exchequer and Chancery courts to promote their landed interests and defend themselves against misjudgements at common law. The Exchequer Court was often used as a court of appeal. Most suits in the Chancery Court came from those areas that in the past had formed part of the Marches. Sir William Gerard doubtless exaggerated in his treatise on Wales in 1576 – a year before he quarrelled bitterly with Sidney – when he declared that the Welsh 'were as civil and obedient to law as are the English in England'.[31] He attributed this situation to the success of the Council in the Marches where 'the people found place to resort unto, to have upon complaint their wrongs heard and remedied: the country growing to more civility, suits increased.' It is estimated that about 2,000 suits were heard by that court by the 1590s and that they increasingly dealt with civil rather than criminal matters. Despite the weaknesses in the Council's procedures, the significance of Gerard's comment lies in the fact that Wales was by then securely under the control of one officially acknowledged legal body. When he consulted the Privy Council in his capacity as lord chancellor to discuss the most effective way of restoring peace in Ireland, he could suggest no better way than to pacify by conciliation as had been the case in Wales.

Litigation was a common feature among the gentry and the professional classes. Property owners and businessmen had become aware of law and legal procedure. Legal chicanery, backbiting, bribery and corruption served only to enrich greedy lawyers. William Vaughan of Tor-y-coed, Carmarthenshire, reflected critically on the litigious procedure and stated that, if the economic condition of Wales were improved, there would be better-quality husbandry, less oppression and fewer reasons to go to law. 'These days,' he maintained, 'we are rearing two-legged asses who do nothing but bicker the one and the other in the law.' 'If reasons for the suits were to be dissolved men would practice husbandry diligently at home...', he continued, emphasising the need to improve agrarian practices in Wales.[32] William Harrison had little regard for the Welshman as a litigant and described him on his way to London: 'though he go bare-legged by the way and carry his hosen on his neck (to save their feet from wearing) because he had no change'. Commentators also resented the usurer in a society that could ill-afford the services of London moneylenders who placed a continual burden on poverty-stricken gentry increasingly finding it difficult to make ends meet. 'From my part,' Ellis Wynn informed his brother Sir John Wynn of Gwydir who had fallen into the clutches of usurers, 'I would like you to respect your reputation and property, and leave that thirst of purchasing more that cannot ever be quenched...because we believe here [the Chancery Court] when a man purchases money to purchase lands he does very little good for his reputation and less for his material benefit.'[33] Other sources refer to this malaise in a backward community. George Owen referred to the multiplicity of attorneys employed at Ludlow, and a number of poets in the late sixteenth and early seventeenth centuries drew attention to the avarice of lawyers and usurers alike. Bribery was also common practice, not only in courts of law, but in appointments to public office and other preferments. It is remarkable that so much criticism was levelled at crooked officials in a period when increasing emphasis was being placed on legality and material advancement. The number of lawyers was multiplying – many of them from Welsh families – and litigation became as important as administering law. It did not, however, necessarily imply a rise in the number of those who took suits to court, but rather indicated a possible increase in legal actions designed to delay or forestall an order in another court or presentation in the wrong court. Nevertheless, the law industry was buoyant enough.

The dissolution of the monasteries led to a greater amount of land being placed on the market, thus increasing the opportunities of extending landed power. The gentry had become expert in dealing with the affairs that led to their increased hold on church and monastic property, and Court of Augmentations records, for example, illustrates how far-sighted and ruthless they were in expanding their estates. In a flexible society, where expertise in law offered chances of promotion, sons of gentry entered the inns of court not only to increase their legal knowledge, but also to acquaint themselves with qualities of gentility and to enable them to apply their legal knowledge in office. Of the 299 individuals in the three south-western counties of Wales in the period 1540–1640 who held offices as sheriffs and justices of the peace, 81 had attended either university or the inns of court. 'And because of his excellent understanding and skill in the laws...', it was stated of Hugh Owen of Gwenynog, Anglesey, a self-taught lawyer, before his conversion to the Old Faith, 'his neighbours from all parts came to him as if to the most renowned lawyer to obtain counsel freely and to have their deeds drawn up and accurately recorded'.[34] Most of those who professed the common law were Welshmen, Humphrey Llwyd observed: doubtless an exaggeration, but none the less an indication of the dominating influence of law and the legal profession on the lives of Welsh gentry. Whether educated formally or not, an increasing number of Welsh gentry familiarised themselves with jurisprudence and legal processes in order that they might express opinions on politics and deal aptly with their private business.

It is in the context of estate-building that the practice of law became popular during the course of the sixteenth century. William Owen of Henllys in Pembrokeshire published two editions of an abridged version of English law printed in 1521 and 1528, and his son George Owen referred to legal commentaries in his own writings. Knowledge of the law improved the gentry's understanding of constitutional affairs and parliamentary procedures. Legal obligation was also considered vital to the task of serving the state and, in that respect, could cause conflict between the central authorities and their local agents. The performance of local duties entailed respecting and fulfilling the needs of the state as upheld by the law. Henry Herbert rebuked the Caernarfonshire deputy-lieutenants for neglecting their duties and demanded that they attend more diligently to urgent affairs. He also urged them to maintain peace and security in their province when dealing with military affairs 'because what you do now must be considered coming from your nature and good disposition to promote any act to serve Her Highness and your country's safety....I believe it would be harmful to your credits, according to your abilities, if you were unprepared to accomplish your functions.'[35] These are key words that illustrate the views of the most prestigious in county society who were sensitive to the need to preserve their prestige with the government. In a letter issued from the Council in the Marches in December 1585, urging officials to perform their duties diligently, the dangers of non-compliance were swiftly recounted. It indicated that the Council itself was insecure, but was aware of the consequences of misgovernment in local communities. Maladministration was often the stock-in-trade of prominent local landowners who served also in a public capacity. A notable example is Morus ab Elisa of Clenennau, the constable of Eifionydd and a forward-looking if modestly placed squire who, in 1551, was accused of murdering a neighbour and rival for land in the township of Gest, but as a result of strong local connections and corrupt practice was acquitted of the charge.[36]

The earl of Essex manipulated local government in south-west Wales for his own uses, his practices savouring of the retaining that characterised the old aristocracy now on the way out. The bitter rivalries between factions in Glamorgan later in the century and the high-handed practices of individual county leaders again indicated personal ambition, and one of them – Edward Kemeys of Cefnmabli in Glamorgan, a notorious briber – held the office of sheriff of his county on four occasions at ten-yearly intervals. Similar wranglings occurred between the principal families of Merioneth, Anglesey, Denbighshire and Montgomeryshire. In 1599, for example, the Salusburys of Denbigh were accused of being maintainers of murders,[37] and in 1602 there were objections voiced to the three nominees for the shrievalty in Merioneth – Huw Nannau, Gruffudd Vaughan of Corsygedol and Lewis Anwyl of Parc, Llanfrothen – because they were related to the murderer of Thomas ap John ap Humphrey at Bala three years previously.[38] It was not unusual, of course, for individuals of this kind to 'use' the system for their own benefit, and rivalries between individuals – even kinsmen – and families were quite common, especially since jockeying among them for the privilege of being county or borough Member of Parliament became a more common feature by the end of the sixteenth century. They should not, however, be exaggerated because they seemed not to have affected the routine of life in the countryside and the urban centres. What they did was to illustrate the ability of powerful gentry and freeholders to maintain their 'credit' because they had no rivals and because the government depended entirely upon their services. The framework of Tudor regional government survived because the gentry were aware that it functioned primarily in their own interests. They were also constantly reminded of the nature and significance of the responsibilities placed upon them. The office of *custos rotulorum* in Quarter Sessions – introduced in 1543 – represented the superiority of law since it was responsible for defending and preserving legal precedence and ensuring the strict enforcement of legal practice according to a body of acknowledged legal custom. Despite regional differences, a uniform system of government and law was practised throughout the country. It was legal awareness of this kind that accounted for the survival of the Tudor Settlement and for the continuation of gentry participation in the process of governing. Law became an instrument by which individuals sought redress against the oppression of their masters and by means of which the community withstood high-handed activity as happened in the 1570s when Gwynedd freeholders fiercely opposed the earl of Leicester in the Forest of Snowdon affair.

Law, Order and the Community

Another dimension to legal practice in the regions was the emphasis on preserving the 'body politic' of the realm. This aspect assumed prominence in periods of political stress when the nation's defences were strengthened, and the situation became increasingly more critical in the latter decades of the century. The appointment of deputy-lieutenants in 1587 led to an intensive effort to strengthen coastal defences which uncovered inefficiency and often a lack of initiative on the part of some officers, particularly when they confronted problems that featured chiefly among backward rural communities. 'How can your minds be united in the matter of common defence,' Henry Herbert declared to two such officers, 'when they are divided by private quarrels?'[39] Commissioners were occasionally unwilling to perform their duties, as occurred in Carmarthenshire in 1578 because two of the four appointed were unable to undertake their tasks. In 1597 the Cardiganshire deputy-lieutenants espied a Spanish ship off the Aberdyfi coast but, like the vice-admiral, were powerless to organise any attack upon it since, it was reported, men could not be pressed to serve on that occasion because their superiors had 'no authority to levy her Majesty's subjects to risk their lives at sea on so dangerous a service'. At about the

111

same time George Owen was concerned about lawless behaviour, particularly cattle-stealing, at Cwmystwyth in the Pumlumon area of mid-Wales. He blamed local Crown officials, principally the sheriffs and justices of the peace, some of whom 'either negligently or wilfully suffer many things to pass their hands with less care than they ought to do' and who 'with more diligence and industry will not follow such bad people and their harbourers'.[40] These areas were situated where three judicial circuits of Great Sessions converged, bordering on marcher terrain where old loyalties and animosities persisted among freeholders subjected to royal government and officials. Rowland Lee had attempted years earlier to suppress the depredations of Arwystli felons – 'a cluster or company of thieves', as he called them – and endeavoured to persuade Cromwell not to appoint justices of peace in Wales from among Welsh freeholders. 'As there is yet some bearing of thieves by gentlemen, if this statute go forward,' he explained, 'you will have no other but bearing and little justice, as you may judge by the demeanour of Merionethshire and Cardiganshire, for though they are shireground they are as ill as the worst part of Wales.'[41] The words, of course, were in character, but in context drew attention to the threats of continued lawlessness in the more exposed areas of Wales. Lewis ab Owain, sheriff of Merioneth and baron of the exchequer, an influential and seemingly controversial figure in public affairs, was assassinated at Mallwyd in 1555 on his return journey from Welshpool assizes by the notorious 'Red Brigands of Mawddwy', a band of freeholders dissatisfied with their lot after the Tudor legislation.[42] Traces of disaffection and instability of this kind, of which Dr David Lewis so readily complained, existed among communities of the eastern borders extending from Ysbyty Ifan in the north to the south-east. Evidence does appear to suggest that this, in part, may well have been the survival of old marcher practices and the persistence of kindred or seignorial loyalties, but also, in part, and possibly more significantly, the establishment of a land system that denied younger sons their common rights in land inheritance.

Landowners and professional men from different income groups were attracted to the commission of the peace. Indeed, the consolidation of the office of justice of the peace led to an inordinately large increase in the size of county commissions, above the eight stipulated by statute in 1543. In 1573–4 there were 24 justices in the Pembrokeshire commission, of which 9 were resident; in Carmarthenshire 29, of which 17 were resident, and in Cardiganshire 23, of which 8 were resident. On 23 June 1605, Orders in Council were issued designed to regulate the court's procedure and to enforce full attendance at quarter sessions.[43] The £20 qualification had not been introduced into Wales, and as early as 1580 the Council in the Marches deplored the practice of granting commissions to unfit persons.[44] In 1621 Lord Keeper John Williams threatened to exclude from commissions those who had less than £20 in land.[45] According to the Orders in 1605, justices of the peace were not only required to fulfil their duties efficiently but also to supervise the duties of other officials.[46] In 1623 Sir Francis Nethersole reported the proposal to dismiss superfluous justices in each commission to reinforce the efforts in 1611 to dismiss those among them who failed to pay their debts.[47] It was reported in 1622 that the Privy Council was engaged in compiling an expurgatory index of magistrates that exceeded twenty or even thirty in some counties.[48] This policy was given further impetus in 1615 when a proclamation demanded that all noblemen, esquires and gentlemen should live in their country residences 'for the better maintenance of hospitality'.[49] Those who refused to spend nine months in their counties were liable to lose their commissions. Such a requirement, if it had been acted upon, might well have benefited the cultural life of the Welsh countryside. All these efforts, however, seemed not to have had any significant effect since the number of justices extending from those at the top end of the social scale, down to quite modest freeholders, were eager to maintain their precedence in their respective communities. In Caernarfonshire and Merioneth, for example, the social structure largely dictated the commission's composition. The number of squires with incomes of over

£300 a year was small, but they did exert a considerable amount of local influence. Those on a lower income level obtained commissions with greater ease and gave them further prestige, particularly in isolated communities. Circumstances were not easy, however, in such areas where the scarcity of magistrates placed heavy burdens on one official, as happened in 1618 in the exposed western parts of Denbighshire.

Most justices of the peace were appointed from among the freeholders valued at between £50 and £100 a year. While it is true that income levels rose gradually during the sixteenth century, the impact of inflation, bad agricultural conditions and inefficient husbandry adversely affected living standards. Some freeholders were reasonably well-off. The Nannau family of Llanfachreth in Merioneth was worth £300, and in the same county the Vaughans of Corsygedol, Prices of Rhiwlas and Salusburys were comfortably placed. Robert Salusbury of Plas Isa, Llanrwst, and Ffowc Vaughan of Bronheulog, Llanfairtalhaearn, valued at £200 a year and also 'learned and discreet', were considered worthy of appointment as magistrates in Denbighshire in 1618.[50]

The type of social conditions with which local officials were required to deal reflected the impoverishment of many communities. Opposition to governmental controls is invariably tied to the effects of economic hardship, which also accounted for grievances and the threats to law and order. This was indicated in the increase in poverty, the unemployed and the wandering rogues, all of which led to a substantial body of legislation placed on Tudor statute books, particularly from mid-century onwards. The cornerstone was the Statute of Artificers (1563), designed to ease the situation by laying down maximum wages and compelling men to offer their labour for a specific wage. It was intended to provide labour at a reasonable rate and to establish a more flexible wage-structure in a period of inflation. The effects of unemployment threatened stability in the localities, and Poor Law statutes were tightened to enforce employment and suppress unnecessary wandering. In 1567 the commission that legalised the Caerwys *eisteddfod* required the justices of the peace to distinguish between professional poets licensed to practise their craft legitimately and the wandering bards, described as 'vagrant and idle persons' who had 'grown into such an intolerable multitude within the Principality of North Wales' that they caused disquiet among the landed gentry and affected the livelihood of professional poets.[51] Local government records illustrate the hardship suffered when individuals were brought before the courts charged with petty thefts and other misdemeanours. These problems caused alarm in the towns and rural districts alike, and the Council in the Marches urged local officials to attend more diligently to their duties to suppress any signs of discontent. It was awkwardly placed in 1585 when it appealed to local officials to support its efforts to command the loyalties of Welshmen who had either taken the law into their own hands or had gone elsewhere to seek redress of grievances.[52] The loss of control was a cause of serious concern, as was the reluctance of local officials to comply with the Council's wishes. A series of bad harvests exacerbated the situation. During the critical year 1586–7, for example, the Council was commanded to impose some order on the sale of corn, and two years later John Penry complained of the adverse effects of bad harvests in 1585. The winter of that year, he maintained, 'destroyed all their cattle well near, so that now the very sinew of their maintenance is gone.' Many that lived well and thriftily,' he continued, 'are fain to give over both house and home, and to go abegging.'[53] The Poor Law statute of 1598 took further steps to alleviate the situation as it affected the deserving poor and took order to punish sturdy beggars. The growth in population and land hunger led to an increase in the number of landless men, the majority being destitute paupers and labourers wandering to escape the dire effects of economic recession. The problem by then had become acute in the towns of Wales, which were unable to contain them let alone control the situation adequately.

Most of the information available for the functions of the justices of the peace in Wales in the period to 1640 is extracted chiefly from the corpus of Caernarfonshire Quarter

Sessions records, the only ones to survive almost continuously in the Welsh counties. They serve to show how a small number of prominent gentry, aided by a band of modest freeholders functioning as high and petty constables, overseers of the poor and bailiffs, grappled with the problems of government in inhospitable and rugged terrain and areas of limited economic resources. 'The country is poor,' it was observed in 1595, 'and the most rugged unpassable barren country in all Wales with wild roads and many harbours and landing places upon its long promontory.'[54] Poor Law records illustrate the hardship created by bad harvests and plagues, and the constant demands by the Crown for financial aid caused some disquiet in the localities. A Book of Orders compiled on 20 May 1618 for the hundred of Nanconwy has survived, showing how Sir John Wynn and Thomas Vaughan of Pantglas, Ysbyty Ifan, set about dealing with the poor in petty sessions.[55] Details were given of those granted relief in each parish, those allowed begging licences, the numbers of children apprenticed, and the alehouses, highways and bridges in the hundred.

The years of famine between 1621 and 1623 and 1629 and 1631 had adverse effects, for bad harvests led to imposing severe restrictions on the quantity of malt that could be used for brewing. In 1622–3 the Privy Council spearheaded yet another drive to suppress unlicensed alehouses so that barley could be used to relieve the poor. Since much of it was consumed to make strong ale and beer unlicensed and unnecessary alehouses were to be suppressed and others permitted only to brew moderate ale and beer.[56] The Caernarfonshire quarter sessions records (since they are the only ones to survive from this period) are particularly valuable in that they reveal economic conditions among the poor and unemployed in one of the most austere counties in north Wales. Magistrates in Cymydmaen, Afloegion and Dinllaen in Llŷn complained that there was an insufficient amount of corn to last until the harvest, the region 'exceeding poor, past belief because their cattle whereon they live, for the four last years bare no price and bread corn is exceeding dear whereof they have great scarcity'. In 1623 Thomas Glyn, sheriff of Caernarfonshire, refused to accept contributions collected in Cymydmaen, Nanconwy, Arllechwedd Isaf, Creuddyn and the borough of Conwy for military purposes because of their impoverished condition and because he knew that the Privy Council could not demand payment without parliamentary consent.[57] In 1636 Harry Lloyd, a vagabond, was reported by the Tudweiliog parish constable in Caernarfonshire for having 'fained colour and pretence of surgery or physic' and creating fear among country-folk because he exercised 'wicked and unlawful arts such as fortune-telling, palmistry, common haunting and familiarity with wicked spirits at night'.[58] Moreover, Ithel ap John, a native of Treuddyn in Flintshire, a maltmaker by trade, had his house and possessions destroyed by fire, and the Caernarfonshire justices of the peace decided that they would do their 'best endeavour' to relieve him and his large family.[59] Sir Peter Mytton, chief justice of North Wales, arranged a benevolence to assist the destitute children of Agnes ferch David who had been convicted of theft. In a letter to the county magistrates he compassionately appealed to them to be merciful and charitable towards them and he enclosed ten shillings to clothe them for the winter, charging the magistrates 'to do good works and to be careful for the good government of your country'.[60] His benevolent spirit may well have been aroused by his first marriage to an orphan girl, but it is doubtless the case that justices of assize and magistrates were disposed to be more lenient with deserving cases in times of hardship. In 1624, because of the extremity of the famine, justices of assize dismissed prisoners upon their own recognisances.[61] Even in years of abundance, measures were taken to suppress wandering rogues and vagabonds and control the exorbitant prices being charged for essential foodstuffs. In 1626, for example, Lord Keeper John Williams ordered Robert Devereux, *custos rotulorum* of Staffordshire, and the justices of the peace to regulate the 'troops of rogues' and popery and to supervise excessive prices.[62]

The royal proclamation in 1631 established a commission to investigate methods of dispensing poor relief and the

117

punishment of sturdy beggars and vagabonds in parishes. The system was to be more ruthless and the commission was granted wide powers of interrogation which compelled justices of assize and magistrates to assist in reducing the localities to some order. Deputy commissioners were appointed to assist in compiling orderbooks containing detailed instructions regarding the procedure adopted. Magistrates were to assemble monthly to receive reports from churchwardens and overseers of parishes to administer matters relating to the poor, arrange apprenticeships for children of the age of seven upwards, and dispense relief. In such dire circumstances it was impossible for impoverished communities, like Isaled and Isdulas in Denbighshire, for example, to pay dues continually, and in 1637 they expressed reluctance to pay more tax than was expected to repair St Paul's in London.[63] It was testified that they refused 'to undertake the like sums or any other sums whatsoever by way of annual or yearly payments,' and the document was signed by three magistrates. In this respect local government in Wales was characterised by an independence of thought and action, a feature that became more evident as pressure upon magistrates increased to comply with the Crown's wishes in matters relating to defence and finance. Following the dissolution of Parliament in 1626, and the impeachment of the duke of Buckingham, the Crown demanded a 'free gift', but the proposal was replaced by a Forced Loan. Commissioners were appointed in each county and granted powers to assess freeholders for this purpose, and it is hardly surprising that records reveal that there were many defaulters in Wales.

The Crown's insolvency had increased to become a serious burden on the localities. In 1622 the first stage of the Thirty Years War came to an end and James I imposed a benevolence to assist his son-in-law Frederick, king of Bohemia. The heavy demands led to a grievance being voiced in one northern county that the tax was 'too high a pitch for our poor country...and by alledging the poverty of the country we must leave longer time...for that money to be paid'. Often magistrates pleaded the cause of under-privileged communities when they considered that the demands of the central government were excessive.[64] After inspecting military preparations in Wales in 1600, the privy council declared that 'the choice of men out of the Welsh counties is so bad as it would seem they were picked so as to disburden the counties of so many idle, vagrant and loose persons rather than for their ability and aptness to do service'.[65] A harsh comment indeed on the inefficiency of officers and the economic plight of many areas. Distraint of Knighthood left north Wales in arrears to the tune of £900 in 1639 and the receiver despairingly reported that he had little hope of recovering the debts. Furthermore, when Ship Money was imposed on the counties between 1634 and 1639 problems of collection hit several counties very hard. The counties and corporate towns of north Wales were required to provide one ship of 400 tons furnished with men, tackle, ammunition, victuals and other necessities. The expense amounted to £2,000 in the first year when Wales, for administrative purposes, was attached to Cheshire, Lancashire and Cumberland, but, owing to a miscalculation, the following year's demand leapt to £10,500 (£4,000 for north Wales and £5,000 for south Wales, and Monmouthshire contributing £1,500). Wales's overall contribution had increased fivefold. The decision to force counties to pay individually to the exchequer in London replaced the scheme whereby the Council in the Marches, having obtained due quotas from the counties, settled for Wales. Essentially, the problem appeared to be twofold: the difficulty of ensuring that the tax was paid and accounted for by county officials, and of safely conveying the sums collected to London.[66] Often matters did not work out to the government's satisfaction. For example, when Anglesey magistrates were directed to levy £111 to provide a ship in 1639, Owen Wood, the sheriff, informed the Privy Council that the winter season was a 'dead' time for the collection of taxes and that revenues could only be raised in the following summer when the cattle trade would be more active. 'The poor country,' it was stated in 1638, 'affords no commodity to make moneys of but a few cattle and sheep which are not vendible till the beginning of summer, and therefore at this time of the year collections are most difficult.'[67] Also in 1638 Thomas Whitley, sheriff of Flintshire, when submitting his incomplete accounts, expressed his concern that the county could not sustain continual financial demands. Hugh Lloyd, sheriff of Denbighshire, also expressed anxiety concerning the pestilence in London and delayed forwarding payments conveyed by drovers. Two years previously the Merioneth sheriff complained to the Privy Council that local collectors of the tax were dishonest, and there was evidence that some officers refused to collect it because they feared intimidation.[68] A tragedy occurred in 1635 when John Scourfield of New Moat, Pembrokeshire, was drowned at Eynsham ferry when he was conveying Ship Money to London and £43 was lost of a total of £713 10s. 0d.[69]

Finance matters were not the only problem that beset justices of the peace in their quarter sessions because, besides legal commitments, multifarious duties relating to highways and bridges, the administration of the Poor Law, regulation of alehouses, weights and measures and other duties consumed much of the time that gentry would otherwise have devoted to running their estates. Although recusant activity continued to cause concern in the early seventeenth century it was not the serious threat that it had been under Elizabeth. However, magistrates kept a vigilant eye on any movements that might endanger national security. 'As they issue from the head and body of the state,' Edward, Lord Zouch, lord president of the Council in the Marches, declared in 1603, when referring to the government's directions to muster troops and disarm papists, 'so the execution rests upon your hands as if in so general a service there were no member to be exempted.'[70] He was determined to assert his authority soon after his appointment to the office, and defined security in the realm in the context of establishing order and justice in the provinces. 'I protest,' he maintained, 'that the desire of a peaceable government and the due execution of the law is all I seek...to neglect which would be the overthrow of the commonwealth and of private estates.' In a period when the power of the Council in the Marches was waning it was only rarely that it rose to the occasion to assert its authority with any degree of success, particularly when a prominent squire disregarded that authority. That occurred, for example, in 1615 when Sir John Wynn of Gwydir, after being found guilty of oppressing his tenants in Dolwyddelan and Llysfaen, and other transgressions, was ultimately subjected to its jurisdiction. Although the fine of 1,000 marks was reviewed and drastically reduced, the fact that the Council had been able to impose a penalty at all on such a powerful figure was itself considered an achievement.[71]

Bonds of Loyalty

In any attempt to assess the degree of success achieved by the Tudors in establishing law and order in Wales, certain factors need to be borne in mind. First, there was no large-scale opposition to Tudor legislation, partly because a system of government and administration had already been practised in the Principality and partly because there was no longer any strong aristocratic leadership in Wales that might transform discontent into a strong rebellious force. The Tudor settlement was tailored to meet the needs of a different type of leader, one who was gradually becoming more favourably disposed to executing the law rather than fostering a spirit of discord. Secondly, religious developments in the sixteenth century and the creation of the Protestant state served to consolidate the power of the Crown and its institutions. Although too much credence should not be given to the testimonies of George Owen, Thomas Churchyard and Nicholas Robinson in their praises of Tudor government in Wales, too much emphasis should not be placed on the inability of the government to come to terms with the situation. It is clear that, by the 1580s and 1590s, the Tudor settlement had been well-established and that the majority of Welsh gentry were no longer prepared to endanger a structure that they had helped to create and from which they had benefited so much. Thirdly, exercising public office represented the solidarity of the nation state in the localities. However unscrupulous and aggressive the gentry might be in their relations with others, high and low, fundamentally they were well aware where their interests lay and how dependent they were on a monarchy that eagerly promoted them. Lastly, the strength of regional government sustained a sense of unity in local communities. Despite the weaknesses in the chain of command, the machinery of government continued to be effective, and among those who managed the system two types of loyalty can be identified: to the Tudor monarchy and to the Welsh heritage. The one grew out of a close attachment to royal institutions and the other from the inextricable bond between the gentry and their Welsh roots. It was these bonds that sustained loyalty among the Welsh gentry to the Stuarts in the decades up to the outbreak of Civil War. Concepts of hierarchy and authority continued to govern the legal and administrative life and, in theory, emphasis was still being placed on the organic structure of the community within the Tudor state. The framework of that state continued to function effectively in the reign of James I and his son Charles.[72] Public functions and relations were geared to maintain the unity of the sovereign realm. At local level the county community became an essential component in regional government and the Council in the Marches, even after 1601 and the death of Henry Herbert, continued to coordinate administration in the Welsh and border shires. When James I came to the throne he inherited in Wales a strong system of local government where links had been established between the central government and the localities despite the fact that bad communications and inefficiency often impaired the smooth-running of county affairs, particularly in the less accessible counties. Local government officials had served their apprenticeship under the watchful and stern eye of the agencies of the central government, and the royal Court and country residence became the two main symbols of their authority.

Despite evidence of negligent behaviour, the Welsh gentry, as their correspondence shows, were aware of their responsibilities when attending to their duties. Family quarrels and factious rivalries seemed not to have disrupted the course of justice unduly, as was the case, for example, in Glamorgan and Merioneth during the latter half of the sixteenth century. Courts were held at regular intervals and care was taken to appoint men who were best suited to the task of running them. Concern was often voiced when it was feared that law and order was likely to be at a discount if manpower was not maintained on local commissions. 'The country,' it was stated in 1618, referring to the border areas between Caernarfonshire and Denbighshire, 'being disfurnished of governors doth more and more grow in disorders and diverse complaints do come daily of several felonies of late committed in sundry parts of that country which will grow to a head if they be not shortly suppressed.'[73] That area was still regarded as being subject to much turbulence, and doubtless the squire of Gwydir expressed anxiety about his own and his house's safety as much as about the peace and good government of the neighbourhood. In Caernarfonshire in 1620 it was further complained that high constables in the hundreds were not sufficiently confident to undertake the tasks of supervising highways and bridges and other affairs unless they were given clear directions by the justice. Since they worked among the lower orders in country society, continual hazards led to inefficiency and reluctance to act.[74] Indeed, securing compliance among freeholders acting as constables and petty constables in parishes was no mean task. Some protested that they were not able-bodied, others that they had not the resources to serve in that capacity. The nominated high constable of Arllechwedd Isaf in 1630, for example, claimed that his rank and status did not warrant his appointment. He described himself as being illiterate and considered the duties well beyond his capacities.[75]

Although the sense of county community was strong there also existed among the gentry an equally powerful allegiance to neighbourhood. The Welsh poets sang to prominent gentry in local office from both sides, viewing them as representatives of their countries as well as extolling their virtues as custodians of community life in their hundreds, townships and hamlets.

He who was regarded as 'ruler and chief magistrate among us' was noteworthy principally for his prominence in an even wider context, even a region, as was the case with Sir John Wynn who served as justice of the peace and in other capacities in three shires simultaneously, and he was concerned that the family interest was maintained in local affairs. Since he had decided not to travel to Caernarfon in winter he obtained a commission of the peace in the county for his heir and namesake [76] and Sir John Bodfel, his son-in-law, in Anglesey.[77] Eight justices, according to Wynn, had died in the county in 1610, and it was considered essential that there should not be any delay before commissions were obtained for his sons: 'The example is ordinary,' he observed, 'that the father and the son be in as is Mr Glyn and his son Sir William Glyn, who were both together in commission, Thomas Gruffudd and William Gruffudd in Anglesey; in Flintshire, Mr Thomas Mostyn and his son Sir Roger, Sir Thomas Hanmer and Sir John his son, and so in diverse countries.'[78] His reference to individuals emphasised how prominent worthy families had become in their respective regions. In 1575 the sheriff of Pembrokeshire reported that he had suggested the names of six of the 'aptest' squires in the county worthy to be appointed as magistrates because, in most cases, their fathers had already served in that capacity, and therefore the nominees were 'of the best credit in the county'.[79] Other ambitious families of this kind were the Prices of Newton, the Pryses of Gogerddan, the Vaughans of Corsygedol, Llwydiarth, and Golden Grove, and the Stradlings, Mansels, Perrotts, Morgans and Lewises in South Wales. Holding public office had become so much a family matter that commissions were often privately arranged, thus revealing close-knit kindred affinities and a dynastic approach to office-holding on a county basis. Superimposed upon this close allegiance to the local community there continued to be a strong bond of loyalty to the Tudor and Stuart monarchies as the mainstay of order and justice.

The centre of government activities in Wales in the early seventeenth century continued to be Ludlow Castle. Despite the difficulties that beset the Council in the Marches, it still maintained the allegiance of the Welsh gentry. Its authority in the old counties of the Principality was not as effective as it was in eastern counties of Wales and the border English shires. Its power in counties such as Glamorgan, Radnorshire and Denbighshire explains the continued instability in those areas traditionally associated with marcher jurisdiction. The Principality had, over three centuries, largely governed itself and had been securely controlled by royal institutions and officials. The Council itself, despite the increasing pressures placed upon it early in the seventeenth century, still retained much of its prestige and, in the last years of Elizabeth I's reign, Welshmen began to appear as members such as Sir John Perrott, Sir Thomas Jones of Abermarlais and Sir Richard Pryse of Gogerddan. It had maintained its power during Sidney's long period of office, and by the close of the Tudor period had increased its authority. It was the 'four-shire controversy' that in part affected its standing and power. However, compared to Star Chamber, it is calculated that, at the end of the reign, for each Welsh shire there was an average of 4.0 cases heard in the London court and 17.0 for each border shire. This has led Penry Williams to conclude that the Council had obtained a greater volume of business in Wales compared to the border shires which opposed its jurisdiction. That view, however, should be treated cautiously since it is based largely on conjecture. After a period of a sharp fall in business, between 1604 and 1615, when income from fines fell by 70 per cent following the controversy that embittered relations between the Council and the border English counties, its authority was remarkably restored, and the value and amount of fines it imposed were increased. Indeed, its volume of business was maintained until 1636 when the total number of fines was higher than at any other time previously. In Charles I's reign its business exceeded that of Star Chamber, and it was estimated that it dealt with about 1,200 suits a year, mostly civil cases. Such activity increased profits, revealed a degree of buoyancy that would not normally be expected in the Council's period of decline and, at the same time, reflected a more litigiously orientated society. Whether that increased business came mainly from Wales rather than the border shires is not clear, and Dr H. A. Lloyd argues that this may not have been the case.[80]

The Council, however, was largely self-destructive in that higher fees were exacted in order to line the pockets of sinecure officials whose main interests lay at Court. New officials obtained positions such as attorneys, clerks, servers of process, under-clerks and so on, all of which led to increased fees. Wrongful judgement – the incidence of which should not be exaggerated – revealed more the pressure of work on the Council rather than deliberate mismanagement on its part. The fines were less than those imposed in Star Chamber, but were exacted for trifling suits that stifled the Council's business. All in all, to the mid-1630s the Council held its own, but the increased pressure from the border counties and the opposition of Westminister lawyers as well as the persistent absenteeism of John Egerton, earl of Bridgwater, appointed lord president in 1631, did not help much to reform that institution in its most critical period.

How efficiently, therefore, was Wales governed in the decades leading to the Civil Wars? The confused and tense situation in the late 1630s did not imply that the period of personal government, despite its frustrations, was necessarily a failure, nor did the king's demands seriously interrupt the smooth running of local administration. Doubtless, the functioning of regional, county and lower courts maintained stability in areas that otherwise might have been permanently disrupted by economic and social upheaval. The Crown was evidently aware of the need to maintain a tight hold on affairs in the provinces and used what resources it had to retain Welsh allegiances. It was assisted by the very nature of government, which had as its base that firm alliance that had survived well over a century between gentry and the Tudors and Stuarts. The solid phalanx of county governors had deepened even further their affiliation with the localities, thus strengthening their links with the Crown. Regardless of the impending constitutional crisis, which harassed the most politically articulate gentry wishing to protect their own interests, a broad spectrum of families continued to display loyalties that led Charles I to expect and to exploit the widespread support that he enjoyed in the Principality.

4

RELIGION AND SOCIETY

In the year when the House of Commons legislated to assimilate Wales to England, the Reformation Parliament was in the last stages of establishing the king's authority on a new foundation. Two years earlier, in the Act of Supremacy, he was proclaimed to be 'Supreme Head' of the Church and state, and papal power in England was destroyed. Religious houses – and later friaries – were dissolved and, sanctioned by Parliament, the supreme legal and jurisdictional authority in the Church was vested in Henry VIII. However, that did not imply that the Church had abandoned its medieval structure. Much of it survived, but it was now formally controlled by the monarchy. Despite the revolutionary nature of those changes, the Church as an institution continued to be conservative. The Crown's sovereignty was defined in the preamble to the Act of Appeals, which referred to the 'empire' over which Henry governed in England and Wales. This *imperium* sprang from divine authority, as had the Pope's jurisdiction, and was exercised through Parliament and the privy council. In an ecclesiastical context the *potestas jurisdictionis* of the Pope was transferred to the Crown. Henry did not claim the *potestas ordinis*, but rather sought to exercise a new authority that gave him episcopal power to administer canon law within the realm. Since royal supremacy was divinely ordained, he claimed powers as the 'Vicar of Christ' in the kingdom. Under his authority, the Church in England and Wales became the

Ecclesia Anglicana; it also acquired a new role, with the Crown assuming full authority in religious and secular affairs.[1]

The four dioceses in Wales were in the province of Canterbury and there was no need for any formal legislation to legalise the king's authority over an institution that had already, over the centuries, formed a part of the Church in England. Although the condition of the Welsh Church was unsatisfactory, it cannot be said that the quality of religious life was worse than in other poor dioceses – particularly in the north of England. The value of Welsh bishoprics was well below the average in England. According to the *Valor Ecclesiasticus* (1535), they were assessed as follows: Bangor (£131), Llandaff (£144), St Asaph (£187) and St David's (£457).[2] St David's income, however, was just above that of Rochester, the poorest English diocese. Temporal and spiritual incomes were low and were leased out to lay families. Clerical standards were poor, only 6 per cent of parish clergy were valued at more than £20 a year, and the average stipend of unbeneficed clergy was £4 a year. Pre-Reformation bishops were non-Welsh and often non-resident. It was an impoverished Church, remote and conservative, with large parishes and parishioners who were illiterate and superstitious. Old Catholic customs were still being practised, and in the early stages of the Reformation government agents referred to the persistence of ancient practices in all parts of the country. Dr Ellis Price of Plas Iolyn, who was responsible for destroying the image of Derfel Gadarn in Llandderfel, Merioneth, clearly informed Cromwell that he had taken orders 'for the expulsing and taking away of certain abusions, superstitions and hypocracies' within the diocese of St Asaph. He marvelled at the fact that pilgrims had been 'sore allured and enticed to worship the said image insomuch that there is common saying as yet amongst them that whosoever will offer anything to the said image...he hath power to fetch him or them that so offers out of hell when they are damned'.[3] Remarkable powers indeed, and in other parts of Wales commissioners investigating the condition of religious houses in 1535 commented adversely on most of them; this indicated that they were not performing their duties to the extent they had in the past, and that they were in serious decline. In fact, their total value stood at £3,178 and approximately 250 men and women lived in these monastic institutions on the eve of dissolution, with the Cistercian establishment at Tintern only having the minimum complement of nine monks.[4]

Bishop William Barlow and the Early Reformation

The first major stages of the Reformation in Wales occurred in the diocese of St David's. William Barlow, prior of the house of Austin Canons at Haverfordwest and later appointed bishop of the diocese in 1536, was a strong character opposed to traditional Catholic practices. He was an aggressive priest who spared no words in severely criticising the low standards of religious life in the diocese. He was appointed a royal visitor in 1535–6, and in one of his many references to the inadequacies of regular and secular priests he informed Cromwell that 'among them all so many in number and in so large a diocese is there not one that sincerely preacheth God's word, nor scarce any that heartily favoureth it, but all utter enemies against…the king's gracious acts established upon the verity of God's word'.[5] Other sources corroborate what he had to say about the quality of religious life generally in the diocese, and it appears that Barlow – ardent Protestant though he was – was sincere enough in his comments on the abuses that hindered the Church's progress. The well-known strictures by Dr John Vaughan of Narberth in Pembrokeshire, another Crown commissioner, on Monmouth Priory and other houses doubtless delighted Cromwell who sought for all kinds of information – authentic or fabricated – to justify his course of action: 'While you have monks there,' Vaughan maintained, echoing the views of others, 'you shall have neither good rule nor good order there.'[6] Verdicts on houses such as Basingwerk, Valle Crucis, Aberconwy, Tintern, Brecon, Cardigan and Haverfordwest were not favourable either. References to the ruinous state of buildings and depleted numbers of monks and impoverished conditions paved the way for Cromwell to formulate his policy to dissolve them. Having said that, not all religious houses were completely derelict. The abbot of Aberconwy, for example, endeavoured to offer hospitality on the eve of dissolution although it housed but four monks at the time. 'I keep 40 persons, besides poor people and strangers, at no small cost this dear year when corn is so scant in these parts,' Richard Price, the abbot, reported to Cromwell in June 1536 in an unsuccessful attempt – amounting to a bribe – to influence his decision on the house's fate.[7] The condition of St John's Austin priory at Carmarthen, according to the report, was favourable, and the Franciscan Friary, which had the largest number of brothers, appeared to be more prosperous than any other institution of its kind in Wales.

While it would be wrong to be over-sentimental about the conditions and circumstances of these houses in 1535–6, it is well to bear in mind that some houses did try, albeit in vain, to keep up appearances. They were the last visible signs of papal power in the countryside, but were by then hardly the centres of hospitality, piety and learning that they had been. The impact of economic recession, plague, revolt and social change had hit them hard in western Europe from the latter part of the fourteenth century onwards, and the *Valor* provided a sad commentary on a mode of life that had, in the past, represented all that was worthy in medieval civilisation. Consequently, in 1536, the 47 religious houses in Wales – all valued below £200 a year – were dissolved and their possessions were surrendered to the Crown. The majority were Cistercian settlements and only three abbeys – Whitland, Neath and Strata Florida, which were daughter churches of English settlements – were allowed to continue temporarily on payment of large fines, but they were all dissolved by 1539. In 1538 the friaries came to an end, and in 1540 the centre of the Order of St John at Slebech in Pembrokeshire finally closed its doors. Leases already agreed to were confirmed by the Crown, usually on terms ranging from 40 to 100 years.[8] Subsequent to the dissolution, other monastic properties not already farmed out by monks were leased, usually for 21 years, to landed speculators, many of them attached to the royal household, and to prominent gentry, such as Sir John Price of Brecon, Geoffrey Glynne of Bangor and Dr John Vaughan of Narberth. Leasing eventually led, from 1540 onwards, to sales of monastic properties, and by Elizabeth I's reign a large proportion had been disposed of – with the most conspicuous beneficiaries being gentry with vested interests in religious change and, surprisingly, staunch Roman Catholic families such as the earls of Worcester at Raglan, the Carnes of Ewenni and the Owens of Plas Du, Llŷn, who considered self-interest rather than conscience to be their guide in these matters.

The condition of the Church in Wales on the eve of the Reformation reflected the malaise that affected religious life generally. William Barlow's episcopate (1536–48) corresponded to a formative period in the early development of the Reformation in Wales, from the dissolution of the monasteries to the changes that laid the basis of the Protestant state in the reign of Elizabeth. He came to office through the patronage of Anne Boleyn, then marchioness of Pembroke, and his correspondence with Thomas Cromwell amply revealed a hostile and intolerant attitude towards the unreformed Church. Besides conducting a thorough reformation of his diocese, he had three main aims: to establish a grammar school to improve the quality of education among clergy and laity; to destroy superstition, corruption and other evils and introduce a system of regular preaching in the diocese; and to move the cathedral from St David's to Carmarthen. The school, known as Christ College, was opened in 1541 and maintained by part of the revenues of the collegiate church at Abergwili. He considered that moving the Bishop's Palace from St David's to Carmarthen – more specifically to the site of the dissolved Franciscan friary – would be advantageous to the task of reforming the diocese. The town was appropriately placed, for it was the largest urban centre in Wales situated in a rich agricultural area, a town with good trading connections and a literate and strong English-speaking community. Carmarthen was also a centre where powerful gentry families, members of which were aware of the religious changes of their day, had purchased town houses. Although Bishop Richard Rawlins had completed repair work on the cathedral during his time at St David's, his successor Barlow criticised him for his conservatism. Despite the opposition of his chapter, Barlow pursued a radical policy. He failed in his bid to move the cathedral to Carmarthen, but succeeded in moving the Bishop's Palace to Abergwili and, doubtless under pressure, surrendered Lamphey, the richest of the episcopal lordships and manors, to the Crown. This transfer revealed the impoverished state of the diocese which could no longer maintain the lavish hospitality that had been the custom in the past, and royal policy aimed at reducing the wealth and power of the episcopate. Lamphey was not the only palace to be sold in the sixteenth century, chiefly to landowning families. It was the powerful Richard Devereux, to whom Lamphey was transferred, who gained most at the Church's expense in the diocese of St David's. In that respect, Barlow's stay in the see heralded the rise of an influential lay family in his diocese and the introduction of Protestant reform into Wales. He represented the first generation of iconoclastic reformers in Wales who attempted to cleanse the Church of popish customs and to deprive it of its possessions, partly to his own advantage.[9]

It was a period when powerful laymen became increasingly involved in ecclesiastical affairs. In the diocese of Bangor, for example, in the years 1524–36 faction lay at the root of the rivalry between the powerful Sir Richard Bulkeley I of Beaumaris and William Glyn, archdeacon of Anglesey (formerly suffragan to Bishop Thomas Skeffington), and his ally Edward Gruffudd of Penrhyn, the heir to another powerful north Wales family. The intense quarrels illustrated how religious affairs in the diocese were used as a cover for deeper political and family motives.[10] At St Asaph, Bishop Robert Wharton kept up appearances by letting episcopal lands on long-term leases. At Llandaff as well, concern was expressed about the condition of the diocese and, between 1517 and 1537, George de Athequa, handicapped by his absenteeism and inability to speak English – let alone Welsh – did little that was beneficial to improve the quality of its clergy, and his absentee successor Robert Holgate also neglected the Church.

In view of indifferent leadership and the unreformed state of the Church, the situation faced by Barlow and other first-generation Protestants called for drastic measures. The Church did not possess the resources needed to improve its standards and was unable to defend its position. It is hardly surprising, therefore, that there was no opposition to the religious changes that occurred in Henry VIII's latter years, and during the reign of his son Edward, when significant innovations were introduced in doctrine and discipline. Simple parishioners, in the first instance, were hardly affected by such doctrinal changes. It took time for changes to occur in individual parishes and Catholic practices persisted. The gentry, most of whom had adopted the New Faith by the latter half of the century, controlled their tenants and stemmed any opposition to royal policy that might threaten their own position among the lower orders. A Church isolated from the main centres of intellectual activity and religious reform was moribund and unlikely to spur on a conservative and monolingual peasantry to revolt without strong religious leadership. Moreover, the Crown had destroyed the old aristocracy in Wales so that no traditional leadership survived to defend the Old Faith as occurred in England with the Pilgrimage of Grace (1536). In view of gentry loyalties to the Crown and the fact that pilgrims often came from afar and were not in any position to organise a coordinated and effective revolt against the closure of shrines, it seems that strong Roman Catholic resistance was not possible in Wales. It was only gradually that the Welsh people accepted the new religious dispensation; it was formal legislation and gentry leadership rather than any strong active allegiance to it on behalf of a conservative peasantry that ensured the success of the Protestant faith in the long term.

The Definition of Doctrine

One of the most remarkable bishops in the period down to the accession of Elizabeth was Anthony Kitchin (Dunstan) of

Llandaff (1545–63), who was among the last abbots to be consecrated a prelate in the Roman Catholic Church. His shrewd manipulation of religious circumstances enabled him to adapt himself to religious change to suit his own purposes and to safeguard his position. His control over his diocese indicated how aggressively ambitious bishops could maintain their power in times of religious crisis.[11] He sold many episcopal farms and let the remainder on long-term leases. Between 1547 and 1559 the Church faced a challenge that drew it two ways within a decade, first towards extreme Protestantism and then towards the Old Faith. In the period between 1547 and 1553 the inflow of Protestant reformers from the Continent increased, as did also the pillaging of church buildings. Vestiges of papistry were destroyed, and a Protestant doctrine was imposed on the realm by means of the two English Books of Common Prayer compiled by Thomas Cranmer, archbishop of Canterbury, in 1549 and 1552. There were revolts against the first edition in Cornwall and Devon, demanding that the Mass, the Six Articles and the monasteries should be restored. The first version was also criticised by Protestants because its contents compromised with the tenets of the Old Faith. Zwinglian leaders opposed it because they considered that the Communion was no more than a reformed version of the Mass. When the earl of Warwick (who became duke of Northumberland in 1551) assumed power after the duke of Somerset in 1549, the government proceeded to attack the Old Faith violently; churches were violated and pillaged by unscrupulous landed proprietors, the doctrines of Luther and Calvin became more widespread, and anti-Catholic forces increased. In the second Book of Common Prayer in 1552, doctrine was defined more clearly and in greater detail with strong Zwinglian influences. Transubstantiation was rejected and a second Act of Uniformity was enacted to impose the new doctrine on the realm. Cranmer was not entirely satisfied with the situation since he believed that the people had not been given sufficient time to understand – let alone accept – the changes, and Edward VI was blamed for that by the Strasbourg reformer Martin Bucer.

Cranmer failed to introduce any further reform, but the king's Council accepted the Forty-Two Articles in 1553. They were moderate and condemned the most obvious deficiencies in the Church. Declarations were made in favour of justification by faith, and a definition of 'good works' was avoided. This was Cramer's last attempt to establish a *via media* in religious matters.[12]

What was the situation in Wales? If reformers were aware of the need for better instruction for the clergy of England, it was all the more urgent in Wales. In addition to doctrinal matters, there were serious problems of communication. The humanist Sir John Price of Brecon in 1546 referred to the prevalence of 'extreme darkness for lack of knowledge of God and His commandments' among his fellow-Welshmen and to the ignorance or apathy of the clergy in such matters although it was their responsibility to care for 'those souls which would go to perdition because of their shortcomings'.[13] William Salesbury, undisputably the greatest Welsh Renaissance scholar of his age, was also well aware of the depressed religious condition of the Welsh because of their ignorance of the New Faith. His ardent appeal in his preamble to *Oll Synnwyr Pen Kembero Ygyd* in 1547 reveals the dire state of religion on Edward VI's accession.[14] Earlier in the same year he published *A Dictionary in Englyshe and Welshe* with the intention of teaching English to the Welsh people. This was so that they could become acquainted with learning and with the contents of the Bible which had been published in English, but he realised that ignorance was a barrier. The clergy had received very little instruction to assist simple parishioners in understanding the tenets of the New Faith, and Barlow and his colleagues in the Welsh Church appear to have accomplished little in this respect. While it is true that in March 1538 Barlow complained of his canons' 'slumbering negligence towards the preferment of God's Word', he was more immediately concerned about the condition of the cathedral church, 'lurking in a desolate corner', and opposed to the attempts of the canons to 're-edify' it 'without any profitable effect saving to nourish clattering conventiles of barbarous rural persons'.[15] It was an age of self-seeking and religious faction. Pre-Reformation bishops before Barlow's time, were largely negative in their approach and they placed greater emphasis on their own material interests. Their ignorance of the Welsh language was also an obstacle in any attempt to reform the clergy. It was probably to that language and allied features that Barlow referred when he mentioned the 'uncivility' of the Welsh people.[16] When he planned to erect a free grammar school in Carmarthen his intention was to provide a 'daily lecture of holy scripture, whereby God's honour principally preferred, the Welsh rudeness decreasing, Christian civility may be introduced'. At St Asaph, Robert Wharton took no interest in reforming the clergy; neither was Arthur Bulkeley, the brother of Sir Richard Bulkeley I of Beaumaris, a reformer although he publicly declared his desire to safeguard the spiritual interests of his diocese. It appears, however, that he was the first bishop for over a century to reside at Bangor, and it is possible that, had circumstances been more favourable, he might have attempted some further reforms besides urging his clergy to give religious instruction to their parishioners.

In his Latin preamble to *Kynniver llith a ban* – a Welsh version of the Epistles and Gospels to be read at Communion on Sundays and holy days – William Salesbury expressed his desire to seek the support of the Welsh bishops (and the bishop of Hereford) to authorise the work to be used in churches.[17] His aim was to provide translations of central parts of the scriptures contained in the Book of Common Prayer because he believed that there was need for them to be regularly used in parish churches. He was aware of the spiritual needs of his countrymen, and he lightly chastised the bishops for not attending to their duties and the clergy for being unable to withstand the 'wolves of Rome'. In view of such depressed conditions, Salesbury took it upon himself to improve the situation. He was a pioneer among anti-Catholics in Wales, and in 1550 he published two polemical works: the first to justify clerical marriage, and the second, *The Baterie of the Popes Botereulx,* as a fierce attack on the Catholic altar. In fact, it is in this work that he attacked Roman Catholic doctrine directly. He presented the work to Sir Richard Rich, the lord chancellor, whom he served at the time, praising him for his attempts to suppress false religion. The need for a translation of the scriptures into Welsh – in an age when so much emphasis was placed on the vernacular languages – was evident in some of his works, particularly the preamble to *Oll Synnwyr Pen Kembero Ygyd*. It was an entirely different matter, however, to convert that ideal into reality since clerical inadequacies and the gross ignorance of the people stood in the way.[18]

The Catholic Reaction

The progress of the Reformation was again interrupted in the reign of Mary Tudor between 1553 and 1558, for she was determined to restore the Old Faith to the position it had occupied in 1529. The policy was unsuccessful for various reasons, but it must not be thought that Wales gradually drifted back to the Old Faith because Protestantism had not been understood nor accepted before her accession. According to Catholic poets, composing their verse in free and strict metres, it appears that the Welsh people, totally bewildered by the sudden changes in religious policies and being Roman Catholic at heart, warmly welcomed her policies. Although some opposition to Mary's accession arose from among the Herbert family, earls of Pembroke and the Devereux family, later earls of Essex (both supporters of the duke of Northumberland), it did not last long. There was some support also for Sir Thomas Wyatt's revolt in London in 1554, but not sufficient to have any impact in Wales. The anti-papal legislation of Henry VIII and Edward VI was repealed, the Protestant bishops dismissed and imprisoned, the Mass restored, and Cardinal Reginald Pole was sent by the Pope to receive the realm back to the Old Faith. Married clergy were dismissed and papal supremacy was reasserted. This sudden reversion was readily accepted by Parliament, but it refused to restore monastic lands – which, by then, had largely been incorporated into the landed estates of lay proprietors. The first to lose his position in Wales for defending clerical marriage and for his heresy was Robert Ferrar, bishop of St David's in March 1554. He was a moderate Protestant and the first to be consecrated according to the new English liturgy in 1548. He was a Yorkshireman who came to the diocese under difficult circumstances and without much local support. He attempted to reacquire Lamphey, but clashed with the Devereux family, and also embittered relations between himself and the Barlows in his bid to acquire the tithes of Caeriw. His quarrels with George Constantine, the registrar of the diocese, Humphrey Toy and other powerful laymen in Carmarthen frustrated him further. They accused him of being too mild in his approach to religious reform and too tolerant of Roman Catholic practices. After being deprived of his bishopric soon after Mary's accession, he was imprisoned and suffered martyrdom in March 1555 in Carmarthen market square. Although not the type of Protestant anxious to promote the Faith with all the ardour of a front-line reformer, Ferrar nevertheless refused to recant.[19] It is hard to say what impact his death had, but his enemies used religious scruples chiefly to serve their own interests since some of them, ardent Protestants though they were, continued to hold office under the new Catholic queen. The spoils of office rather than the horrors of persecution drove them into accepting a regime that their consciences were disposed to reject. When the two other Protestant martyrdoms in Wales are also considered in the context – Rawlins White in Cardiff (1555) and William Nichol in Haverfordwest (1558) – it cannot be said that they had made any great impact other than to warn people in populated areas, where Protestantism was growing, of the consequences of heresy under a Catholic monarchy.

Details of deprivations appear in the diocesan registers of St David's and Bangor, and it appears that one in eight and one in six lost their livings in each diocese respectively. It was not a matter of clerical marriage alone that caused opposition so much as the effects whereby they set their livings on lease to their personal and their family's advantage, a situation that often led to disputes over the leasing of tithe and glebe involving deprived clergy. With regard to royal policy and allegiance to the Crown, the clergy were flexible enough. In this respect, Anthony Kitchin of Llandaff is a classic example among his colleagues of a prelate adaptable to circumstances. Dr Ellis Price of Plas Iolyn, a powerful layman, adopted a similar outlook. Kitchin served two kings and two queens and Price held a variety of offices in north Wales over a long period from 1535 to his death in 1594. In contrast, the term of office of Marian bishops in Wales was very short, with the most important among them being Thomas Goldwell, bishop of St Asaph, who was actively involved in attempting to restore the Old Faith. He had served Cardinal Pole on the continent before returning to England after his promotion to become papal legate in England in 1553. After Goldwell's appointment to St Asaph, he refused to accept Henry VIII's religious policy, restored pilgrimages to St Winifred's well at Holywell, and denounced clerical marriages in his see. He retained close connections with Rome, and in October 1558, shortly before Mary's death, was appointed her legate in the Roman curia. During his three years at St Asaph, Goldwell attempted to restore papal power, and it is possible that if Mary had survived he would have laid the cornerstone of Catholic recovery in Wales. At St David's, Henry Morgan, a native of Pembrokeshire and an ecclesiastical lawyer, set about the same task. He was orthodox and he deprived about eighty clergy in 1554–5 because they had married. This caused problems, especially when canons of the cathedral church sought to obtain their incomes for the year after they had been deprived. In most cases, the marriage custom among clergy in Edward VI's reign merely legalised cohabitation – although it was prohibited under canon law.

At Bangor, William Glyn, a native of Anglesey, organised synods twice annually in his diocese to ensure that the clergy were performing their spiritual duties as required. He was 'a great scholar and a great Hebrician', according to Sir John Wynn of Gwydir in his *Memoirs*,[20] and was highly regarded by the contemporary Catholic poets, Siôn Brwynog and Lewis

Daron. It was a period when a spate of poetry, composed in free and strict metres, expressed support for the old religious rites. Siôn Brwynog, in a famous strict-metre poem (*c.* 1550), comprised the two faiths and found solace only in the old services. 'There is coldness in our times,' he maintained, 'the churches are as cold as ice'; he also deplored the speedy desecration of altars and revered Catholic observances.[21] There had been a growing feeling of dissatisfaction with religious tendencies and the statutory imposition of a new code of religious practice. For the common people, Mary's reign had restored the status quo, but Catholic scholars in her time desired a more positive approach to reform within the Church. Among them, Gruffydd Robert and Morus Clynnog, archdeacon of Anglesey and the bishop-designate of Bangor respectively, were the most ardent, and they took a prominent part in spearheading the Catholic Reformation on the Continent where they took refuge after Mary's death. Roger Smith, Owen Lewis and Morgan Phillips were other exiled reformers. Smith, at Douai – a Mecca for some Welsh Catholic scholars – translated into Welsh a part of St Petrus Canisius's catechism *Summa Doctrinae Christianae* in 1609. Owen Lewis also settled at Douai, and before moving to Rome served as a canon of the cathedral of Cambrai and as archdeacon of Hainault. He also became the vicar general to Archbishop Carlo Borromeo in Milan before being appointed bishop of Cassano in southern Italy. It was in Milan that he met Gruffydd Robert, who served as Borromeo's confessor. It was there that Robert – arguably the greatest of Welsh Roman Catholic scholars of his age – became fully acquainted with Italian Renaissance culture; and it was also there that he published his Welsh grammar – *Dosparth Byrr ar y rhan gyntaf i ramadeg Cymraeg* – in 1567. In the following year, again in Milan, a Welsh version of Ioannes Polanco's *De Doctrina Christiana* was printed, entitled *Athravaeth Gristnogavl*, which is attributed to Morus Clynnog.[22]

Another Catholic leader on the continent was Robert Gwyn of Penyberth, Llŷn, who fled to Douai but subsequently returned to Wales where he was sheltered by Hugh Owen of

Plas Du, another dangerous recusant. It was this Robert Gwyn who translated Robert Parson's *Christian Directory* and who probably wrote *Y Drych Cristianogawl* (1586). This dealt with the 'last four things', and was clandestinely printed in Rhiwledyn cave on the Little Orme between Llandudno and Rhos-on-Sea on the land of the Pue family of Penrhyn Creuddyn, powerful recusants in that area. This cave seems very small to have sheltered at least eight recusants, including Robert Pue and William Davies, a missionary priest martyred at Beaumaris in 1593, and no remains of Gothic print have been found. Surviving traces of charcoal, however, may indicate the wooden floor and the spot where the altar was built. Morgan Phillips also moved to Douai. He was the precentor of St David's, and a keen disputant in his student days at Oxford. It was with his assistance that William Allen set up the seminary at Douai.[23]

During Elizabeth I's reign, Welshmen of this calibre on the Continent were in the forefront of Roman Catholic reform and had the intention of restoring Wales to the Old Faith. It was during Mary Tudor's short reign that the foundations of this campaign were established. With a Catholic queen on the throne, the prospects seemed to be favourable, and it was at that time that the division between two small religious groups, keen to win over the loyalties of the Welsh people, became more distinct. They shared some common interests and concerns, not least their desire to elevate the Welsh language as a vehicle of Renaissance learning and to see published a purified version of the scriptures in the Welsh language. Religious reform, however, could never be achieved on the basis of intellectual ambitions alone. In the last resort, the success rate depended largely on the degree to which an illiterate peasantry could be won over to the New Faith. One thing is clear: the majority of the peasant population in Wales had not accepted (and could never accept) a faith that did not appeal to them. In this context, more important was the attitude of the gentry who exercised power over the lower orders and who were regarded as the natural leaders of peasant communities.[24]

The Elizabethan Church and the Protestant Faith

It is in the context of radical religious changes that emphasis was placed on the need to achieve religious uniformity and solidarity in the state, a factor that assumed increasing importance after the accession of Elizabeth during the remainder of her reign. Her first task was to settle the problems of the Church, and with the aid of Sir William Cecil she reorganised it so that it might become acceptable by the majority of the populace and established the independence of the realm. The main points at issue at the time were the need to strengthen the kingdom's defences, reform religion and establish royal supremacy on a Protestant basis. As the daughter of Anne Boleyn who had been reared in the household of Catherine Parr, her father's last wife, she was a symbol of the breach with Rome, and of English independence of foreign Catholic powers and, to the papists, illegitimate.

In politics and religion much depended at the outset of her reign on the queen's attitudes and intentions. Her choice was not easy: if she accepted the Old Faith she would be obliged to declare her illegitimacy and seek the Pope's permission to accede to the throne. It was not part of her nature to establish a Church independent of the state. She wished to emphasise the links between religion and political supremacy and knew that she could never turn the clock back to 1529, not even 1547. Her people probably would have favoured a return to her father's religious policy, but that was not practicable in view of the momentous changes that had occurred in the years 1547–53. Protestant reformers had left an indelible impression on England and Elizabeth's task was to devise a way of settling religion acceptable to the majority. Her choice was to support the Roman Catholic faith, or introduce Protestantism, or reach a compromise situation between them. She was a secular monarch and had personally very little interest in theological matters. Her main concern was to protect the welfare of the realm she had inherited. She also emphasised the need to care more for the 'commonweal' than to nourish a religious conscience, and thus directed her policies towards establishing and maintaining religious uniformity to ensure the safety of the realm. For a variety of reasons, the easiest policy would have been to support the Old Faith, already *in situ* when she came to the throne. This would spare her the opposition of Catholic claimants – thus reducing the threat to her throne. Elizabeth, however, considered that maintaining the independence of her realm, and establishing unity and uniformity within it, were factors of paramount importance. Like her father, but under different circumstances, she was aware of the *imperium* that legislation in the Reformation Parliament had established in the 1530s and that she wished to maintain. Most of her counsellors were Protestants, and reformed missionaries from Geneva and Frankfurt were again heard expounding the New Faith. The Mass was celebrated at her coronation service, but she walked out when the celebrant insisted on the elevation. She also unequivocally declared that she did not wish 'to make windows into men's souls'. It is in that spirit that Elizabeth embarked upon her task to solve the religious problem on her succession.

Since convocation was not prepared to undertake a reform of the Church, the government set about restoring religious order in the realm. Convocation stood firmly by transubstantiation, the Latin Mass and the supremacy of Rome. The foundations of the Church were established on government measures in Parliament designed to reform religious worship, and three versions of the Act of Supremacy (1559) were drafted before Parliament accepted it. Henry VIII's legislation was restored and Crown officials and the clergy had to take an oath acknowledging the queen as 'sole superior governor of the realm in all spiritual matters or causes, ecclesiastical and temporal'. According to the Act of Uniformity, in the same year it was ordered that the second Book of Common Prayer (1552) should be used in services. The passage of that Act was not easy either, but it succeeded because of the weakness of Catholic opposition to it in the House. In the Lords it was passed only by three votes because of episcopal resistance.[25]

The Elizabethan settlement was generally accepted: it had been imposed by the will of the government despite the stiff opposition among Catholic leaders and the tepid support of Parliament. There were strong Catholic sympathies in the Church, and its leaders were not favourably disposed to abandon the orthodox faith. It was the government that chose the path of Protestantism and laid the foundations of the Elizabethan state Church. Serious problems arose, but gradually – although the Church failed in its prime objective to unify the realm in religious matters – it was now becoming recognised as one of the chief institutions of state. It became a cornerstone designed to create unity in the realm, and together with the Crown, Parliament and the law, the Church was acknowledged as a formative pillar of Elizabethan government.

In Wales, the new religious proposals were accepted, as in the past, without protest. Ecclesiastical commissioners were sent around its four dioceses and those of the border to administer the oath of uniformity and supremacy to the clergy. About a dozen of the higher clergy refused to take the oaths, some of them fleeing abroad, and only Bishop Kitchin of Llandaff – as adaptable as ever – submitted among the Catholic prelates. The vast majority of laymen outwardly conformed but, at that time, there must have been much soul-searching among many gentry with divided loyalties and torn consciences. Most of the royal commissioners were the stalwart leaders of the Protestant Church in its first generation, such as Richard Davies and Thomas Young, two commissioners in 1559 and two bishops who were eager to plant the seed of the New Faith in Wales. They were well aware of three underlying features in that Church – its impovershed condition, its conservatism and its limited resources – which emphasised the problems confronted by the new leaders in the poorest dioceses. Its resources were weak enough in a mountainous country with no large and prosperous towns, no capital city and no university. The Renaissance had not struck deep roots there and the influence of the printing press was non-existent, and very modest indeed even after 1546 when the first Welsh book was printed. The spiritual condition of the Church was feeble, and the task of conducting a reform programme was a major undertaking even for bishops appointed specifically for that purpose.[26] The vast majority of the population was monolingual and illiterate, and the language of the new as well as the old liturgy was equally lacking in meaning for them. In addition, grasping lay landed proprietors sought all ways to benefit from the acquisition of church lands, tithes and other ecclesiastical emoluments. The attack on the Church intensified, and by Elizabeth's reign what Crown leases remained of old monastic properties applied only to tithes and rectories. In a period of growing inflation, the Crown exacted high entry fees, a trend that continued down to the 1580s and 1590s when leases for three lives and low entry fines became customary.

One feature that posed a serious threat to the Church and to the growth of Protestantism in Wales was the conservative nature of the Church. Communities continued to cling to superstitious practices that the reforming spirit in the Catholic Church itself had rejected. These shrines, relics and pilgrimages, however, were not considered to be the most serious problems, but represented deep-seated social and economic weaknesses that hindered the Church from making more rapid progress. The threats of strong recusant families and their followers was another factor, and records show the amount of support for the Old Faith that the Council in the Marches was expected to suppress. Prominent recusant families commanded considerable support in their respective areas – the Edwardses of Plas Newydd, Chirk, the Pughs of Penrhyn Creuddyn, the Herberts of Powys Castle, Welshpool, the Morgans of Llantarnam, the Turbervilles of the Vale of Glamorgan, the Owens of Plas Du, Llŷn and the earls of Worcester at Raglan. Their persistence protected pockets of recusant activity and frustrated the progress of the new Church. It was often claimed that there was much negligence among regional officials in pursuing their duties, tracking down heretics and suppressing political dissidents. Roman Catholicism was suspected chiefly because of its serious threat to organised stable government. In 1570 the Bull *Regnans in Excelsis* excommunicated Elizabeth and absolved her subjects from their temporal allegiance by declaring her deposed. Consequently, they were regarded as traitors by the Crown, and not merely heretics, and were subject to heavy penalties.[27]

The popular free-metre verse, to which reference has been made, illustrated how alien the New Faith was in mid-century to ordinary peasant folk, and in some quarters opposition was intensified. Among the most productive was Richard White, the Llanidloes schoolmaster and first Welsh Catholic martyr (in 1584), whose carols mocked at the Protestant form of worship. He scorned the 'sad trestle' and the 'wrinkled cobbler distorting his lip to eat the bread in place of Christ'.[28] In his view, Protestantism was discreditable because it had abandoned 'the virtue of Christ's sacrifice' and had 'rejected the miracle of the Lamb's passion'. He also harshly condemned those who suppressed the images of saints, and he deplored the replacement of traditional priesthood with a lay ministry. In his poem applauding William Morgan for translating the scriptures into Welsh, 'Sir' Thomas Jones, the vicar of Llandeilo Bertholau in Gwent who had a strong Protestant bias, described the penurious condition of the peasantry in the age of papistry.[29]

England's prime contribution to the Protestant Reformation was the religious settlement that was legislated – not without considerable opposition – in Parliament in 1559. As 'supreme governor' of the Church, Elizabeth ruled the institution from outside, and it was made subject to her 'governorship' as ordained by statute in Parliament. It united Calvinistic theology with the medieval organisation of the Catholic Church. The followers of the reformed faith – regardless of their diversity in matters of interpretation – emphasised the authority of the Bible, and declared that the prime objective of the Church was to preach the gospel and not to administer the sacraments. Since the lives of simple parishioners had been spiritually impoverished with the disappearance of the Mass, the new institution was intended to replace it with sound Protestant preaching and teaching.

Fundamentally, the Elizabethan Church was legally bound to the concept of the national sovereign state, its chief aim at the outset being to establish firm foundations for the *Ecclesia Anglicana* formulated by the queen, Parliament and Convocation.

The Problems of the Church in Wales

The major danger of such developments was the increasing threat of foreign invasion. Military organisation once more became a priority in a kingdom without a standing army and at a time when it stood in peril of being attacked by Catholic forces from the Continent via Ireland. The war with France and Scotland continued after Elizabeth came to the throne, and relations with Spain were deteriorating. The queen's dealings with foreign powers were cautious. Her expediency, in times of crisis, kept her kingdom independent, particularly in the years surrounding her excommunication and the Jesuit threat in the 1580s and 1590s. When war broke out against Spain in 1585, the demand for improved coastal defence increased and officials were summoned to perform necessary duties to safeguard the realm from invasion. In Wales, emphasis was placed again on the vulnerability of the western coasts, particularly Pembrokeshire, Llŷn and Anglesey, and the defence of the Protestant state was identified with political unity. In her role as head of the Church and defender of the faith, the queen directed her government to preserve the royal supremacy, strengthen the defensive structure of the realm, and establish uniformity. In that context Welsh religious affairs were brought within the orbit of English politics and promoting the New Faith in the country assumed a political dimension.

In view of social and economic difficulties, how could that be successfully accomplished in Wales? In addition to the efforts of church leaders to reform their clergy, the principal objective was to promote the translation of the Bible into vernacular. When the legislation to that effect was enacted in 1563, the prime motive was religious uniformity. Although the most important measure in Elizabeth's second Parliament in that year was the Act to confirm the monarchy's powers in Wales, it was the provision of the scriptures, in the long term, that had wide-ranging national repercussions. Both measures had similar motives, but in view of Wales's linguistic and religious features, the provision of the scriptures departed from the spirit of the Tudor settlement in 1536.

Efforts had been made two years previously by Thomas Davies, bishop of St Asaph, to use the Welsh language in Welsh services. He succeeded Richard Davies, and in a Diocesan Council he directed that the 'epistle and gospel' be read at St Asaph in Welsh after they had been read in English, and that children should 'hear read and have declared the catechism to them in their mother tongue in their churches every Sunday, with answers, and in the English tongue...on Sundays and Holydays'.[30] It appears that the translations of Sir John Price, and particularly William Salesbury, were used for that specific purpose, but it is not known to what extent similar arrangements were made in other Welsh dioceses. What is recorded, however, is that in 1565, when Thomas Huet (the translator of the Book of Revelation which appeared two years later) was chancellor of St David's the chapter laid out 4s 8d for three 'sawter bocks' for the church and 5 shillings for three books of General psalms.[31] It seems, however, that it was at St Asaph that the first attempt was made to introduce the Protestant faith on a liturgical basis among the people, and Thomas Davies – possibly at the instigation of his predecessor – was the pioneer among prelates of his generation in the field.

The preamble to the Act that provided the scriptures emphasised three major aspects of Tudor diplomacy: the need to establish uniformity in religious practice, a uniform creed, and an effective mode of communication. These strands were conveniently woven together through the agency of the central government's policy. The duty of each subject was to acknowledge royal supremacy: it was considered that accepting the New Faith in theological and doctrinal matters was a significant step forward towards extending it into Wales.

The preamble emphasised the central role of the Bible and Book of Common Prayer, and the measure was designed in order that the Welsh people 'might much better learn to love and fear God, to serve and obey their Prince and to know their Duties towards their neighbours'.[32] Emphasis was placed on discipline and obedience as the basic criteria of order. Harmony would never be achieved in the state unless uniformity was established in religious practice and belief. Although the legislation in 1536 did not declare that English was to be imposed as the language of religion, the spirit of the Tudor settlement seemed to imply that there should be uniformity in language as well. That was the purpose of the last section of the statute of 1563 which declared that copies of both English and Welsh versions of the Bible and Book of Common Prayer were to be placed side by side in all parish churches so that those who 'do not understand the said language [English] may, by conferring both tongues together, the sooner attain to the knowledge of the English tongue'. William Morgan, Dr David Powel and Morus Kyffin referred to the opposition to the task of providing the scriptures in Welsh. According to Powel's evidence, it might have been William Hughes, later bishop of St Asaph, and one of William Morgan's supporters in translating the whole Bible, who, at an early stage in his career – when he was the duke of Norfolk's chaplain – was partly responsible for the inclusion of that clause. The urgent situation at the time, however, demanded swift action, namely that the Welsh language should be used officially to promote the New Faith regardless of the long-term policy. Although the crucial last clause would have had no impact at all on the vast majority of parishioners who were ignorant of the written form of both languages, the provision of Protestant teaching and instruction in due course served to strengthen religious allegiances in Wales, and it is hardly surprising that the preamble to the Act betrays elements of nationalism, anti-popery, xenophobia and a firm attachment to the Protestant monarchy.

One serious threat to this policy was the persistence of Roman Catholic recusancy, particularly among the most articulate sections of society. John Jewel, bishop of Salisbury, published his *Apologia Ecclesiae Anglicanae* in 1562 in which he attacked the dogma of the Old Faith and challenged its leaders to establish the truth of their beliefs in scripture and readings from the early church fathers. It was a conscious attempt to further the aims of government. In 1563, Convocation agreed to the Thirty-Nine Articles based by Matthew Parker, archbishop of Canterbury, on the Articles of 1553. His discipline and erudition displayed in *The Advertisements* of 1566 contributed substantially to the character of the Anglican Church, which elevated it to a position above being merely a religious compromise and political tool. Although the Act of 1563 was expected by humanist scholars to make significant strides forward in promoting the New Faith, it was enacted principally as part of the policy to strengthen the Protestant state.

The success of the new Church in its early years depended largely on the way it was organised, the strength of its mission, and the support that it obtained. It depended in England and Wales on wise leadership among the bishops and higher clergy, with Richard Davies at St David's and Thomas Davies at St Asaph representing two fundamental aspects of the ecclesiastical structure at the outset. While Richard Davies promoted intellect and learning in the Church, Thomas Davies devoted himself almost entirely to establishing canon law and administration in his diocese.[33] Leadership among the rank and file, on the other hand, was largely characterised by indifference. There was a change in missionary activity by the end of the century owing to a marked increase in educational facilities, which gradually improved the quality of the priesthood. The mission reached its highest point when there was an appeal for more preachers among priests. Huw Lewis, the circumspect vicar of Llanddeiniolen, Caernarfonshire, was dissatisfied with the condition of the priesthood which he considered to be harmful to the progress of the Church. The bulk of the population lay in spiritual misery, he observed in the preamble to his translation of Miles Coverdale's *A Spiritual and most Precious Pearl* in 1595, because of the lack of books, and bishops and clergy were 'lazy in their office and calling who do not preach and interpret God's word to the people, rather they live silent and harshly like dogs who do not bark, bells with no tongues or a candle under a vessel'.[34] His evidence suggested strongly that the condition of the clergy had not improved by the end of the century, although it appears that more graduates and preachers were being ordained in Welsh dioceses – a sign that the quality of the clergy was gradually improving before the Stuart succession.

Doubtless the poverty of the Church had seriously affected clerical incomes and pluralism and non-residence had increased. Secular clergy suffered heavy pressures because much of their property had been farmed out to laymen. Bishops were forced to stretch their meagre resources, which sadly affected their pastoral work. Laymen acquired leases of episcopal and capitular property, parsonages, endowments of rectories and vicarages were leased out, and rights of advowson were granted which resulted in low clerical stipends. In addition, commissioners of concealment sought rewards by all methods possible, especially leases, and benefited from the despoliation of the Church. Simony and nepotism were common practices when higher clergy tried to maintain their incomes in times of financial stress. In 1586 it was reported that in Brecknock there were many spiritual livings or parsonages impropriated with no preachers.[35] It appeared that negligence was a common feature among the clergy and local government officials. Similar responses were found in the other Welsh dioceses, particularly regarding the poor quality of the clergy. Huw Lewis, the Gwynedd cleric, and Morus Kyffin, who translated Bishop John Jewel's *Apologia Ecclesiae Anglicanae* into Welsh in 1595, were eager to defend the principles of the New Faith, but greater emphasis was placed on improving moral standards among the Welsh people through the Welsh language.[36] Evidence shows that some effort was made to replenish the dioceses with suitable literature, although the material cannot be precisely identified. Bishop Rawlins, for example, collected an extensive library and Marmaduke Middelton, with the consent of his chapter, sold old copes in order that books and 'other ornaments' might be purchased for use in the cathedral church. In 1562, William Phillips, a vicar choral at St David's, was backward in reading (especially the Old Testament in English) and was compelled to read twenty Psalms and two chapters of the Old Testament daily until Thomas Huet was satisfied with his standard. Moreover, in 1571 Huet destroyed 'certain popish books, as mass books, hymnals, grants, antiphoners and such like' concealed by the sexton, and also sent manuscripts suspected of being subversive to Richard Davies and they were not returned. When it is considered that such records might well have contained valuable information about Catholic rites and customs appertaining to the Old Faith, Huet's rash action on this occasion was doubtless the opposite to his praiseworthy contribution to biblical translation.[37]

Protestant Humanism and Translation of the Scriptures

Rather than interpreting the Church's role in society, greater emphasis was placed on the practical extension of Protestantism in the parishes. To accomplish this among the Welsh gentry and other educated laymen, efforts were made by leading Protestant humanists to identify the Elizabethan Church with the Christian traditions of the early British people. The chief interpreter of this theory was Richard Davies, and his *Epistol at y Cembru*, the extended preface to the translation of the New Testament into Welsh, contained fulsome – albeit spurious – arguments in an effort to prove that the early Britons were privileged in being the first to receive the Christian faith and that Protestantism represented its revival and restoration. Davies related how St Joseph of Arimathea had introduced the apostolic faith into Britain soon after Christ's resurrection. It was corrupted after St Augustine introduced the Roman faith in AD 597, and thus began a long and gruelling period of Saxon oppression of the Welsh people. This continued throughout the Middle Ages

153

down to the sixteenth century when the ancient faith re-emerged. The most evident manifestation of this revival was the translation of the scriptures, which Davies and his fellow-humanists were convinced existed in the early Christian period. Some manuscripts containing parts of scripture in Welsh had survived from the Middle Ages, and to him that fact (misleading though it was), as well as other testimonies, was firm evidence that the Bible in primitive Welsh had existed among the early Britons. He set out to convince his fellow Welshmen of the authenticity of that theory and that Protestantism rather than 'ffydd Saeson' ('faith of the Saxons'), imposed forcibly upon the Welsh, was the true faith of the Britons. 'Remember the times of old,' he maintained, 'enquire of thy forefathers, search their history, thou who has been formerly honourable and of great privileges.'[38] Men will interpret history to suit their needs in their own day and this theory was effective propaganda designed to promote the interests of the New Faith based on an appeal to history and antiquity in the spirit of the Renaissance. The theory was accepted by William Salesbury, Morus Kyffin, Huw Lewis and the Puritan John Penry, and it circulated popularly among humanists in England. One of the most prominent among them, Matthew Parker, was steeped in this tradition and identified the Elizabethan Church as an essential part of the religious heritage. He corresponded with Davies on these matters because he considered the Protestant theory of the early British Church to be effective propaganda relevant to the challenge of the age. Parker was a reputable scholar, and as eager as Welsh humanists to discover, study and preserve manuscripts relating to the historic culture of Britain, many of them lost and dispersed during periods of social and political upheaval in the fifteenth century and the dissolution of the monasteries.[39]

This Protestant tradition was closely associated with the central feature of the Reformation in western Europe – namely, the provision of the scriptures in the vernacular. There were three motives underlying the translation of the Bible into European languages and, in that context, into

Welsh. The invention of the printing press facilitated the speedy publication of standard formal works, the Renaissance promoted lay and clerical education leading to specialisation in the classics and Hebrew at Oxford and Cambridge, and the Reformation emphasised the authority of the scriptures as the foundation of individual salvation.

The importance of the printing press was a matter that concerned all humanist scholars. Richard Davies marvelled at the impact of the 'art of printing' on countries in western Europe. Sir John Price also considered that churchmen and scholars should use the resources for the purpose of improving the moral quality of the people. Protestant and Catholic humanists were aware of the problems incurred when publishing books in the Welsh language. Legislation had not helped it, because in 1536 Parliament had authorised that English only was to be the language of law and administration and, by implication, it could also be made the official language of religion. Moreover, the printing press had very little impact on the Welsh people, the consequence being that only a handful of works were published in Welsh after 1546. The market was so small that it was not considered profitable to do so. The literate classes showed little interest in the language for social and economic reasons, which accounts for the ardent appeals made by humanists for more support and leadership among gentry and churchmen who were gradually losing their grasp on Welsh culture. In his preface to *Cambro-brytannicae Cymraecaeve Linguae Institutiones et Rudimenta* in 1592, Dr John Davies of Brecon issued a challenge to the gentry and aristocracy of Wales to print the manuscripts that illustrated their past greatness. 'One shilling from the purse of each one of us for paper and printing,' he maintained, 'would fill the country with such splendid books.'[40] The rhetorical style of this preface betrays traces of Renaissance culture as applied to Wales. Humanists, however, were aware of the dangers to the Welsh language in an age of increased economic pressure and social reorientation among landed gentry and the nouveaux riches in the towns. Consequently, they endeavoured to make their language more appealing to the natural leaders of society by emphasising how it could be restored to its elevated position as a vehicle of learning. William Salesbury's warning in the mid-1540s was echoed, even more meaningfully, half a century later: 'Take this as a warning from me,' he maintained in one of his most powerful appeals, 'unless you bestir yourselves to cherish and mend the language before the present generation is no more, it will be too late to do this later.'[41] Although the gentry were prepared to associate themselves increasingly with the Reformation, principally because of their vested material interests, they did not necessarily associate it with a need to safeguard the welfare of the Welsh language and its literary tradition at a time when greater importance was being attached to English speech and manners in public life.

To have the Bible and the Book of Common Prayer translated into the Welsh language, however, was one thing: to ensure that the achievements in 1567 and 1588 were worthwhile for the peasant community was another. The danger remained that the majority of clergy would or could not fulfil the demands expected of them by contemporary scholars. Sir John Price had seen the danger well before the scriptures were translated, and Richard Davies and Salesbury, among others, were aware of the pitfalls at the time of publication and afterwards.

In addition to ignorance and illiteracy, the persisting recusant threats in the latter years of the sixteenth and early seventeenth centuries continued to cause the government increasing anxiety. In his letter to Sir William Cecil in October 1567, Bishop Nicholas Robinson of Bangor commented despondently on the spiritual condition of his diocese on his appointment after the death of Rowland Meyrick. He blamed priests for neglecting their duties and for their inability to offer strong leadership in their parishes. He also believed that a famine of the Word arose more out of ignorance and lack of guidance than of any inclination to reject the faith on the part of the people. He was particularly critical of the vestiges of Catholic practices that persisted in the conservative areas of the hinterland. He revealed that priests were too old to receive education and that there were fewer than six who could preach (or who were licensed for that purpose) in the shires of Gwynedd. Although he expressed his joy on the publication of the New Testament and Book of Common Prayer in the vernacular in 1567, he was equally conscious of the failure of the clergy to further the cause of the New Faith.[42]

Nicholas Robinson was not the only one to describe in similar terms the dire state of religious life. William Bleddyn at Llandaff went even further and, soon after his appointment to the bishopric, accused his prebendaries of abusing the Church for their own benefit. He was painfully aware of the sad state of his diocese, one of the poorest in the realm, and attempted to counsel and chastise his officials accordingly: 'If you had governed the church according to the ancient ordinances and laudable customs,' he declared, '...how easily might we have met the ruins, the debts, the poverty and the contempt.'[43] Their cupidity had frustrated all attempts to reform the diocese and it seemed that all Reformation bishops in Wales, regardless of their good intentions of root and branch reform, were governed largely by their circumstances and were unable to pursue their tasks as effectively as they desired. Even they themselves were subject to constraints and were forced to use what means lay at their disposal to augment their incomes – usually granting rights of next presentation to livings, leasing prebends and episcopal lands and acquiring properties *in commendam*. One of these bishops was the exemplary William Morgan who was elevated to the sees of Llandaff (1595–1601) and St Asaph (1601–4) successively. He had difficulty in making ends meet, but was at the same time a staunch defender of the Church, particularly at St Asaph. According to the 1587 survey of livings and incomes in the diocese, his predecessor, William Hughes (1573–1600), had left the northern diocese in a deplorable condition. In this languishing state of affairs Hughes, albeit a good scholar, held sixteen livings (admittedly at different times) in the diocese *in commendam* and was regarded as a prelate of whom it was said that he 'fleeced rather than fed his flock'.[44] He had assisted Morgan in providing books for the translation of the Bible and had patronised the Welsh poets quite substantially, but his long term of office – over a quarter of a century – at St Asaph spanned the crucial years of Elizabeth's reign and exposed the Welsh Church when it was most vulnerable.[45] Morgan found it necessary to keep a tighter control on church property, which had fallen into the hands of greedy lay impropriators. Indeed, his defence of the Church was remarkably frank and assertive when he criticised impropriations. It may well have been the case that he had personal reasons for defending the establishment, particularly during his quarrel with the formidable Sir John Wynn of Gwydir over the tithes of Llanrwst rectory, but it appears that, in the last resort, he was a protector of the essential values of the Church. Bitter experience at Llanrhaeadr-ym-Mochnant and elsewhere had shown him that the Church was an institution seriously exploited by lay impropriators and ambitious lawyers. 'But if I had continued vicar of Llanrhaeadr I had been in better case than now I am,' he remarked of Wynn, '...Mr Wyn therein showed great love (as then I thought) to me: but (as now I finde) to himself hoping to make a stave of me to drive preachers partridges to his nets.'[46] Richard Davies also felt hard pressed at St David's when opposed by mighty laymen such as Sir John Perrott of Haroldston and the lawyer Fabian Phillips. He was also accused by his less worthy successor, Marmaduke Middleton, of being a nepotist and simonist. Davies had fallen victim to the very system that he served and doubtless was guilty of leasing episcopal properties to lay gentry, but he was equally aware of the dangers in allowing too much freedom for those who had so much to gain from exploiting the Church: 'But the lust of the world's goods has drowned Wales today,' he remarked, 'and impoverished every special quality and good virtue.' 'Time will not permit now to unfold the harm which the lust of this world's goods had wrought,' he maintained further, 'and the disbelief of the promises of God among all conditions of men in Wales by the lack of the teaching of the Holy Scripture.'[47] In his portrait of Richard Davies ('Diggon Davie') in *The Shepherd's Calendar*, Edmund Spenser drew attention to his opposition to the dogs (officials) which were worse than the shepherds (priesthood) for allowing the wolves (papists) to attack the flock (parishioners).[48] In Davies's Funeral Sermon for Walter Devereux, first earl of Essex, in 1577, he attacked those who oppressed the weak and declared that their evil practices were caused mainly by their lack of true religion.[49]

The translation of the Bible established the foundations of Protestantism in Wales. Although Richard Davies had himself contributed to the publication of the Welsh version of the New Testament and to the Bishops' Bible in 1568, it was the achievement of William Morgan, incumbent of Llanrhaeadr-ym-Mochnant in the diocese of St Asaph, that caused the greatest satisfaction among Protestant humanists in Wales. Despite his critical comments on the standards of the Church, Huw Lewis regarded the appearance of the Bible as a treasure and the 'true and refined Word of God' which would assist the clergy to instruct parishioners in the faith. Although Morgan, like his fellow humanists, favoured the use of one language in the realm, he considered that the spiritual needs of the Welsh was a far more urgent matter, and he explained his standpoint clearly in his Latin dedication of the Bible. He emphasised the religious and devotional rather than the political motives that underlay the venture. 'Moreover,' he declared, 'there can be no doubt that unity is more effectively promoted by similarity and agreement in religion than in speech.' 'Besides,' he continued, 'to prefer unity to piety, expediency to religion, and a kind of external concord among men to that heavenly peace which the Word of God impresses on men's souls shows but little piety.'[50] The availability of the Bible increased the opportunity to supply an effective preaching force in Wales. This was one of Morgan's prime objectives and, a year before the Bible appeared, an ardent Puritan called John Penry drew attention (in *The Aequity of an Humble Supplication*) to the delay in the translation and publication of the Bible. He emphasised to the government the need for a good-quality preaching ministry in Wales, and blamed Parliament for not attending to the spiritual needs of the Welsh people. It is possible that Penry's demand for a better-quality priesthood and the publication of the scriptures may have accounted for the urgent attention given by Archbishop John Whitgift to this matter after a quarter of a century's delay. To issue the Welsh Bible at that time would avoid embarrassment for him, safeguard the interests of the Church in Wales in a period of crisis in foreign relations and at a time of papist and Puritan threats at home, and enable William Morgan to see his work appear in print.[51]

William Morgan was doubtless the priest best suited to undertake the task of translating the Bible, having sat at the feet of the reputable French scholar Anthony Chevallier, or his successor Philip Bignon, at St John's College, Cambridge. Even his inveterate enemy, Sir John Wynn, was obliged to admit that he 'was a good scholar, both a Grecian and Hebrician'. As a native of Nanconwy he was well versed in the language and literature of Wales, and later in his career became a prominent patron of several of the professional poets. It may be that his first appointment to the sinecure living of Llanbadarn Fawr had been made by Richard Davies with a view to encouraging him to undertake the translating, but it is more probable that he had begun the task, aided by Whitgift, in his latter years at Cambridge. However, as he himself recounted, and as Star Chamber and other records amply show, he encountered problems at Llanrhaeadr in completing the work; certainly, if he hadn't had Whitgift's financial support and the assistance of Welsh scholars such as Dr Gabriel Goodman, Dr David Powel, Richard Vaughan and Edmwnd Prys, he would not have completed it. The bishops of Bangor and St Asaph, Hugh Bellot (and possibly his predecessor Nicholas Robinson) and William Hughes respectively authorised the translation for publication and loaned him books. In view of the motive for the legislation in 1563, it is surprising that the government had not pressed for the work of translation to be completed soon after 1567, especially when mounting religious tensions made uniformity a priority.[52] There may well be a grain of truth in the tradition recorded by Sir John Wynn that Davies and Salesbury, who evidently had it in mind to translate the Old Testament, ended their partnership after disputing the meaning of one word because of Salesbury's orthographical peculiarities in insisting on the use of latinised spellings in his works.[53]

The Puritan Scene

It is possible that John Penry's violent attacks on the Church had awakened its leaders to their responsibilities in Wales with regard to scriptural translation, and that indirectly he may have been responsible for the appearance of the Bible in the year of the Spanish Armada. Although eager to improve the moral standards of the Welsh people, Penry had virtually no influence on the Wales of his day. He did not cultivate a following in the Welsh dioceses, not even in his native St David's, and the time he spent in Wales was very slender indeed. There were hardly any signs of Puritan activity in Wales in the latter decades of the sixteenth century.[54] The social structure of the country largely accounted for that, particularly the lack of institutions of learning where horizons would have been widened and religious reform encouraged. There were isolated examples of Puritans, particularly in urban areas such as Wrexham, where it was reported in the 1580s 'pedlars and tinkers...and hot Puritans, full of the gospel' dwelled or visited, possibly as disciples of the Cheshire Puritan leader Christopher Goodman.[55] Rowland Puleston of Bersham (possibly a curate at Wrexham), in 1583 published *Llyfr o'r Eglwys Gristnogedd*, revealing a strong Puritan and anti-papist view, and Walter Stephens, vicar of Bishop's Castle, and Stanley Gower, vicar of Brampton Bryan who was also Sir Robert Harley's chaplain, were two other representatives of Puritanism on the Welsh borders.

While John Penry's spirit of patriotism cannot be denied, his Puritan activity needs to be re-examined and must be viewed within the context of the English Puritan movement in the late Elizabethan era when Jesuit threats and the lapse in the reform movement on the Continent demanded more forceful lobbying of the House of Commons in order that more positive steps might be taken to reform the Church. Indeed, most of what Penry had to say in his three main treatises concerning Wales, stripped of all Welsh references, might easily have applied to England. The Puritan message contained in those works was identical to that found in the writings of Job Throckmorton and the anonymous Marprelate Tracts, which desired to see a drastic reform of the Church. The importance of Penry's works in Wales lies in the manner in which they reveal fundamental weaknesses in the Church in an impoverished and isolated part of the realm. He used his treatises principally to underline the malaise that had afflicted spiritual life and supported the Presbyterian plan presented to the Commons in 1587 to establish a Church on Genevan lines. His comments, which were often laborious, repetitive and exaggerated, consistently attacked the government and its institutions – Parliament, privy council and Council in the Marches – for the depleted condition of the structure and organisation of the Church. His attacks on the bishops were scathing, particularly in the second and third treatises, but he was at all times careful to avoid mentioning any prelate by name and the details he offers of individual dioceses are often superficial and vague. He considered that it was the threat of papistry – in England and on the Continent – and bad economic conditions that had brought famine to the common folk. This he interpreted as being God's vengeance on a country that had disregarded divine commandments. He believed in the need for a powerful preaching ministry determined to offer the gospel of salvation, which could not be achieved until the major abuses in the Church – namely pluralism, impropriations and evil leadership, all of which had stifled the Church's progress – had been destroyed: 'except you grant free passage unto my gospel,' he maintained, 'the navy of the Spaniard which I discomfited before you, shall come again and fight against this land, and waste it with fire and sword'.[56] In view of the political situation at the time, Penry's words, threatening though they were, had a ring of truth about them; however, he achieved little in Wales. Indeed, the only comment on him in Wales by a contemporary was the remark made by George Owen challenging Penry's observations on the dearth of preachers in Wales. The 'shameless man,' he said, had written 'to the slander' of the whole of Wales and had misled his readers because, from his own knowledge of the situation in Pembrokeshire, Owen was aware of a number of beneficed preachers in the country.[57]

John Penry's importance lies in his positive literary contribution in the formative years of the Puritan movement in England and to the propaganda that eventually gave it political edge in the seventeenth century. In 1593 he was put on trial on a charge of treason, having allegedly violated the Act of Uniformity (1559), and his plea to Sir William Cecil to spare his life because of his love for his fellow-countrymen had no effect. He was hanged at St Thomas a Watering in London in May 1593 at the age of 30.

Early Seventeenth-century Recusancy, Puritanism and the Church

What, therefore, was the position of the Anglican Church in Wales in the early seventeenth century? When Francis Godwin, bishop of Llandaff, came to office in 1601 he complained about the same basic problems that had hindered its progress, particularly papistry, impropriations and the quality of the clergy.[58] In addition, he showed concern for the condition of his cathedral church which he described as being almost in ruins. The recusant problem was serious in the border areas, especially on diocesan boundaries where it was possible for adherents of the Old Faith to survive.

In Llandaff, the official recusant number in 1603 was 381, principally in the Vale of Glamorgan, where the Turberville influence was strong, and in Monmouthshire Catholics accounted for about one-fifth of the population. Together with Lancashire that county was considered to have the largest recusant population in the whole realm. The majority lived in the north-east and southern parts of the county, in parishes such as Abergavenny, Llandeilo Bertholau, Raglan (where the Worcesters reigned supreme) and Llanfihangel Llantarnam, the seat of the Morgans. Elsewhere, the diocese of St Asaph had 250 recusants, and the two westernmost dioceses, Bangor and St David's, had 32 and 145 respectively. The larger number for St David's was accounted for by its physical extent stretching as far east as the boundaries of Hereford and Llandaff dioceses and the concentration of recusants along those borders.[59]

Most of the Catholics whose names are recorded on gaol files of great sessions and recusant rolls came chiefly from among the lower middle class gentry and yeoman-freeholders. The total of 808 for the whole of Wales is surprisingly small in view of the estimated population of the country in the late sixteenth century of 212,450. Records, however, do not reveal all, and there were probably many others whose sympathies lay with the Old Faith but who conformed publicly in their own interests. Recusant gentry houses enjoyed a following among tenants and freeholders: the famous 'Llŷn recusancy case' in 1578, for example, centred on the activities of Thomas Owen of Plas Du, and in the Chirk area close ties were established between the notorious Edwards family of Plas Newydd and their dependants.[60] In Anglesey, vulnerable as it was to foreign Catholic invasion, the exploits of the turncoat Hugh Owen of Gwenynog in 1625 caused much anxiety to Lewis Bayly, bishop of Bangor, who regarded him as 'a most dangerous fellow' who had 'given over his place, disposed of his lands and converted his estate into money and went out of his country and no man knew why'.[61] This Hugh Owen, a gentleman of some repute, abandoned his living and offices to join the earl of Worcester at Raglan and eventually translated Thomas à Kempis's *De Imitatione Christi* into Welsh. His influence, in Bayly's opinion, was harmful to the Anglican Church: 'the rest of that faction [i.e. papists] are here so audacious that they never durst be so bold if they knew not of some invasion or conspiracy intended'. By this evidence there seemed to be coordination in the movements of Catholics in different parts of the country for the collection of news affecting their fortunes.

In west Wales in the early years of the seventeenth century anxiety of a different nature, but with similar implications, was expressed when immigrant individuals and families moved into Carmarthenshire and Pembrokeshire and spread Catholic influences. It was this fear that lay behind Sir James Perrott's letter to Robert Cecil, earl of Salisbury, in 1612. He was particularly concerned about the dangers that this movement posed for Milford Haven and the whole county. 'For Pembrokeshire,' he declared, 'it hath not many recusants...but...diverse do resort unto them and that they have intelligence with the recusants of Monmouthshire where there are many not only of the natives but of strangers coming out of other parts of Wales and England that reside there, and no doubt keep intercourse with them of Pembrokeshire and the adjoining counties.'[62] It appears again that such contacts were being maintained between recusant communities in different parts of the country. It was comparatively easy to move westwards to south-west Wales over land and sea. The Jesuit Robert Jones – 'the firebrand of all' as he was called – was typical of the itinerant priests who hardened resistance among recusants to the established order. By 1605 his organisation established in Monmouthshire extended along the borderlands, enabling him and other priests to maintain contact with the Catholic gentry. Lady Frances Morgan of Llantarnam, one of Jones's adherents, provided financial aid to maintain two Jesuit priests in north Wales and two in south Wales and, with the aid of the Jesuits John Salusbury of Rug and Charles Gwynne of Bodfel in Llŷn, to set up the headquarters of the Welsh Jesuit College of St Francis Xavier at Cwm in Llanrothal.[63]

It appears that although there continued to be strong Catholic allegiances in Wales and the borders, their survival depended largely on the degree of isolation in those areas, the political climate at the time, the ability of leading families to maintain opposition and command sufficient support as well as the contacts that were established between leaders and their followers in highly concentrated Catholic areas. One thing is certain: that the Old Faith was not the potent force in Wales on the eve of the Civil Wars that it had been half a century earlier, that the government had gradually gained the ascendancy, and that it was becoming more obvious that the counter-movement to Protestantism had not been successful. Many factors accounted for that situation: Wales was largely neglected, partly because it was considered – according to an over-optimistic report from Douai in 1602 – that Wales was safe, and that there was a need to concentrate on propagating the faith in more vulnerable areas. There were insufficient numbers of priests to conduct the mission, and that itself suffered serious drawbacks when confronted by opposition that had the full power of the state behind it. Although some signs of revival did occur in the reigns of James I and his son Charles, the Watson and Gunpowder plots had very little impact on Wales and the imposition of the penal laws in 1604, 1606 and 1610, for example, did not help the recusant cause.

Nevertheless, Roman Catholic adherents were, by the very nature of their political and religious allegiances, posing a serious threat to the unity of the realm. Gervase Babington, one of Godwin's predecessors, had earlier realised that recusancy was not easy to uproot in his diocese, but did attempt to undermine the influence of the most powerful families who clung to old religious traditions. In 1591 the Council in the Marches was warned by the Privy Council to be vigilant on the borders of the dioceses of Hereford and St Asaph where, it was said, 'there was great back-sliding in religion...especially in the confines of the shires between England and Wales such as Monmouthshire and the confines of the Welsh shires bordering on them'.[64] In March 1602 Lord Zouch, then in charge of the Council at Ludlow, also referred to excessive numbers of papists of some substance in arms and money.[65] Bishop Richard Parry at St Asaph despondently informed Robert Cecil, earl of Salisbury, the lord treasurer, of the poor condition of his clergy, the extent of impropriations and the constant threat of papistry in the eastern parts of his diocese. His letter clearly admitted that the diocese was unable to support a powerful preaching ministry because stipends were insufficient to maintain a learned and dedicated clergy.[66] Parry had succeeded to a diocese that was, in terms of communicants, the second largest in Wales and materially one of the most impoverished in the realm. In the mid-sixteenth century the diocese was valued at only £187 a year and Parry was obliged to confess that he kept for himself a number of benefices to maintain a reasonable income. The livings of bishops had not kept pace with the rise in prices and, like his contemporaries, Parry was forced to lease episcopal lands to powerful lay squires. Sir Richard Lewkenor, chief justice of the Chester circuit, expressed his anxieties concerning the persistence of recusancy in Wales and the borders. In November 1601 he informed Cecil of the increase in the numbers of Catholic adherents and justices of the peace, and also complained of their contempt in neglecting muster duties once they had obtained their 'press' money.[67] The penalties imposed on them, he said, were far too lenient. They preferred to pay a fine of 40 shillings or suffer a term of imprisonment rather than serve in the English army in Ireland, and Lewkenor considered that the government should apply the penal laws relating to forfeiture more strictly. A year later he complained again that recusancy was on the increase, although there were indications that efforts had been made to 'plant' suitable preachers in Welsh parishes.

In its second and third generations the Church continued to grapple with its problems and its leaders were aware of the need to maintain an all-out attack on the forces of resistance. It also had its sources of strength, though. In the first instance, evidence suggests that by the closing decades of the sixteenth century, despite the despairing comments of leading humanist writers, the quality of education among the clergy was improving.[68] The bishops showed a greater concern to improve standards in spheres of activity that had given the Church bad publicity in the past. Serious efforts were made to control the spread of Roman Catholicism, William Morgan at St Asaph repaired part of the cathedral church, and at Bangor Henry Rowlands was similarly occupied and granted endowments to aid charity and educational work. These bishops endeavoured to combat the most threatening economic forces that had stifled the medieval Church. Under such circumstances it is hardly surprising that church leaders found it difficult to win over the allegiance of all sections of the community and establish uniformity.

The Church, nevertheless, possessed resources that have not received the attention they deserve. The cornerstone of the new Church was doubtless the translation of the scriptures, and its early impact was seen in the few religious books that appeared soon after its publication and in the manuscript compositions of the professional poets. In their poems to individual Protestant leaders and the queen, they constantly drew attention to the tenets of the faith and the stability of the new Protestant state as reflected in the availability of the Bible. Prose works were published to provide instruction for the clergy in the principles of the faith so that they could plant the seed in their parishes. Among them the works of Morus Kyffin and Huw Lewis in 1595 are noteworthy. In 1599 William Morgan published a revised version of the Book of Common Prayer and it was his intention to revise the New Testament as well; however, that work, assuming that it was completed, has not survived. In 1606 Edward James, vicar of Llangatwg-iuxta-Neath, translated the homilies into Welsh – published in English in 1547 and then 1563 – with the intention of giving simple parishioners the opportunity of hearing godly and learned sermons being read to them to confirm their knowledge and understanding of the basic tenets of the faith. In 1603 Thomas Salisbury, the London publisher, produced Edward Kyffin's translation of a selection of the Psalms of David, again with similar intentions. In the same year William Middleton produced versions of the Psalms, published by Salisbury for the same purpose. Gradually, such works did have a limited but significant influence on the clergy. To what extent they were widely circulated is not known but it appears that, in the early decades of the seventeenth century, the Protestant faith was beginning to root itself in the Welsh communities.

Having said that, it would not be wise to identify Wales as being Protestant by the Stuart succession. The Church was in its period of growth but, as in England, still handicapped by its deficiencies. Potent though recusant forces appeared to be in certain areas, they were not the most serious obstacles to the Church because Catholic missions had not proven their strength nor their endurance in Wales. The Catholic reform movement failed in Wales more because of its own weaknesses than because of the strength of Protestantism. The new Church used its capacities to protect a new image, chiefly with the support of the government and John Whitgift's guidance as well as the efforts of the small band of Protestant leaders. Once the Church was established, it set about strengthening its doctrinal position and attending to the problems of communication and evangelisation.

Although the Anglican Church failed to achieve uniformity it had acquired a firm foundation. In an unstable political era it saved the realm from becoming embroiled in civil war in the latter half of the sixteenth century. In *The Laws of Ecclesiastical Polity* (1593) Richard Hooker emphasised the historical tradition of the Church and its attachment to the principles of stability, and that also was John Jewel's testimony in his *Apologia Ecclesiae Anglicanae*. William Morgan referred to the need to extend and defend true religion by spreading the gospel, and he identified that with Elizabeth I's achievement in maintaining and protecting the sovereign realm from external threat. He applauded the 'grace incomparable...and the veritable peace' that she enjoyed more than her fellow sovereigns abroad. The queen's greatest favour to Wales, in his view, would be to recommend the translation, thereby uniting the desires of Protestant leaders in England and Wales.[69]

In the context of the early British Church the Elizabethan Church, in the opinion of its protagonists, was elevated to a position of honour. This was considered to be its raison d'être. 'Sir' Thomas Jones sang two free-metre poems, one to greet William Morgan on the completion of his task and the other in praise of the queen who had maintained the realm's independence after the defeat of the Spanish Armada.[70] Both poems contain a unity of purpose since the translation of the scriptures and the defence of the realm were considered to be essentially two strands of the same tradition. During the early decades of the seventeenth century before the outbreak of the Civil Wars, however, the Church experienced two opposing developments. The first development integrated it into the religious life of Wales, but the second gradually drew away from the main body a minute but growing Puritan section. Puritan activity became more conspicuous in the 1630s in the diocese of Llandaff, and it is an interesting feature that religious dissent was stronger in the border areas – particularly in the south-east. This is explained partly by physical conditions and partly by the strength of leadership and the ability to slip in and out of Wales as circumstances required.

The majority of the landed families a century after the Acts of Union were well-aligned with the Stuart Crown and their estates were firmly based on the Tudor settlement. They formed the social group from among whom it was expected that support for the Anglican Church would emerge. The Church, moreover, was firmly in their grasp. In England, of the 9,244 livings, 3,849 had been impropriated by laymen. In the diocese of Llandaff in 1603, of the 177 parishes some 98 had also suffered the same fate, and since 1563, 31 chapels of ease had disappeared. 'If impropriations and non-residencies were not tolerated.' John Penry declared, 'a teaching minister might live well by the Church.' 'Is it not intolerable,' he questioned further, 'that some of our gentlemen should have 6 impropriate livings?'[71] Although the clergy were lax, for the most part there existed a resolute prelacy that was unable to come to terms with dire economic circumstances. In that context, churchmen were often the Church's worst enemies. Lewis Bayly, regardless of his frequent malpractices, had certain misgivings about the diocese in his care. 'I have planted grave and learned preachers over all my diocese,' he explained in 1630, a year before his death, 'and suffer none to preach but such as are conformable, and have preached myself every Sunday until I became impotent.'[72] His concern on an earlier occasion about the ruined cathedral church of

Bangor revealed how eager he was to enlist the support even of grasping laymen to renovate it. Since the house of Gwydir had profited from discovering lead deposits on the estate, in 1626 he appealed to Sir John Wynn to offer some of it 'towards the repairing of your mother church of Bangor which this rainy weather, for want of a better mantle, weepeth that it makes my heart bleed to see her.'[73] The main problems, however, were the inadequacy of preachers and the poverty of the Church which, in part, involved less expenditure on church buildings. In his preface to *Car-wr y Cymru* (1631), Oliver Thomas, an ardent puritan preacher and teacher, referred to the apathy of the clergy and urged them to instruct their parishioners to read the Bible 'in their own houses and to meditate constantly with the family'. Such an appeal revealed what was essentially the puritan ethos relating to the role of the *paterfamilias* and private devotions in maintaining the unity of the Christian household.[74]

In 1620 the revised edition of Morgan's Bible appeared under Bishop Richard Parry's name although it was Dr John Davies of Mallwyd, the celebrated late-Renaissance humanist scholar, who accomplished the task. Of greater importance to Puritans was the small edition, known popularly as the 'Little' or 'Five-shilling' Bible (because of its price), that was published a decade later by Sir Thomas Myddelton and Rowland Heylin, two prosperous London–Welsh entrepreneurs. It was the first family Bible to appear, and with it was bound the Book of Common Prayer, the Psalms and the *Psalms in Verse* by Edmwnd Prys. One clergyman who highly recommended this publication was Rhys Prichard, the austere vicar of Llanymddyfri whose career in the Church extended over almost half a century. Although a staunch Anglican, he preached the individual's inward experience of God, a disciplined life and sanctity. He expounded the doctrines of justification by faith, predestination and the doctrine of grace which were manifested chiefly in his numerous devotional carols composed in the vernacular, probably between 1615 and 1635, for the benefit of simple parishioners.[75] Essentially, they were abbreviated versions of his sermons and were intended to offer moral guidance to simple country folk. His aim was to advocate the individual's moral duties and responsibilities, emphasising the brevity of life, the inevitability of death, and the need for repentance. It is conceivable that the popularity of Rhys Prichard's verses encouraged the illiterate in his parish to read in their own language, but his importance, however, lies essentially in the fact that he represented a small group of clerics who, while remaining within the Church, considered that it needed to foster deeper spiritual experiences if true reform was to be achieved. They bridged the gap between the formality that characterised first- and second-generation priests of the Elizabethan Church and the more introspective evangelical approach that emerged among individual priests in the early decades of the seven- teenth century. How much impact the views of Rowland Puleston, Stanley Gower and Walter Stephens had on their respective communities it is impossible to tell, but to them may be added Robert Powell, vicar of Llangatwg-iuxta-Neath, an ardent preacher and a follower of Edward James; Marma- duke Matthews, incumbent of Pen-maen in Glamorgan who later went to America; Ambrose Mostyn, a member of the Talacre branch of that family in Flintshire, and a lecturer in the parish of Pennard in Glamorgan; and Lewis Bayly, bishop of Bangor, who in 1611 published his notable *The Practice of Piety*, which was translated into Welsh by Rowland Vaughan of Merioneth in 1630. This popular work contained strong Puritan thoughts in its sections on moral discipline, prayer and meditation, and on the doctrines of grace and election.[76]

Puritanism, however, made very little progress in Welsh parishes in the early seventeenth century. That was largely the result of social and economic factors and, although efforts were made to raise clerical standards when advowsons were acquired by Feoffees for Impropriation, it had no effect on the heartland of Wales. The 'lecture' system set up between 1620 and 1636 that allowed unbeneficed men to 'teach, preach and catechise' achieved very limited success. This was because of the restrictions increasingly imposed upon it as a result of the opposition to Puritan tendencies among the preachers.[77] Two of the trustees were John Miles, who later became a pioneer of Baptist causes in south Wales, and Rowland Heylin who, as stated above, along with others financed the popular Bible in 1630. Some Welsh towns, such as Wrexham, Swansea and Haverfordwest, did allow Puritans to preach publicly, but their influence was confined and sporadic. It is conceivable, though, that the 'lineaments' of a Puritan movement existed on the Welsh borders in the 1630s, centred upon the activities of Oliver Thomas in north-east Wales (an area influenced by Cheshire Puritanism) and William Wroth, the rector of Llanfaches, in the south-east, who had close connections with Bristol and London separatists.[78] Thomas was an ardent preacher, and his *Car-wr y Cymru*, to which reference has been made, expounded some of the basic tenets of the Puritan faith. There appeared to be strong connections established between Wrexham, Brampton Bryan – the seat of the Puritans Sir Robert and Lady Brilliana Harley – and Llanfaches, and also between these places and the Puritans of Bristol and London. By the close of the decade, London Baptists had settled in the Olchon valley in western Herefordshire and were later to have greater impact in south Wales. Much of this activity arose in reaction to William Laud's elevation to the archiepiscopate of Canterbury in 1633, the subsequent revival of the Court of High Commission, and the drive to further Arminianism and High Church principles.

In a period when Puritan sentiments in Wales might well have been suppressed, it is a clear fact that persecution gave the movement a new and possibly more meaningful lease of life. Immediately before Laud's promotion, a spate of Puritan literature, including the popular edition of the Bible, was published, and some Anglican priests displayed religious inclinations frowned upon by church leaders. In 1635 William Wroth, William Erbery, vicar of St Mary's Church in Cardiff, and his curate, the headstrong Walter Cradock, were summoned before High Commission, and Erbery and Cradock were deprived of their positions. Evan Roberts of Llanbadarn Fawr, an ejected cleric, a close associate of Oliver Thomas, and arguably the first Welsh nonconformist, was also deprived of his living in the diocese of St David's in the same year.

It is with the support of a small band of Puritan leaders that William Wroth, who retained his living, established the 'gathered' church – the first independent church in Wales – at Llanfaches in November 1639 on the 'New England' pattern.[79] Among his associates at the time were Henry Jessey, independent minister in London who was present at the opening of Llanfaches, Ambrose Mostyn, Richard Symons, Richard Blinman, Morgan Llwyd, Oliver Thomas and Vavasor Powell, some of them young converts who were to assume a formative role among second-generation Puritan leaders during the following two decades. They served their apprenticeships in the late 1630s and 1640s in the fringe eastern and southern areas where first-generation Puritanism established roots that eventually spread into the less hospitable heartland areas of the Principality. In that formative period this 'Antioch of Wales', as Llanfaches church was described, became the power-house of Puritan activity. 'Let all the English counties about them testify,' Erbery declared, 'and tell how many saints from Somerset, Gloucestershire, Herefordshire, Glamorganshire etc., came in multitudes with delight to Llanfaches.' In view of the hazards that accompanied his task, Wroth conducted his pioneering work at the centre of the Puritan network and achieved remarkable progress within the network of relations between dissidents in Wales in the 1630s.[80]

Hastened by Puritan activity and the need to safeguard the Church from further losses at the hands of grasping laymen, attempts were made to protect church property. While it is true that the value of ecclesiastical properties and tithes had increased between threefold and fivefold by the close of the sixteenth century and that the Church had an opportunity to revive itself on that count, by then the processes of impropriation and appropriation had gone too far to permit any significant impact on church reform while the lower clergy still endured miserable conditions. Diocesan records of most of the Welsh sees reveal that attempts were made to achieve some recovery, but counter to that, by the 1630s, the Church had suffered humiliation and had been deprived of much of its possessions. There was little occasion for anti-Puritan activity in the Welsh parishes and only incidental examples are recorded, but efforts were made to improve standards within the Church to offset any further challenge. This can be seen as early as 1604 when the thirty-fourth canon established the standards of education expected of the clergy. Soon pluralism was denounced and investigations conducted regarding the financial plight of poor curates. Between 1632 and 1634 it was declared that bishops should reside in their dioceses and further attempts were made to control impropriation, recover patronage of livings to the Crown, and reduce the length of leases of church properties. All these pronouncements were intended to re-edify a Church that had itself been largely responsible for its own disabilities. In the circumstances of civil war and an imposed Puritan regime, it discovered – to its disadvantage – that too little had already been done too late to reform the institution from within.[81]

5

POLITICS AND FACTION

The dissolution of the marcher lordships as political units in 1536 drew to a close a long and gruelling period in the history of Wales and the borderland. Power in the new Welsh counties from that time onwards was more firmly controlled by Welsh landed gentry who obtained a dispensation to conduct public affairs and establish law and order in the localities. One prime aspect of the Tudor settlement was the privilege of parliamentary representation, which gave the governing families the opportunity to broaden their interests in the field of politics and administration. Representation was regarded as a significant part of the settlement offered to gentry, who had formally been granted equality in public offices. The honour that accompanied the office was the highest in the *cursus honorum* of the landed gentry. The franchise was similar to the practise in England, the vote being granted to the 40-shilling freeholder in the shire and the free burgesses in the boroughs. Thomas Cromwell's motive was to extend to the gentry the political rights enjoyed by their counterparts in England. Each county and shire-town obtained one Member of Parliament, except Merioneth, which had no borough member, and Monmouthshire which was given two knights of the shire, making a total of 26 Welsh Members of Parliament.[1] In 1543 the prosperous town of Haverfordwest was created a county borough with its own Member bringing the total to 27.[2] Although this arrangement lacked equality in terms of actual

176

representation since in England the custom was to send two knights of the shire and two burgesses for the shire-town, economic considerations restricted the numbers of Members of Parliament in Wales. The principle of representation, however, had been recognised at the time, probably on the recommendation of the king's private advisers in Wales who were doubtless aware of the capacities of the Welsh counties and boroughs to sustain membership.

Welsh Involvement in Politics

The government was eager to see Welsh participation in the affairs of the realm in the House of Commons, and the period extending between the 1540s and the opening of the Long Parliament in 1640 revealed increased involvement among the most eligible gentry in public affairs in addition to their local government duties.[3] The expansion of Tudor government and the part played by the provinces in matters that engaged the central administration led eventually to a more vigorous approach to parliamentary functions. Doubtless, the most valued of the privileges granted to localities in Wales was parliamentary representation, particularly as knight of the shire, a privilege that enabled the greater gentry to reinforce their mastery over their communities. Not only had the Acts of Union imposed jurisdictional and administrative unity upon Wales, but they had also linked it to the assumption of wider responsibilities in the House of Commons. The creation of new shires enabled the system to operate with relative ease, and representation revealed a degree of autonomy in that the views of Welsh members were largely governed by their own interests, thus creating distinct political principles.

The delegated authority was entrusted to a select group of prominent and homogeneous gentry, a feature that became more conspicuous in the latter half of the sixteenth century. In their capacity as landowners they maintained the fabric of the social order, thereby promoting their own interests and, at the same time, performing their duties to the central government. The Privy Council, by Elizabethan times, was concerned with political and administrative matters rather than counselling the Crown in cases of redress brought before it. Its main responsibilities were managing royal affairs, including the defence of the realm, securing compliance to the government in matters regarding law and order, dealing with foreign affairs, and managing the finances in the localities. In their role as maintainers of peace and security, the greater gentry furthered their own ambitions and acquired the experienced needed in the event of being elected to Parliament. Although officials were brought in from outside to fill certain posts, public administration was usually the preserve of unpaid county gentry – although some of them enjoyed salaried positions. The closing of the ranks in office-holding locally was reflected as well in the manner in which gentry and professional Members of Parliament – representing the boroughs – responded in the House of Commons.

Undoubtedly, landownership was the chief source of political influence and an essential component in the power structure. Participation in politics was largely the monopoly of the gentry. Another reason why this privilege was protected was the social attractions and the possibilities of political advancement, although that was not achieved to any significant extent unless they were also lawyers or experienced administrators. Gradually, London's attraction as a centre of conspicuous consumption and seasonal festivities for members of eligible families enhanced their civility.[4] Deference was paid to the standards maintained by English gentry, and Welsh gentlemen were drawn within their orbit by marriage and via the adoption of the appropriate code of conduct. Welsh Members of Parliament, however, like some of their colleagues in the remoter parts of England, requested leave of absence from the Commons, chiefly because of the travelling distance from London, their involvement in estate business and local government, periods of illness, and bad economic conditions. More important, perhaps, was their diffidence and inexperience of the broader features of political life. They were serving their apprenticeship and, although attempts were made in the latter

178

half of the sixteenth century to improve attendance and ensure that there should be no absence from the Commons without licence, it seems that it had no lasting effect on those Welsh Members of Parliament who failed to meet their commitments. Although Tudor Parliaments gave rise to political debates on religious and constitutional affairs, in the first three decades after 1536 most of these issues failed to make Welsh Members of the House of Commons more directly involved in parliamentary business. In their view, greater importance was attached to personal status and establishing their relations with their supporters and patrons.

On the eve of the Tudor legislation of 1536–43, the Welsh gentry were given some experience of the type of service that Members of Parliament were to offer because Sir John Price of Brecon, Sir Richard Bulkeley and others, who were later to be returned to Parliament, attended the Royal Court to advise Thomas Cromwell as to the best way of proceeding with the task of settling Wales. They reassured the Crown and its ministers that they represented a solidly loyal band of gentry willing to serve, and their support revealed the alliance that existed – and flourished – between the gentry and bourgeoisie at the expense of the old aristocracy. Their acquisition of the benefits of English citizenship had enhanced their material prospects as well as linking them to the centres of power in the realm. With the growing authority of Parliament, especially after the changes of the 1530s that emphasised the supremacy of Crown in Parliament, membership of the House became an added mark of prestige. 'We at no time stand so high in our royal estate as in the time of parliament,' Henry VIII declared in 1543 when confirming parliamentary privilege of freedom from arrest, 'when we as head and you as members are conjoined and knit together in one body politic.' Parliament's contribution amounted to a revolution since Tudor government was based on establishing royal supremacy set up by the enacting power of Parliament.[5]

Welsh Members attended for the first time Henry's Parliament in 1543 and participated in the proceedings that formulated the 'second' Act of Union. Although there is no record that they contributed to the debates, doubtless they were aware that their power *de jure* had been established by the Tudor settlement. Nevertheless, the contribution of Welsh Members of Parliament to parliamentary business before the late 1560s is not well documented and was probably negligible, but following the increase in parliamentary business and growing tensions in foreign relations they began to assert themselves and to participate – chiefly in matters relating to the localities. They manned parliamentary committees and a 'Welsh interest' began to emerge. They became familiar with parliamentary procedure and were made more aware of the social benefits that they obtained by their stay in London. They also combined two distinct cultures in their activities, for while they were essentially Welsh in outlook, at the same time they acquired political education through active participation in local government and the establishment of closer contacts with the Council in the Marches at Ludlow. This Council lay at the heart of the educating process since it enabled an increasing number of Welsh gentry – usually with legal backgrounds – to obtain practical instruction in the management of administrative affairs, Ludlow Castle became a centre where the rudiments of courtly life and political education were obtained. It introduced eligible young squires into privileged circles, assisted in cultivating useful social contacts, and established its reputation as the 'metropolis' of Wales. Deference was paid to acknowledged concepts of gentility since it was considered that, among 'gentlemanly company…a young man might have learned as much good behaviour and manners as should have stuck by him ever after while he lived'. The ties of matrimony and legal associations with the borderlands of Wales enabled Ludlow to reinforce its influence as the norm of polite society for progressive Welsh and marcher gentry. A. H. Dodd observed that membership of a wider community that followed the Tudor settlement 'made the sense of common political obligation something like a normal habit of mind' among the privileged order.[6] It instilled in them a sense of territorial loyalty and established closer links with Ludlow that survived to the death of Henry

Herbert, earl of Pembroke, in 1601. They became increasingly aware of the principles underlying the collection of taxes, the defence of the coastline and the maintenance of law and order. It was a protracted and often frustrating process, but it enabled Welsh Members of Parliament to consider their privileges as representing something more than mere personal achievement. What they acquired in terms of regional domination was applied to broader issues in the realm.

Electioneering and Politics

In the early decades elections were uncontested; where they did occur in Elizabeth's reign and after, they revealed family and regional rivalries. Normally, one prime family was given the privilege, but where contests did occur the main issue was to safeguard reputation rather that assert political principle and to protect family interests when rivals threatened to assume superiority and seize political power in the county. In Anglesey, the Bulkeleys reigned supreme. In adjoining Caernarfonshire, the Wynns and their satellites were in the ascendant and, in Carmarthenshire, the Vaughans of Golden Grove. In Monmouthshire, the earls of Worcester, whose interests were privately protected in the Act of Union, virtually monopolised one of the two seats granted to that county. Where there was a group of substantial houses eligible for county election, as was the case in Glamorgan, aristocratic patronage played its part; in that county the earl of Pembroke manipulated the situation to ensure that no contests occurred to preserve family interests. The government, through its regional agencies, tried to ensure that suitable persons were elected to Parliament, and often the lord president of the Council in the Marches would recommend individuals to serve such as, for example, Richard Mytton, lord of Mawddwy – who was nominated for Merioneth in 1541,[7] and Sir Rhys Gruffudd of Penrhyn for Caernarfonshire soon after Mary Tudor's accession in October 1553.[8] The sheriffs of the counties were to ensure that responsible men, Roman Catholic in sympathy, were returned – 'grave men and of good and honest behaviour, order and conversation, and especially of Catholic religion, which sort of well-ordered men are most meet to consult upon the good order and state of the realm'.[9] In April 1572 Robert Dudley, earl of Leicester and lord of Denbigh, was offended because the burgesses of Denbigh had proceeded to elect a burgess Member of Parliament without his consent, and instead directed them to elect Henry Dynne, his own nominee: 'In respect I am your lord and you my tenants,' he declared, 'as also the many good turns and commodities which I have been always willing to produce you for the benefit of your whole state.'[10] It is clear that the elections, although not as spectacular as some were to become by the end of the century, were not matters to be dealt with lightly because they always revealed vested interest and patronage. Much depended on the sheriff ensuring that the election process was carried out as expeditiously as possible. It was his responsibility to organise the county court for the election and he also declared and returned the result. Corrupt practices often decided elections where contests occurred, the return depending largely on the sheriff's honesty.

Parliamentary elections – particularly those for the county – revealed how self-seeking and irascible the gentry class could be. Whether Welsh Members were as active and as politically conscious in all parts of Wales, as has been suggested, is a matter of debate. H. A. Lloyd expresses doubts that this was the case with regard to the constituencies of south-west Wales before the Civil Wars. There were exceptions, of course, such as Sir John Perrott of Haroldston, who became the dominant squire in Pembrokeshire 'more feared of the gentlemen and freeholders of the county'.[11] He was a remarkable figure whose authority touched on all aspects of public life in the region. His extensive control of patronage and clientage enabled him to maintain an army of retainers. Far from being a thing of the past, the practice of *arddel*, in defiance of the law, continued to be used to maintain his power and protect the lord's interests. He was not the only one among his contemporaries prepared to use armed force if necessary to ensure that they gained the ascendancy, with most of their aggression being demonstrated at electioneering times. In 1588 the Denbighshire election had not been smooth, and in Merioneth in 1571 the rivalry between the Llwyn and Rug families largely involved John Salusbury's desire to secure for himself a reversion of the lease of the royal township of Dolgellau. The sheriff and justices of the peace were directed to ensure that no upheaval would occur in view of the 'great labour and suit' in the matter. It was also feared that a well-conducted election might be ruined 'by outward signs and tokens of brag', on behalf of contending factions.[12] Again, in Denbighshire in 1601, the rivalry between the Trefors of Trefalun and Lloyds of Bodidris, tied together by a marriage alliance, and the Salusburys of Lleweni, in the eastern and western parts of the county respectively, caused prolonged animosities. Sir John Lloyd was a belligerent fellow and a supporter of the second earl of Essex, for which he was summoned to Star Chamber in 1601 charged with corrupt management of musters.[13] In the October polls of that year at Wrexham, according to the case presented against him in Star Chamber, he brought with him 100 armed retainers to support Sir Richard Trefor, another figure of considerable magnitude in north-east Wales, and the brother of Sir John Trefor, a naval administrator and political survivor who was accused of corrupt practice in office. Sir Richard Trefor's quarrel with the Salusburys extended back some years, and in 1588 he felt sufficiently confident to challenge them in the county elections. His military career led him to become embroiled in an affray at Ruthin in 1600 when his attempt to recruit forces for service in Ireland was frustrated by the Salusbury faction. The tense situation forced the sheriff, Owen Vaughan, to abandon the election, and it was in December of the same year that Salusbury was eventually elected. He was also opposed by his kinsman, Captain John Salusbury of Rug, the head of a cadet house that contested the ascendancy in western Denbighshire.

Situations of this kind exposed a number of factors that characterised the late Elizabethan political scene: the survival of old methods of seeking and maintaining political domination; persistent provincial rivalry among opposing landed families; the impact of such rivalries on communities; the ineffectiveness of local government officials, largely because of their involvement in such broils, in establishing law and order; the use that rival families made of public positions and authority to achieve their own personal ends; and lastly, the malaise that continued to trouble government agencies in Elizabethan times. A case in point is the prolonged rivalry between the Owen families of Bodowen and Frondeg and their followers and the Bulkeleys of Beaumaris, which represented an alliance of traditional Welsh gentry against a common enemy regarding borough and county representation. The struggle to maintain Newborough – the centre of the western families – as the county town ended in 1549 when Beaumaris replaced it, supported by the powerful Bulkeley faction. It is hardly surprising that of the five members representing the borough in the years 1553 to 1559, two of them were close relatives of Sir Richard Bulkeley, one other had married into the family, and the remaining two were tenants of a patron of William Bulkeley, Sir Richard's uncle, a merchant and Member of Parliament for the borough in 1554. And that was not all; there was also a contested election to Mary's first Parliament in October 1553 when William Lewis of Prysaeddfed was returned by a corrupt sheriff, and another in January 1556 when the western gentry planned to have the quarter sessions held at Newborough instead of Beaumaris.[14]

The situation in Merioneth was equally tense, even though there was not one dominant family in what is regarded politically as the 'cinderella' of the Welsh counties. Physical isolation, the absence of commercial towns, and the decay of Harlech intensified infeuding among up-and-coming families of moderate means. Electoral influences were less, communities were not as exposed to conflicting loyalties, and the allegiance to the local squire was strong. Thus arose factions from a complex of relations. Whereas early in Elizabeth's reign royal officials – such as Dr Ellis Price of Plas Iolyn and Lewis ab Owain of Llwyn – were dominant in administrative and parliamentary affairs, in the middle and later periods of the reign, in the shadow of the fierce Llwyn versus Rug dispute, there emerged older families such as Nannau, Rhiwgoch, Corsygedol and Ucheldre, all of which achieved some prominence by the end of the century.[15]

Broad political divisions began to emerge in electioneering affairs less than half a century after the Tudor settlement, such that it became clear that personal ambitions overrode all other considerations and that membership of Parliament was a mark of personal ascendancy rather than public service. The 1588 election in Montgomeryshire saw the return of William Herbert of Parc – who had achieved prominence of local affairs in the county – to Parliament, although the outcome of the election was disputed in Star Chamber where it was claimed that the sheriff, Herbert's son-in-law, had favoured him.[16] Moreover, the Cardiganshire election in 1601 led to some upheaval because of the double return for the Cardigan borough. William Awbrey of Brecon was elected at Aberystwyth and William Delabere at Cardigan, the latter eventually being returned.[17] In Anglesey in the 1540s and 1550s, as noted above, claims to primacy caused disputes between the Bulkeleys and the more traditional families. This indicates that the system was still in a state of flux, that the squirearchy had not finally come to terms with the proper means of achieving respectability in their county community, and that the overriding ties of kindred, in a political context, continued to hinder a smooth-running election system. Most polls in Wales, however, were conducted in a peaceable enough manner chiefly because, for most of the Tudor century, only one dominant county or borough family emerged to claim the privilege. Some families outshone others in the political life of their county or boroughs. In south-west Wales, for example, in the period 1540–1640, a total of 48 local families were represented in Parliament, including the Joneses of Abermarlais and Vaughans of Golden Grove in Carmarthenshire, the Perrotts of Haroldston and Haverford-west in Pembrokeshire, and the Pryses of Gogerddan in Cardiganshire.[18]

Sir James Perrott towered among his peers, his parliamentary career extending between 1597 and 1614 as Member for Haverfordwest and for the county in 1624. He was the illegitimate son of Sir John Perrott who was equally active and powerful and served on the committee on the queen's marriage and the succession. His interests took him into the field of national politics, he being the only parliamentary representative in south-west Wales of his time to have 'enjoyed anything approaching a parliamentary career'. He spoke on a variety of matters such as the union of England and Scotland, religion and law, and served on many committees including the Committee of Privileges in 1607. His voice was also distinctly heard declaring his opposition to the Crown. A man of Puritan inclinations, Perrott was regarded as a figure of political integrity and displayed a breadth of intelligence and understanding of parliamentary affairs that enabled him to involve himself in matters that lay outside the concerns of his immediate neighbourhood.[19]

In the period before 1570 little is known of the activities of Welsh Members of Parliament. Edward Carne of Ewenni, Member for Glamorgan, was the only one among his colleagues to introduce a Bill in the Commons – in 1554, for the 'true making of Welsh friezes' (a kind of Welsh cloth).[20] It is from 1567 onwards, when important changes occurred in procedure, that Welsh Members became more actively engaged in the business of the House, particularly after the establishment of parliamentary committees. They were placed on a variety of such committees and they all served on the subsidy committee in 1584. They attended more regularly, only three cases of leave of absence being recorded between 1571 and 1603. In that period, when eight Parliaments were held, thirty or more Members gained experience of sitting on committees. Although little is known of their active participation in debates, the Elizabethan era saw the rise in parliamentary affairs of Sir William Morgan of Pencoed (Monmouthshire), Sir Richard Bulkeley (Anglesey), John Herbert of Neath Abbey (Glamorgan), Sir William Herbert of St Julian's and Sir Gelly Meyrick (Carmarthenshire), all representing the most prominent landowning fraternity in Wales. They showed concern in parliamentary business, and by the end of the reign were eager to participate further.

Faction and the Political Scene

The Elizabethan political structure in Wales was largely dominated by faction and the role of the aristocracy in regional government. The Leicester, Cecil and Essex groups at Court had their impact on Wales, but the allegiances were not as clear-cut as they may appear. Five families dominated the situation in Wales down to the early 1590s. Among the prominent gentry, Sir James Croft of Croft Castle in Herefordshire emerged as an influential figure in Welsh border politics.[21] More dominating were the aristocratic families: the earls of Worcester were the most powerful in Monmouthshire and Gower, the earls of Pembroke in Glamorgan, the earls of Essex in Carmarthenshire, and the earl of Leicester in north Wales. The senior branch of the Herberts of Raglan were the Somersets. Elizabeth, grand-daughter of Sir William Herbert, second earl of Pembroke of the first creation, married Sir Charles Somerset who was created earl of Worcester in 1513–4. The centre of his power was Raglan Castle and he held extensive lands in Monmouthshire, Tretŵr, Crickhowell, Gower and Swansea. After the death of the third earl in 1589, the successor, Edward, was a Catholic who still found favour at Court and established himself as a power. This family, however, was not as dominant as the earls of Pembroke, stemming from the same family; they enjoyed the most power. That family descended from the illegitimate line of Herberts. William Herbert advanced his fortunes by allying himself with the earl of Warwick against the duke of Somerset. He held extensive lands in Wiltshire where, at Wilton, the family seat was established, and he obtained the lordship of Cardiff and other lands in Glamorgan. In 1550 he was appointed lord president of the Council in the Marches and was reappointed in 1555; he was elevated to earl of Pembroke in 1551 and,

187

having abandoned his support for Warwick, by political shrewdness held on to power under Mary and Elizabeth. His successor, Henry Herbert, played a significant role in Welsh politics, followed Leicester and married his niece, the daughter of Sir Henry Sidney. Walter Devereux, steward of Builth and chief justice of South Wales, by means of his son and deputy Sir Richard, obtained Lamphey palace, which increased his prestige in Pembrokeshire. His grandson and namesake was created earl of Essex in 1572, and his great-grandson, Robert Devereux, second earl of Essex, although absentee, continued to maintain the family's influence in Pembrokeshire and Carmarthenshire. He was closely allied with Leicester who was his stepfather.[22] After his father's death in 1576, Essex became attached to the Leicester group, the most powerful of the contending factions. He enjoyed influence at Court, and among his supporters was the influential magnate Sir John Perrott of Haroldston who, although not especially rich, was a power to be contended with in Pembrokeshire.[23]

In 1563 Robert Dudley obtained lands in Denbighshire, and in the following year the earldom of Leicester and lordship of Denbigh. He was given a commission to investigate encroached lands in north Wales on behalf of the Crown, and he built up his power in Wales principally through the support of Sir Henry Sidney and the Wynns of Gwydir and their allies. Morus Wynn and his son John were employed by him as intermediaries in his dealings with the conservative Catholic freeholders in Llŷn and Eifionydd. He was also supported by Dr Ellis Price of Plas Iolyn, Sir John Huband, Steward of Arwystli and Cyfeiliog, and Sir William Gerard.

After Leicester's death in 1588, the Essex faction assumed power that coincided with Sir John Perrott's return in disgrace from Ireland, his imprisonment, the charge of high treason against him, and the forfeiture of his estate. The death of Henry Herbert and the execution of the second earl of Essex in 1601 left the third earl of Worcester as the only dominant aristocrat in Wales. By then, gentry families had also attached themselves to other factions outside Wales – the Trefors with the Sackvilles and later the Howards, the Pulestons and Wynns with Sir Thomas Egerton, and the Salusburys with the Cecils. Within their respective regions the Edwardses of Chirk, Wynns of Gwydir, and the Herberts and Worcesters had their own supporters, particularly among their own kin, the Herberts in Glamorgan, Swansea and Cardiff, Monmouthshire and Montgomery. Indeed, faction was complicated by the role of family connections: kindred relations could unify and also divide a family, and the Pembroke, Essex and Leicester groups manipulated local government offices, especially the commissions of the peace, largely for their own benefit. In such a situation the county gentry, regardless of their allegiances to powerful families, endeavoured to assert their independence, their connections with tenants enabling them to strengthen alliances from below. Among them Sir Richard Bulkeley opposed the earl of Leicester in the Forest of Snowdon dispute and the Pembroke faction was rivalled by the Mansels and Stradlings who feared that their power was being undermined in Glamorgan.

Matrimonial connections also played a central role in parliamentary elections. On the marriage of Barbara Gamage, heiress of John Gamage of Coety, to Robert Sidney, younger son of Sir Henry Sidney in 1584 (a successful union for the Pembroke faction), Robert Sidney's candidature as knight of the shire for Glamorgan was promoted by the Sidneys. The consequence of this was that he was elected, at the tender age of 21, to represent the county.[24] Ellis Wynn of Gwydir (a Chancery clerk and younger brother of Sir John Wynn), although he failed to obtained the Caernarfonshire seat in 1598, sought the support of Lord Keeper Sir Thomas Egerton, who had a strong following in parts of north Wales.[25]

Local prestige in the public careers of some Welsh gentry was soon converted into regional domination through their elevation as members of the Council of the Marches, a position normally reserved for members of the most eligible of landed families. This is illustrated in the few Welsh squires who were appointed in Elizabeth's reign, such as Sir William Herbert of Swansea, Sir Thomas Mansel, Sir John Perrott, Sir Thomas Jones, Abermarlais, Dr Ellis Price, Plas Iolyn, Sir Richard

Trefor, Trefalun and Sir Richard Pryse of Gogerddan. They became members of a body that was to reveal traces of serious decline in the early decades of the seventeenth century. There were feuds within it and its fees were rising, thus lessening its popularity. Moreover, the control exercised by the Council was weakening, its finances declining, and the opposition of the border shires to its jurisdiction increasing. The opposition to Sir Henry Sidney was also stepped up, led by John Whitgift, Sir James Croft, Fabian Phillips and Sir William Gerard.[26] Efforts were made to remedy the major weaknesses: regulations were formed to control the growth in litigation and delays in the Council's procedure investigated. However, some lingering problems remained, mostly relating to poor finances and abuses among the Council's officials. Factious rivalries also exacerbated the situation, and by 1581 there was a marked opposition to the Leicester influence. When Henry Herbert became lord president in 1586 he possessed personal attributes that might be advantageous in reviving a flagging Council and was himself aware of the political climate and the continuation of feuds and factions. His early reforms created enemies who had connections at Court. His absence from Ludlow prevented him from continuing his programme, and the failure to achieve permanent reform led to an attack, led by Sir James Croft from the border shires, on the Council's ineffectiveness.

Other factors threatened the Council, particularly the rise of Robert, second earl of Essex, after Leicester's death. Croft and Perrott and the legal faction among members of the Council aimed at overriding the lord president's authority. Whitgift and Phillips were also creating animosities, but Essex, once he had achieved power, began to manipulate commissions of the peace – chiefly in south-west Wales – with the aid of Sir John Puckering, chief justice of the Carmarthen circuit of Great Sessions and later lord keeper. Essex, evidently eager to strengthen his position, maintained friendly relations with Egerton and Richard Broughton, who was a skilful lawyer. Of his most powerful adherents, Sir Gelly Meyrick doubtless was the most influential – especially in Wales, because of his close friendship with the Essex household, his landed possessions, and his ability to maintain good relations with the local gentry.[27] In north Wales, Essex formed a group of supporters in east Denbighshire among the Trefors of Trefalun and Salusburys of Rug and their allies as opposed to the Salusburys of Lleweni who clung to the Cecils.[28]

The amicable relations between Essex and Pembroke eventually ended in 1595 at a time when Pembroke became isolated at Court and his failure to arrange what appeared to be a propitious marriage with the Cecil family. One example of the feud between them was, contrary to Pembroke's wishes, the appointment of Sir Gelly Meyrick as deputy-lieutenant for Radnorshire, and he joined Roger Vaughan of Radnor, who was already in office and an Essex supporter. Essex's power had indeed increased in south-west Wales, Herefordshire, Denbighshire, Radnorshire and Pembrokeshire. A large contingent intended to join in a *coup d'état* in February 1601 but turned back, and he and Meyrick, his most faithful servant, were executed, Pembroke's troubles, however, were not over because he was involved, aided by Henry Townshend, in a disagreement with the Ludlow lawyers concerning the restrictions on the numbers of lawyers who were allowed to practise in the Council and intrusions upon the common law and allied affairs. Sir Richard Lewkenor, chief justice of Chester who was appointed to the Council in 1600, directed Pembroke's opposition to the lawyers. Pembroke, however, never recovered enough power in the years before his death in January 1601 to be able to make a comeback. Gradually, the opposition to him in the Council grew stronger. The lawyers there were very powerful, and he failed to secure favourable appointments to it.[29]

The deaths of Pembroke and Essex did not restore harmony immediately in Wales. Essex's enemies revived their power in the localities and the bitter rivalry between the Salusburys and the Trefors continued in Denbighshire. The Catholic problem again became acute, leading to the unpopular demand for military service in the Irish wars. The delay in appointing a new lord president had serious effects on defence organisation and strengthened further the power of the quaternity of lawyers at Ludlow, especially Sir Richard Lewkenor, justice of Chester, and Sir Henry Townshend. However, Sir Robert Cecil, earl of Salisbury, appointed Edward, Lord Zouch, a friend and ward of the Burghleys, to the post, and reluctantly he undertook his duties (he preferred living in retirement in the Channel Islands where he had served as deputy-governor of Guernsey). Nevertheless, he set about his task with some alacrity and his early days at Ludlow were occupied with the restoration of the authority of his post. Existing tensions in the Council did not help him, and he soon met with the persistent opposition of lawyers and officials, particularly Sir Richard Lewkenor, who resented his power. Zouch was also disliked by Lord Keeper Thomas Egerton who had a strong following in Wales, particularly among the Trefors, Pulestons and Wynns in north-east Wales. Moreover, the earl of Worcester, lord lieutenant of Glamorgan and Monmouthshire, challenged his position, and marcher gentry stood against him. Confronted by such hostility, Zouch would have found his task impossible had it not been for the support of Robert Cecil.[30]

Early Seventeenth-century Developments

On James I's accession, the main threats seemed to be papist activity on the borders and the continuing quarrels in Denbighshire.[31] New problems, however, were to emerge in 1604 when the King's Bench claimed the right to issue writs of *habeas corpus* to the Council, thus undermining its jurisdiction. This gave the English marcher gentry the opportunity to resist the Council's authority over them, which led to an effort on its part to protect its interests and assert its powers. Faction had done much to weaken its stand against opposition and, like the Council in the North, it had been exploited chiefly because it performed its duties under adverse political conditions. Circumstances had changed after Pembroke's death, and the failure of the Essex rising and bid for power in 1601 heralded the triumph of the Cecil faction and the beginning of a new era in Court politics. No longer was aristocratic influence to play a dominant role in the political affairs of the Welsh gentry.[32]

The gradual increase in Welsh membership of the Council in James I's reign signified that the gentry were coming to terms with politics as reflected at Ludlow and acquiring the social niceties which identified them even more firmly with English families and public offices beyond Offa's Dyke. Among its members in 1617 appeared Sir John Wynn of Gwydir (who only two years previously had been forced to submit to its authority), Sir Thomas Mansel, Sir Edward Herbert, Sir Richard Bulkeley, Sir Richard Pryse and Sir Thomas Mostyn.[33] They were all well-tried gentry aware of the pitfalls of regional government and determined to enhance their prestige by associating themselves with the Council. This trend, however, was not as evident as it had been, and Welsh gentry looked more towards London than they did towards Ludlow. The Council itself became less a vice-regal court and more of a court of law; there was also a tendency to take suits to the King's Bench courts at Westminster and, compared to preparations in Elizabeth's reign, there was less involvement with defence matters.

In parliamentary affairs the accession of James I to the throne of England began a period of increased activity for some Welsh Members of Parliament. Their status was a mark of social precedence and they grasped at the opportunity to increase their participation in parliamentary business. They were drawn to act together by a number of public matters causing common concern among them. They established political principles that became more evident during the Parliaments of James I and his son Charles, the most important being their adherence to the Welsh heritage – which bound them together to serve a common purpose – financial and defence matters, and an attachment to the Protestant tradition.[34] This entailed maintaining a firm allegiance to the Crown and its institutions, the most conspicuous being the Council in the Marches. Although it was subject to increasing criticism, it was still regarded by the Welsh gentry as a political fulcrum. It was a focus of autonomy and symbol of unity, and in the early Stuart period – since a substantial number of Welsh gentry were appointed members of the Council – it increased their political and social education. They were concerned to maintain their grip on their localities and to defend the realm from Catholic threat. Most of this activity revolved around the county and its legal and fiscal organisation. In 1604, however, Welsh Members of Parliament were content with the arrival and establishment of a new dynasty that represented a common citizenship. The Acts of Union had accomplished their task: government institutions had achieved remarkable coordination and the land and property structure had been finally settled. Since the Stuarts were viewed as the legitimate successors to the Tudors, enhancing the prospects of landed gentry, there was no opposition to James I's accession.

Wales's parliamentary apprenticeship had ended by the close of James's reign. By then, a sizeable proportion of Welsh members were actively engaged in parliamentary affairs. The counties still returned Members from well-established families such as Sir Richard Bulkeley (Anglesey), John Herbert (Monmouthshire), Sir William Herbert of Powys Castle, Edward Herbert, later Lord Herbert of Chirbury (Montgomeryshire), Sir Philip Herbert, Sir Thomas Mansel (Glamorgan), Sir Henry Williams (Brecknockshire), Sir John Lewis of Abernant Bychan, and Sir Richard Pryse of Gogerddan (Cardiganshire). Few of them, except the Herberts, had enjoyed Court connections, but they had all by then familiarised themselves with and had adapted themselves to parliamentary procedure. Not all heads of families, however, desired to see their sons enter the House of Commons. Because he feared a contested election and a humiliating defeat, Sir Roger Mostyn decided that neither of his two sons should stand for Flintshire in the county election of 1624. If the seat could not be obtained without contest, he declared, then it was not worth having. If a choice had to be made, he favoured the younger son so as to avoid the heir being drawn away to live in London far from his family and estate. 'The times are dangerous,' he asserted, 'and a man knows not to what inconvenience a young man may be drawn unto, and to draw him to live in London, his wife in the country, having no other business there but to attend the parliament may be inconvenient.'[35] A rather conservative attitude maybe, but Sir Roger came from one of the few major gentry families that continued to value residence and homekeeping qualities and their benefits to the community.

One country squire who was Mostyn's direct opposite was the vociferous Sir William Maurice of Clenennau, the Member for Caernarfonshire, described as the 'complete Tudor gentleman'. He often bored the House to tears with his tediously long speeches. He had served earlier in 1593 and for Beaumaris in 1601, but it was in James I's first Parliament that he began to attract attention when the Bill was introduced to recognise the king's title to the throne. He ardently supported the Stuart accession and spoke for the majority of his fellow Welsh Members of Parliament. His interest in crucial issues debated at the time was remarkable: he opposed the monopoly of the Shrewsbury Drapers Company and supported convocation, the Council in the Marches, the collection of royal purveyance, the Great Contract, parliamentary subsidies and royal prerogatives. As a native of one of the most conservative regions of north Wales and steeped in Welsh poetic traditions, he introduced a good measure of Welsh antiquity into his speeches. He was among the first to be knighted by James, and between 1604 and 1610 he spoke formally on 12 occasions on that theme and delivered upwards of forty speeches on a variety of matters.[36] So fervent was his support for the Stuart Crown before and after James's first Parliament that his sister, Ann Wen Bryncir, considered that he deserved just reward. 'And me thinks,' she told him, 'you should desire his Majesty to speak to my Lord Chancellor and my Lord President to use you well and to show you some favour thereby for the great service that you have done in Her Majesty's reign being Knight of the Shire so many years and attending upon her parliament so duly and truly as you have done.'[37] Maurice, perhaps, could expect to be appointed a member of the Council in the Marches or possibly a privy counsellor. He failed to acquire these positions, but continued to exhibit his allegiance to the Crown in the most overt fashion, assuring the king that Welsh prophecies had foretold his accession. His long disquisitions in the House caused much amusement. During one of his speeches he declared that 'the name [of Britain] was not more dearer than our lives'.[38] On another occasion he attempted to further the cause of a Bill to make 'the king to be Emperor of Great Britain', and unknowingly 'moved laughter in the house'.[39] Time and again, he would return to his favourite theme and, in one parliamentary session, he pleaded that 'the king might be wedded to the old widow Britain'. These assertions, absurd though they might appear, do nevertheless reveal vital aspects of contemporary Welsh political thought at a time when the popular concept of the 'Cambro-Briton' represented the transition from the Tudors to the Stuarts.[40] The term 'Briton' and 'British' held a dual significance for the Welsh gentry since they were distinguished as the true Cambro-Britons who not only aimed at preserving their ancient heritage but also defending it.

Despite occasional quarrels, Sir William Maurice supported his kinsman Sir John Wynn of Gwydir and his house in parliamentary elections, particularly in the critical election year of 1620. To that extent he was different from the majority of the backwoods gentry in Llŷn and Eifionydd, in the southern and western parts of Caernarfonshire. The social structure of the county led to the emergence of two political factions, one in the more progressive northern region centred on the towns of Caernarfon and Conwy and the trade and military routes to Ireland, and the other more conservative group of gentry hemmed in the southern and western extremities of the county. In the north the Wynns of Gwydir and their satellites succeeded to the domination once held by the Gruffudd family of Penrhyn, and their extensive connections enabled them to entrench themselves firmly in the political life of north Wales. The family had sent knights of the shire to seven Parliaments since 1547. Its pre-eminence was matched in the south and west by the group led by the

Gruffudd family of Cefnamwlch, and it was a scion of that house, John Gruffudd, a young London lawyer, who contested the county seat in 1620 with Sir Richard Wynn of Gwydir, heir to the estate and a prominent courtier and groom of the bedchamber to Charles, Prince of Wales.[41] It was during the career of John Gruffudd I and his son and namesake that the house arose to challenge Gwydir's ascendancy. John Gruffudd II had strong connections, not only in London, but also with the Trefor household of Trefalun since he had married Sir Richard Trefor's daughter. Trefor's wife enjoyed some influence at Court and the patronage of the Earl of Northampton, then lord president of the Council in the Marches, assisted Gruffudd to feel confident enough to contest the county seat successfully. The election involved much intrigue, the creation of free-holders on both sides on the day, and drumming up support among potential allies, even to the point of poaching in each other's territories. So confident of victory was Sir William Thomas of Caernarfon, one of Gwydir's staunchest allies, despite some serious misgivings among the family's allies at the time, that he eagerly declared to Sir John Wynn shortly before the election: 'Assure yourself your cake shall not burn, if all the power I have can help it; and that I will stick to you even unto the uttermost whatever befall thereof, *contra omnes gentes*.'[42] The cake, however, was burnt to a cinder when John Gruffudd triumphantly carried the polls in December of that year. And that was not all because Gruffudd proceeded to obtain the constableship of Caernarfon Castle and returned to Parliament again in 1626 – when he succeeded his father-in-law as vice-admiral of North Wales – and in 1628. Despite their political activity in other counties in later years, this was a clear sign that Gwydir's power had declined so much that the family was never again to re-establish its old ascendancy.[43]

Political Tensions

It was when fiscal affairs, particularly arbitrary taxation, became a matter of dispute that the localities in Wales began to feel the pinch and to resent heavy demands. In its attempt to fill its depleted coffers, royal policy lay a heavy burden on the remote and impoverished areas that forced local officials and Members of Parliament to express their concern – and often despair – in times of hardship. There were other issues, such as monopolies, which frustratingly engaged the Welsh gentry who often scratched only a meagre livelihood off the land. The monopoly of Welsh cloth enjoyed by the Shrewsbury Drapers Company and the sales of Welsh butter controlled by a syndicate of London businessmen were vexed questions since both hit the Welsh economy very hard. Although they were eventually quashed by Parliament, when the Welsh Members obtained the support of London merchants equally eager to establish free trade, the arguments advanced to seek freedom of trade for the import of Irish cattle weakened Welsh support, again for economic reasons.[44] However, the remarkable unity achieved by the Welsh gentry in Parliament was maintained and, although their allegiance to the Crown never faltered, their attitude towards some of its ministers was critical. Matters of defence and the preservation of the Protestant tradition tied in with the deep fear that the period of peace with Spain after 1604 might endanger all that their forebears had striven to achieve, particularly since Wales was too close for comfort to Catholic Ireland. The opposition to Buckingham intensified with the failure of the Prince of Wales's visit to Madrid to woo the Spanish infanta in 1623. Moreover, the duke of Buckingham's pro-French policy was also viewed with suspicion in Charles I's first Parliament, an issue that forced Sir Robert Mansel to oppose the king's favourite – which eventually led to his losing his place in the Glamorgan commission of the peace.[45] John Williams, appointed lord keeper in 1621, had risen to power under James but, on his son's accession, his influence gradually declined, chiefly because he made enemies of Laud and Buckingham by speaking out against them. He was soon deprived of the Great Seal, and in 1637 lodged in the Tower for using what devices he could to avoid Laud's actions against him in Star Chamber. Buckingham's conduct of the Anglo-

Spanish war in 1624, the negotiations in 1627 that led to war with France, and the danger that a grand Catholic alliance might be formed against England, exacerbated the situation and again revealed grave defensive problems. War broke out with France in 1627; this tarnished further Buckingham's image, particularly after the disastrous expedition to the Isle of Rhé to relieve La Rochelle. Added to all this was the reluctance to pay taxation, which came to a head in the years of personal government in the 1630s. The religious policy involving enforcing of Arminianism and re-establishment of the Court of High Commission raised the question of episcopal involvement in state matters and Laudian high-Anglicanism.[46]

Political struggles also ensued in the relations between the Council in the Marches and its adversaries. In the latter years of the sixteenth century the Council's jurisdiction had been subject to heavy criticism. The King's Bench and Common Pleas courts invaded its jurisdiction and acquired the civil jurisdiction of great sessions. There were moves also to exempt the border shires from the Council's control, Bristol and Cheshire having freed themselves from it in 1562 and 1569 respectively. The king's view of the Council's jurisdiction was clear. He feared that if the marcher shires were to break away then Wales might conceivably revert to lawlessness, and 'revive the ancient enmity between these two people and bring all to the old confusion again, which as nothing could redress at first but that Court'. There were ambiguities as to the definition of 'marches', and the Council had suffered some setbacks. After the death of Henry Herbert, the lord presidency was held mostly by men who lacked presence, and offices were either concentrated in an elite or acquired by absentee courtiers. The Council's efficiency was marred by the multiplicity of officials who lined their own pockets by increasing fees, and fines were imposed on absent defendants and in cases of non-prosecution. All this came to a head in the 1630s when the Council was at its most active, and the increase in civil cases prompted the criticism that the Council was no longer functioning as it should to try criminal cases and establish law and order. Although the increase in civil cases was not new in the mid-sixteenth century, in an age of litigation and intense competition among courts it is hardly surprising that the Council endeavoured to extend its jurisdiction. Nevertheless, it was a target for attack from the marcher gentry who wished to break away from its jurisdiction and who resented the heavy incidence of fines imposed upon them. The Westminster lawyers wished to increase their fees which the Council threatened, and to impose their authority on the Council. Its powers duplicated the jurisdictions of great sessions, and the courts of Common Pleas and King's Bench as well as the ecclesiastical courts. In addition to pluralism and absenteeism, there were charges of malicious suits, disreputable informers, as well as dissension between judges and corruption among the lawyers.[47]

The overriding issue of royal prerogative powers also affected the Council's reputation. As with other similar institutions of government, it became increasingly subject to attack in the 1630s. During the personal government the royal prerogatives were maintained by the Council in the Marches and the north. The earl of Strafford exercised the new policy of 'thorough', and in Wales the earl of Bridgwater was appointed to govern Wales and the border in 1631. His support for the duke of Buckingham had proved his allegiance to the monarchy and the new set of instructions issued increased the Council's membership substantially and enabled him to exercise the role of the lieutenancy of the south-eastern counties of Wales which the Pembrokes had monopolised. Bridgwater's time at Ludlow was best characterised by the lavish attempts made by him to restore the Council's reputation as a vice-regal court, with the celebrated masque *Comus* by John Milton and Henry Lawes performed there in 1634 proclaiming – inappropriately at the time perhaps – the Welsh to be the 'old and haughty nation, proud in arms'.[48] That age had long passed and the nation was about to enter upon a traumatic period that tightened local administration and intensified the demand for financial and military aid. The Bishops' Wars – which had little relevance for Wales – had introduced further threats to the king's position. Moreover, the success of Edward Somerset, fourth earl of Worcester, in enhancing his prestige by reacquiring the lord-lieutenancy in south-east Wales, and the interim ascendancy in 1642 of Henry Somerset, his heir and fifth earl, when he was made a marquis, seemed to suggest a revival of aristocratic faction undermining Bridgwater's authority.[49] This was achieved: Worcester and his son, Lord Herbert, rose in favour by being exempted from the penal laws against Catholics, with Lord Herbert sitting in the Council and acquiring the lieutenancy. This signified a serious breach in Bridgwater's authority. Therefore, when the Long Parliament met, the Council was fiercely attacked and there was little effort in Wales by that time to defend royal prerogative and the Council that exercised it. A full-blown attack was launched on the basis of the Council's authority in the Act of Union in 1543 and, although attempts were made to delay its demise when Star Chamber was abolished in 1641, the Council in the Marches lost its jurisdiction in criminal matters. Richard Lloyd of Esclus, Denbighshire, an up-and-coming lawyer who at the time served as attorney-general for north Wales, from August 1641 until April 1642, was commissioned to use delaying tactics and to suggest alternative proposals to abolition.[50] Those proposals favoured devolution centred on Ludlow: judges of Great Sessions, during intervals between court sittings, were to function under the lord president at Ludlow with powers of the common and equity laws, and it was considered that Ludlow was more conveniently placed for Welsh litigants than London. It was also envisaged that a central records repository might be established at Ludlow and that the Council might be revived as the Prince of Wales's residence. Lloyd's recommendations had much to commend them, but too much had occurred and the Council's power had dwindled to such a point that the civil and administrative jurisdiction it wielded finally collapsed in May and August 1642 respectively. The Council, in fact, had, over the last four decades, trodden on too many toes. Its supervisory role had threatened too many vested interests at a time when the border gentry were asserting their independence, when London was becoming increasingly the nerve-centre for budding lawyers and litigants and when the king's prerogative powers were being seriously undermined.

It was at this crisis point in the history of the Council in the Marches that Welsh Members of Parliament began to consider their own situation vis-à-vis the clash between Crown and Parliament. Their involvement in the events of 1628 had not been significant and the response to the Petition of Right had at best been ambivalent.[51] They were in a dilemma when the institutions they had cherished as the centre-piece of law and stable government were at odds with each other: 'If any blow be given to the body,' one Welsh member asserted, 'the head will feel it, and if there be any violation of the privilege of this house it will concern the whole kingdom.' The failure of the Short Parliament to achieve anything for the king and the fiasco of the Scottish war could only lead to further confrontation in Parliament, hence the summoning of the Long Parliament in November 1640.[52] A small group of Welsh dissidents, such as the Thelwalls of Ruthin, and Charles Jones of Castellmarch in Llŷn, had revealed their opposition to the king, but were dead before 1640. The campaign, however, was maintained by Sir John Vaughan of Trawsgoed who assisted in formulating charges against Strafford, Laud and the 13 bishops who tried to enforce passive obedience on the country. In another direction Sir Thomas Myddelton, a member of a family known for its Puritan inclinations, argued against the Crown in financial and religious matters. Among them appeared Hugh Owen of Orielton, Charles Price and John Bodfel, and one factor that decided their responses was the fear of the Catholic army supposedly raised at Raglan and the fierce Ulster Rebellion of 1641. Nevertheless, in the last resort the majority of Welsh Members supported the Crown, not only because of their innate loyalty to a monarchy that they had regarded as Welsh, but also because their political education in legal and administrative institutions had taught them to respect the Crown as the fount of law and government. There was a deep suspicion of papists, it is true, and there was a decidedly critical mood – reflected in the 1640 elections – in the Short and Long Parliaments.[53] They were inclined more towards supporting the royal prerogatives because they did not feel sufficiently committed to any radical alternatives. It was when opposition came dangerously close to disaster that Welsh members thought and acted otherwise. A decisive Welsh voice in the House opposed the Bill of Attainder against Strafford, and although Parliament took charge in raising an army to reconquer Ireland, regardless of the Welsh concern for coastal defence, its members voted against the Militia Ordinance because it was feared that the army might be used for other undesirable purposes.

The situation on the eve of the Civil Wars drew to a head a number of factors that ultimately decided Welsh support in the ensuing conflict. Basically, the gentry were royalist and always had been, but not, as A. H. Dodd has shown, unconsciously so. They had not served their political apprenticeship over the previous century in vain and were able to weigh the issues and decide judiciously how best the kingdom might be governed. It so happened that, in a conservative and isolated country, the views of the vast majority on central issues differed little since the Welsh gentry of all ranks, for the most part, had benefited most by the rule of Crown in Parliament. Although a small group raised eyebrows when the excesses of royal policies caused concern, parliamentarian supporters were far fewer than royalists. The reason for that is not difficult to find. As had always been the case, the economic factor had dominated Welsh loyalties. The scarcity of large towns with a wealthy merchant middle class deprived Parliament of a strong Welsh entrepreneurial base.[54] Most of the gentry were not involved in faction and politics on the grand scale, and although they were aware of political developments, even to the point of active participation, the majority were modestly placed and reticent. Their firm contacts with the localities guaranteed them the allegiance of a faithful tenantry. Loyalty became increasingly associated with the hierarchy of government institutions embracing the law, administration and the Church. The emphasis was placed on the rule of law as represented by king in Parliament. They resented the fierce attacks on the Church and monarchy, deplored the constitutional upheaval that sadly affected their own political status, and were concerned about protecting their own estates and communities.

On the parliamentarian side, support was largely limited to the few thriving commercial centres and families in south Wales, particularly Glamorgan, Monmouthshire and Pembrokeshire. The towns of Pembroke, Tenby and Haverfordwest, English in speech and commercially tied to Bristol and London, became bulwarks of the Roundhead cause and, higher up the social scale, Philip Herbert fourth earl of Pembroke, who owned Cardiff Castle and extensive lands in Glamorgan, and the more committed Robert Devereux, third earl of Essex, – who was mostly an absentee landowner in south-west Wales – supported Parliament. In all parts of the country there were isolated examples of Puritan gentry who supported the rebels, and others who, for personal reasons, joined the cause not from any conviction but in order to benefit materially. In north-east Wales, Wrexham, dominated by the Myddletons of Chirk Castle, and Chester just over the border, were centres from which Puritans sprang. In a religious context, Puritan leaders and their congregations also actively supported Parliament, notably Morgan Llwyd, Vavasor Powell and Walter Cradock. They travelled extensively, spreading their beliefs and, on the outbreak of war (excepting Morgan Llwyd who actively joined in the parliamentary campaigns), fled to Bristol and London.[55]

On the royalist side the chief motive was doubtless the preservation of the established order. The chief supporters were the earl of Worcester (created first marquis of Worcester), and his son Lord Herbert, who provided the king with financial aid to the tune of £90,000. Archbishop John Williams was a powerful and influential figure. Though disgraced in the earlier part of Charles's reign, he made his peace with the king in 1640; and, after serving a second prison sentence for formulating the 'Bishops' Remonstrance' in December 1641, the year when he became archbishop of York, he fortified

Conwy Castle and was strategically placed to negotiate with the royal army in Ireland.[56] Among the landed gentry there were a number of prominent local families that gave the king support, such as the Salusburys of Rug and Bachymbyd, the Mostyns of Flintshire, the Kemeyses of Cefnmabli and Stradlings of St Donat's. Sir John Owen of Clenennau, great-grandson of the redoubtable Sir William Maurice, became a staunch military commander, and Richard Vaughan, second earl of Carbery, of Golden Grove, was appointed royalist commander in west Wales. Despite their loyalties, Welshmen did not really want to enter the fighting. Apart from their devotion to the established order in government, they had estates and communities to defend, with bitter experiences in Germany having shown some of them the dreadful consequences of war and pillaging.[57]

The king, for his part, was eager to foster Welsh support because the proximity of Wales to Ireland and Chester was a military asset. It was also, as has been said, the 'nursery of the king's infantry' and a source of some – and in some quarters considerable – financial aid. The issues were not always clear and there were many non-committed families who did not realise the urgency of the situation, who were ill-disposed to spend their resources on what they considered to be a futile conflict, or who expected to see matters resolve themselves eventually in the king's favour. Sir John Vaughan of Trawsgoed (later chief justice of the court of Common Pleas), although he appears to have given the king some support, retired from any involvement, in order 'to keep even with the world,' and Sir Owen Wynn third baronet of Gwydir, threatened by sequestration after the Civil Wars, firmly denied that he and his elder brother, Sir Richard, had supported the royalist cause and had taken office under the Crown during the wars.[58] It was no doubt the case that support in the Civil Wars was decided principally by the impact of family pressures and patronage. Specific conditions often dictated the attitudes of particular regions to the conflict: commercial ties, conservatism, family and partisan links; religious fervour and the spirit of adventurism. Non-involvement was one thing, wavering loyalties quite another, and it was a marked feature among some participants. These included Henry Vaughan of Derwydd in Camarthenshire, Edmund Jones of Buckland in Brecknockshire, and notably Sir Trefor Williams of Llangybi in Monmouthshire – whose family interests, personal ambition and position as tenant of the earls of Pembroke (who were at odds with the Somerset family) led him to abandon the royalist cause in the summer of 1645. In the second Civil War in 1648, however, he assisted Sir Nicholas Kemeys to seize and defend Chepstow Castle for the king.[59]

Among the lower orders there was little understanding of issues and a marked lack of interest. The language barrier had prevented Parliament from declaring its case convincingly. The popular poetry that was written seemed wholly to favour the Crown and the old order, but these compositions also revealed apathy as to the outcome of the conflict and the extent of ignorance of the issues at stake among the lower orders. It is in the following decade, when Puritan government and administration was tightly imposed on Wales, that the writers of this popular poetry positively opposed the policies of anti-royal government. 'That black Tragedy,' James Howell declared in 1649, referring to Charles I's execution, '...hath fill'd most hearts among us with consternation and horror'; 'the more I ruminate upon it,' he continued, 'the more it astonisheth my imagination, and shaketh all the cells of my brain'. Howell, despite his many missions abroad, kept in close touch with his native country and was aware of the gentry's attitude and loyalties at that time.[60] As for the staunch royalist families who doubtless shared his sentiments, they withdrew from positions of power but began to creep back gradually in the latter years of the 1650s. Their future role in politics and society, however, was to change dramatically.

CONCLUSION

Exciting though the prospects were for the governing classes in Wales during the century that spanned the Acts of Union and the Civil Wars, it cannot be said that it introduced any startling innovations. While it is true that the Tudor settlement was to have a permanent impact on the national development of Wales, in politics, administration and culture it hardly created a stir among any section of the population. The reason for that is not hard to find. Remote Welsh communities, very much in the clutches of a landed nobility whose natural leadership was the most influential factor, accepted the existing social order. Things might well have been different if Sir Rhys ap Gruffudd, for example, had survived into old age in south-west Wales. His power might have forced Cromwell to adjust his policy, and his Roman Catholic leadership might have mustered successful resistance to the overthrow of papal power in the most conservative areas. Henry VIII and his advisers introduced their package for Wales at the most propitious time for the government and for those who were expected to share the burdens of local administration. The settlement was noteworthy not because of its novelty, but for what it preserved; not only for what it accomplished, but also – in certain respects – for what it failed to achieve. Tudor and early Stuart rule was successful in Wales principally because the ruling classes were identified, albeit in a new political context, with an administrative framework that, in their view, was viable because of its very conservatism. This period focuses attention on three main features that, in different ways, left a deep impression on Welsh society.

(i) The positive achievements of government in early modern Welsh society are not difficult to identify and assess. The Tudor settlement was a remarkable legislative feat in that those who drafted the statutes were aware of the historic background and regarded the legislation as the final stage in a natural constitutional progression that could be traced back to the thirteenth century. Far from creating unity, the Acts of Union preserved and extended the Principality to cover the whole of the marcher lordships. In that context Wales acquired a unified status within the national sovereign state and the Crown reserved for itself special rights – based on the Crown's personal relationship with Wales – to legislate further if the need arose. What was not achieved was the creation of a Principality governed directly by a Prince of Wales nor a Wales inextricably bound in administration and culture to England. The title 'Principality', which survived into the seventeenth century, was purely honorific and did not represent a distinct governmental entity. What had been achieved, however, pleased the governing classes and the Crown and enabled the Reformation settlement, in the latter half of the sixteenth century, to root itself firmly in Welsh soil. It also amply served the interests of landowners. Cromwell would never have entertained a policy of assimilation had he not known that there was a strong economic base to support it and a body of eager administrators to execute it.

The new landed estates that came to fruition in this period created a social unity based on authority, privilege and communal obligations. In due course a select band of gentry emerged, superior in status and means to an inordinately large number of freeholders who, in this period, continued to serve their localities and to cling zealously to clan loyalties. It was the close relationship between all ranks of the gentry and their native communities and between the gentry and the Crown – which were not at all times compatible – that, linked together, created a distinct and integrated social structure. The tight legal and administrative control exercised in the shire communities derived principally from an abiding loyalty to the ruling dynasty and an unbroken affection for the native heritage. The period saw the inauguration of a new Protestant tradition that was designed to consolidate the national state. In religious as well as secular affairs the landed gentry of Wales, for the most part, sought to protect their own personal interests as well as the welfare of the realm. The New Faith, interpreted in a peculiarly 'British' context, fostered a belief in a common religious and cultural heritage which inspired some of the formative humanist writings that reinforced political allegiance to the Tudors and Stuarts. It also assisted in creating and preserving a sense of 'British' identity among the politically articulate, and shaped a concept of Welsh nationhood that survived because of – rather than in spite of – the imposition of English statehood upon the Welsh people. The Tudor settlement with its religious and secular repercussions, gave meaning to that phenomenon.

(ii) In view of the various strands that constitute Tudor policy in Wales, some aspects need to be elucidated. Emphasis was placed on the need to maintain efficient government and foster 'British' patriotism. This factor was quickly grasped by the gentry who eagerly attached themselves to key administrative institutions. They served the Crown to enhance public order and establish security in the realm. Regardless of this aim to establish a lasting bond of unity between government at the centre and the localities in the Tudor and early Stuart era, the question arises as to whether or not political stability was achieved. Given the opportunities that they had to exert their authority, how successful were the governors of Wales in establishing law and order? The mechanics of county and regional government were readily at their disposal. Elements of success were dependent largely on the voluntary contribution of these leaders, and their willingness to align themselves with the Crown. In welcoming the Stuart succession they were not only aware of lineal connections between James I and his predecessors, but also conscious of the common heritage. It is impossible to gauge the degree of success achieved by the Tudors and Stuarts in establishing law and order, particularly in view of the persistence of old customs positively harmful to creating stability in the provinces. What is evident, however, is that the Tudor settlement survived unscathed and that the institutions of government remained in good working order down to the Civil Wars. Periods of inefficiency and gross self-interest there may well have been, but they did not permanently damage the smooth-running routine of local government. Court and other fiscal and administrative records reveal how formally established the course of justice had become by the early decades of the seventeenth century. The masters of the communities had also become the servants of the state which made constant demands on all their resources.

It is only by comparison with other periods that the historian can assess the degree of efficiency achieved in government in Wales at that time. The adoption of more peaceful ways of resolving differences was a gradual and uneven process that depended largely on individual attitudes among gentry leaders and the manner in which they interpreted their role in regional society. It has still to be established whether or not abuses in the old marcher territories stubbornly survived the new shire organisation to a greater extent than in the Principality, but judging by contemporary evidence that appears to be the case. However, despite the persistence of *cymortha*, armed retaining and physical intimidation among the most aggressive squires reveal that the role of laymen in government and the legal knowledge that they acquired served in due course to make litigation and the authority of the courts the prime means of dispensing and obtaining justice. Local institutions of government, albeit deprived by the early 1640s of the authority of a supervisory Council in the Marches, functioned reasonably well in maintaining royal control when civil war broke out.

(iii) One other strand of social development in this period is difficult to assess and has caused divergencies in historical interpretation. Despite the salutary impact of the Tudors in imposing order and advancing the social progress of the Welsh gentry, it is often considered to have had harmful effects on Welsh cultural life. This malaise, it is argued, increased in the succeeding century so that, by the eve of the

Civil Wars, the bardic itinerancy and its patronage (regarded as a prime social function among heads of Welsh families) were in serious decline. The economic climate may have been in the gentry's favour, but the most ambitious, it is said, lost contact with native cultural traditions. That might not have been so serious had it not entailed loss of community leadership as well. In many respects that was certainly the case since the children of arranged marriages between Welsh and English gentry families did not usually become patrons of bards, and the plight of younger sons, who were deprived of paternal inheritance, often drove them to seek a livelihood over Offa's Dyke. It was only to be expected that the Tudor settlement would consolidate the gentry's position, some even among the ranks of their counterparts in England. Although 'cultural apathy' did cause anxieties, mainly among bards and humanists, it was a trend equally damaging in provincial England as well – where individuals estranged themselves from their communities to seek brighter lights elsewhere. The fundamental difference, however, appeared in the character of the cultural tradition that was deprived of their support because, in Wales, it entailed forsaking the mother tongue and the rich literary heritage it had fostered.

More research needs to be undertaken to assess social and cultural attitudes and to examine the extent and nature of mobility among the gentry, and further questions need to be asked: was movement over Offa's Dyke, in many cases, temporary, and were those who were supposedly indifferent to their native culture as negligent as they have been made out to be? Moreover, in that context, how is one to define and quantify the often used and disparaged term, the 'anglicisation' of the Welsh gentry? They certainly had the opportunity to turn their backs on native poetic traditions, but evidence shows that many – even younger sons who returned to establish cadet families – revealed a keen interest in Welsh antiquities and some in the bardic craft. More attention needs to be given to the concept of regional identity, particularly the 'county community' which is a powerful entity in any examination of gentry allegiances down to the mid-seventeenth century. This loyalty arose out of the development of shire institutions and administration, the growing prosperity of rural gentry and the tendency on an increasing scale for younger sons of the gentry to marry local heiresses. Moreover, the gentry displayed a deep interest in history, antiquities and law in a regional context, and the county town became a focus for all social, governmental and cultural activity. Social relationships linked individual members of privileged families together in a bond of affinity which even the lure of life beyond Offa's Dyke could not destroy as family correspondence and marriage ties amply prove. One thing is clear; alienation, when and where it occurred, was often gradual and depended on several more complicated factors than is often realised. Moreover, the bardic tradition that over centuries had overtly manifested and preserved the qualities of gentility, was itself in its period of serious decline. This was because of the rapid increase in the printing press, the medieval conventions stubbornly upheld by the bardic order, and the impact of financial inflation which prevented the gentry from digging deeply into their pockets to support a tradition that they considered to be unnecessary expense. The tradition of eulogy was more suitably adapted to a rural rather than an urban setting, and the trend among landed gentry to adopt a town life in Wales and over the border also restricted its function. More appealing social conditions and opportunities would naturally lead to a broadening of interests and would, in turn, create a yawning gap between the progressive country squirearchy and the bards. Whether that phenomenon was as widespread as has been supposed, however, is questionable.

Certain points need to be considered in this context. First, it might be argued that Tudor policy saved the Welsh language and its literature; that the conscious attempt to promote the New Faith necessitated the use of the vernacular, albeit as a means to an end. It is doubtful, however, whether the government set out deliberately to discourage the social and cultural use of the language regardless of what Thomas Cromwell might have envisaged. Trends in motion before and after the Acts of Union had a lasting impact on the language and, to that extent, the impact of the Acts themselves might have been exaggerated. This leads to another consideration in this context – namely, that in view of bardic and humanist responses to the Tudor settlement, it is not inconceivable that the events of 1536 relating to Wales had the effect of increasing a sense of national consciousness among a sizeable proportion of the Welsh gentry. The bards themselves never referred in any positive way to the legislation, but it is manifestly clear that they endorsed the trends that it set in motion regarding office-holding, estate building and the advancement of a new code of conduct. Their innumerable compliments to those patrons who were sheriffs, justices of the peace, deputy-lieutenants and the like interpreted the status and indeed the offices as being essentially Welsh and their holders as representatives of all that was considered praiseworthy in Welsh society. The Acts of Union themselves did not sever the native gentry from Wales. Other forces were already at work that accomplished the task. Moreover, by the mid-seventeenth century, many Welsh-speaking gentry continued to reside in the countryside, contributing actively to local government and to the King's cause in the Civil Wars, and maintaining close connections with their dependants and collaterals. In a broader political context, since the Tudor inheritance in the seventeenth century was expounded and interpreted essentially against a background of ancient British traditions, there emerged a growing sense of national consciousness among the politically articulate. It may be that historians have adopted too narrow and preconceived a view of the Acts of Union, believing that they were designed to destroy all that was considered worthy in the Welsh cultural tradition. It is misleading to emphasise its negative impact on Welsh life even in that context. The middling and lower ranks of Welsh gentry in 1640 were as aware as their predecessors a century earlier of their cultural background and, regardless of the declining poetic standards, continued to sustain the traditional order. It was from among the ranks of their descendants that the inspiration came which saved and promoted the literary standards of the vernacular and made it the chief means of communication for the majority of the Welsh people in future generations.

What is the significance of the Act of Union and its aftermath in any interpretation of the early modern period in Welsh history? It was an effective catalyst and created a new territorial entity within the realm in an era that led to individual Welshmen achieving prominence in various fields of activity. The Tudor settlement established political cohesion, consolidated country estates, improved economic opportunities, imposed upon Wales the Elizabethan Protestant Church and, regardless of its official policy, provided the conditions that led to the translation of the scriptures into Welsh and the consolidation of the Protestant faith. The period also gave Welsh gentry and parliamentary representatives – already deeply involved in local affairs – a conspicuous role to play in governmental circles in an age leading to civil strife. In this period also were formed the conditions that eventually laid the basis of large-scale industrial development. In that context, the century constituted a watershed that blended the old with the new and paved the way for commercial and entrepreneurial enterprise. In the cultural scene, despite the malaise that had deeply affected the bardic system, the period gave the Welsh language and its literature a new lease of life and direction as a means to establish a new religion and deepen a new sense of patriotism and national consciousness. Although the destabilising effects of the mid-seventeenth century left a permanent mark on the structure of the squirearchy, many essential features of its Welsh character survived.

NOTES

Abbreviations

BL	British Library
Cal. Clenennau Letters and Papers	*Calender of Clenennau Letters and Papers in the Brogyntyn Collection*
Cal. Salusbury Corr.	*Calendar of Salusbury Correspondence*
Cal. State Papers Dom.	*Calendar of State Papers Domestic*
L & P	*Letters and Papers Foreign and Domestic*
NLW	National Library of Wales
PRO	Public Record Office
Trans. Anglesey Antiq. Soc. and Field Club	*Transactions of the Anglesey Antiquarian Society and Field Club*
Trans. Caerns. Hist. Soc.	*Transactions of the Caernarvonshire Historical Society*
Trans. Cymmr.	*Transactions of the Honourable Society of Cymmrodorion*
Trans. Denbs. Hist. Soc.	*Transactions of the Denbighshire Historical Society*
UCNW	University College of North Wales
Y Cymmr.	*Y Cymmrodor*

1   SOCIAL AND ECONOMIC FOUNDATIONS

1.   A. H. Dodd, *Studies in Stuart Wales* (Cardiff: University of Wales Press, 1952), chapter 1, pp. 1–21.
2.   W. H. O. Smeaton (ed.), *Francis Bacon's Essays* (London: Dent, 1906), pp. 40–1.
3.   For background, see F. Emery, 'The Farming Regions of Wales', and T. Jones Pierce, 'Landlords in Wales', in J. Thirsk (ed.), *Agrarian History of England and Wales, vol. IV, 1500–1640* (Cambridge University Press, 1967), chapters 2 and 6, pp. 142–7, 357–81; T. Jones Pierce, 'Agrarian Aspects of the Tribal System in Medieval Wales', in J. B. Smith (ed.), *Medieval Welsh Society* (Cardiff: University of Wales Press, 1972), XII, pp. 329–37; B. E. Howells (ed.), *Pembrokeshire County History: III, Early Modern Pembrokeshire, 1536-1815* (Haverfordwest: Pembrokeshire Historical Society, 1987), pp. 52–93; W. O. Williams, 'The Social Order in Tudor Wales', *Trans. Cymmr.* (1967 Pt. ii), pp. 167–78; F. Jones, 'The Old Families of Wales', in D. Moore (ed.), *Wales in the Eighteenth Century* (Swansea: Christopher Davies, 1976), pp. 27–32; idem, 'Welsh Pedigrees', in *Burke's Genealogical and Heraldic History of the Landed Gentry* (London: 1952), pp. lxix–lxxvi; L. Owen, 'The Population of Wales in the Sixteenth and Seventeenth Centuries', *Trans. Cymmr.* (1959), pp. 99–113.
4.   M. Griffiths, '"Very Wealthy by Merchandise"? Urban Fortunes', in J. G. Jones (ed.), *Class, Community and Culture in Tudor Wales* (Cardiff: University of Wales Press, 1989), chapter 5, pp. 197–235; R. A. Griffiths (ed.), *Boroughs of Medieval Wales* (Cardiff: University of Wales Press, 1978); I. N. Soulsby, *The Towns of Medieval Wales* (Chichester: Phillimore, 1983).
5.   T. Churchyard, *The Worthines of Wales* (London, 1587), pp. 51–2.
6.   R. Flenley (ed.), *Calendar of the Register of the Council in the Marches of Wales, 1569–91* (London: Cymmrodorion Record Series, no. 8, 1916), pp. 105–6.
7.   J. G. Jones (ed.), *History of the Gwydir Family and Memoirs* (Llandysul: Gomer Press, 1990), p. 52; J. B. Smith, 'Crown and Community in the Principality of North Wales in the Reign of Henry Tudor', *Welsh History Review*, III (1966), pp. 165–7; J. G. Jones, 'The Wynn Estate of Gwydir: Aspects of

Its Growth and Development *c.* 1500–1580', *National Library of Wales Journal*, XXI (1981), pp. 141–5.

8. N. W. Powell, *Dyffryn Clwyd in the Time of Elizabeth I* (Ruthin: Coelion Trust, 1991), pp. 4–8.

9. R. Stephens, *Gwynedd, 1528–1547; Economy and Society in Tudor Wales* (Ann Arbor, Michigan, 1979), pp. 27–31, 79–80.

10. G. Owen, *The Description of Pembrokeshire*, ed. H. Owen (London: Bedford Press, 1906), I, p. 190.

11. J. G. Jones (ed.), *History of the Gwydir Family and Memoirs* pp. 16, 31–2; F. Smith Fussner, *The Historical Revolution, 1580–1640* (London: Routledge & Kegan Paul, 1962), pp. 26–59, 92–116, 250–2.

12. F. Jones, 'An Approach to Welsh Genealogy', *Trans. Cymmr.* (1948), pp. 303ff.; J. G. Jones, *Concepts of Order and Gentility in Wales, 1540–1640* (Llandysul: Gomer Press, 1992), chapter 3, pp. 104–48.

13. BL, Harleian MS, 1961. See also NLW, Peniarth MSS, 128, 183, 212; Mostyn MSS, 1, 111, 145; UCNW, Bangor MS, 5943; Christchurch (Oxford) MS, 184.

14. For the general background, see D. J. Bowen, *Gruffudd Hiraethog a'i Oes* (Cardiff: University of Wales Press, 1958); Jones, *Concepts of Order and Gentility*, pp. 68–73.

15. C. Davies (ed.), *Rhagymadroddion a Chyflwyniadau Lladin, 1551–1632* (Cardiff: University of Wales Press, 1980), p. 39.

16. Rice Merrick, *Morganiae Archaiographia*, ed. B. Ll. James (Barry: South Wales Record Society, 1983), App. 2, pp. 147–64; R. A. Griffiths, 'The Twelve Knights of Glamorgan', in S. Williams (ed.), *Glamorgan Historian*, III (Barry: S. Williams, 1966), pp. 154–68; idem, 'The Rise of the Stradlings of St Donat's', *Morgannwg*, VII (1963), pp. 37–47; G. Williams, 'The Stradlings of St Donat's', in S. Williams (ed.), *Vale of History* (Barry: S. Williams, 1960), pp. 85–95; A. L. Rowse, 'Alltyrynys and the Cecils', *English Historical Review*, LXXV (1960), pp. 54–76.

17. A. O. Evans, *A Memorandum on the Legality of the Welsh Bible, and the Welsh Version of the Book of Common Prayer* (Cardiff: W. Lewis, 1925), pp. 107–8.

18. James (ed.), *Morganiae Archaiographia*, p. 68.

19. J. E. Neale, *The Elizabethan House of Commons* (London: Jonathan Cape, 1955), pp. 114–21; Dodd, *Studies in Stuart Wales*, pp. 182–4; H. G. Owen, 'Family Politics in Elizabethan

Merionethshire', *Bulletin of the Board of Celtic Studies*, XVIII (1959), pp. 185–91.

20. W. J. Smith (ed.), *Calendar of Salusbury Correspondence, 1553–c. 1710* (Cardiff: University of Wales Press, 1954), pp. 1–19, no. 26, p. 31, no. 52, p. 38; idem, 'The Salusburys as Maintainers of Murderers: a Chirk Castle View, 1599', *National Library of Wales Journal*, VII (1952), p. 235.

21. NLW, MS, 9052E, 324.

22. J. M. Traherne (ed.), *Stradling Correspondence* (London: Longman, 1840), LVIII, p. 66.

23. NLW, MSS, 9052E, 348; 9055E, 724.

24. Smith, (ed.), *Cal. Salusbury Corr.*, no. 321, p. 148.

25. J. Leland, *Itinerary in Wales*, ed. L. Toulmin Smith (London: George Bell, 1906), *passim*.

26. Churchyard, *The Worthines of Wales*, pp. 106–7.

27. Owen, *The Description of Pembrokeshire*, III, p. 57.

28. A. M. Everitt, *Change in the Provinces: The Seventeenth Century* (Leicester University Press, 1969), pp. 5–15.

29. B. R. Parry, 'Huw Nanney Hen (*c.* 1546–1623), Squire of Nannau', *Journal of the Merioneth Historical and Record Society*, V (1972), pp. 185–206.

30. T. Jones Pierce 'The Clenennau Estate', in Smith (ed.), *Medieval Welsh Society*, VIII, pp. 229–49; E. N. Williams, 'Sir William Maurice of Clenennau', *Trans. Caerns. Hist. Soc.*, XXIV (1963), pp. 78–97; C. A. Gresham, 'The Origin of the Clenennau Estate', *National Library of Wales Journal*, XV (1967–8), pp. 335–43.

31. J. E. Lloyd and R. T. Jenkins (eds), *Dictionary of Welsh Biography* (London: Honourable Society of Cymmrodorion, 1959), s.n.; F. Jones, 'The Vaughans of Golden Grove: I: the Earls of Carbery', *Trans. Cymmr.* (1963 Pt i), pp. 96–139; A. D. Carr, 'The Mostyns of Mostyn, 1540–1642', *Publications of the Flintshire Historical Society Journal* (Pt i), XXVIII (1977–8), pp. 17–37; (Pt ii), XXX (1981–2), pp. 125–44; idem, 'The Making of the Mostyns: the Genesis of a Landed Family', *Trans. Cymmr.* (1979), pp. 137–57.

32. Lloyd and Jenkins, *Dict. Welsh Biog.*, s.n.; A. D. Carr, 'Gwilym ap Gruffydd and the Rise of the Penrhyn Estate', *Welsh History Review*, XV (1990), pp. 1–20.

33. A. D. Carr, 'The Making of the Mostyns', in *Trans. Cymmr.* (1979), pp. 137–42.

34. Griffiths, *Boroughs of Medieval Wales*; D. H. Owen, 'The Englishry of Denbigh: an English Colony in Medieval Wales',

Trans. Cymmr. (1974–5), pp. 61–4; idem, 'Tenurial and Economic Developments in North Wales in the Twelfth and Thirteenth Centuries', *Welsh History Review*, VI (1972), pp. 117–35.

35. Lloyd and Jenkins, *Dict. Welsh Biog.*, s.n.; Smith, (ed.), *Cal. Salusbury Corr.*, pp. 7–8.

36. T. Jones Pierce, 'The Gafael in Bangor Manuscript 1939', in Smith, (ed.), *Medieval Welsh Society*, VII, pp. 195–227; E. G. Jones, 'Some Notes on the Principal County Families of Anglesey in the Sixteenth and Early Seventeenth Centuries', *Trans. Anglesey Antiq. Soc. and Field Club* (1940), pp. 48–61; D. C. Jones, 'The Bulkeleys of Beaumaris, 1440–1547', in ibid. (1961), pp. 1–20.

37. Lloyd and Jenkins, *Dict. Welsh Biog.*, s.n. Also G. Williams (ed.), *Glamorgan County History, IV, Early Modern Glamorgan* (Cardiff: Glamorgan County History Trust, 1974), pp. 77–83; idem, 'Rice Mansel of Oxwich and Margam (1487–1559)', *Morgannwg*, VI (1962), pp. 33–51.

38. Jones, 'Wynn Estate of Gwydir', pp. 141–5.

39. E. Roberts, 'Teulu Plas Iolyn', *Trans. Denbs. Hist. Soc.*, XIII (1964), pp. 41–2; J. Y. W. Lloyd, *History of the Princes, the Lords Marcher, and the Ancient Nobility of...Powys Fadog* (London: T. Richards/Whiting, 1881–7), V, p. 406.

40. Williams, 'Rice Mansel of Oxwich and Margam', pp. 41–2.

41. M. Gray, 'Change and Continuity; the Gentry and the Property of the Church in South-east Wales and the Marches', in Jones, *Class, Community and Culture in Tudor Wales*, pp. 11–15.

42. See E. G. Jones, 'The Lleyn Recusancy Case, 1578–1581', *Trans. Cymmr.* (1936), pp. 97–123.

43. Davies, *Rhagymadroddion*, p. 70.

44. NLW, Llanstephan MS, 124, 312; J. G. Jones, 'Changing Concepts of Gentility in Mid-Tudor Wales: Some Reflections', *Brogliaccio 1 de Lettera*, XIII (1977), pp. 25–37.

45. P. Smith, *Houses of the Welsh Countryside* (London: HMSO, 1975), pp. 228, 265; R. Gwyndaf, 'Sir Richard Clough of Denbigh *c.* 1530–1570', *Trans. Denbs. Hist. Soc.* (Pt i), XIX (1970), pp. 24–65; (Pt ii), XX (1971), pp. 57–101; (Pt iii), XXII (1973), pp. 48–86 (esp. pp. 67–85); idem, 'References in Welsh Poetry to Sixteenth and Early Seventeenth Century New and Rebuilt Houses in North-east Wales', ibid., XXII (1973), pp. 87–92. See NLW, Llanstephan MS, 124, 355 (Wiliam Cynwal); Brogyntyn MS, 5, 302 (Simwnt Fychan).

46. J. C. Morrice (ed.), *Barddoniaeth Wiliam Llŷn* (Bangor: University of Wales, 1908), I, pp. 1–3.
47. ibid., XXVIII, pp. 72–4.
48. *Royal Commission on Ancient Monuments in Wales and Monmouthshire: Caernarvonshire East* (London: Royal Commission on Ancient Monuments, 1956), pp. 58–64; A. and H. Baker, *Plas Mawr* (London: Farmer and Sons, 1888), pp. 17–20, 23–7, 30–1; R. Williams, *The History and Antiquities of the Town of Aberconwy and Its Neighbourhood* (Denbigh: Gee Press, 1835), pp. 83–4.
49. Traherne (ed), *Stradling Correspondence*, p. 66.
50. E. G. Jones (ed.), 'History of the Bulkeley Family (NLW, MS, 9080E)', *Trans. Anglesey Antiq. Soc. and Field Club* (1948), pp. 22–3.
51. Jones, *Concepts of Order and Gentility*, pp. 65–99.
52. R. Kelso, *The Doctrine of the English Gentleman in the Sixteenth Century* (Mass.: Peter Smith, 1964), pp. 70–110.
53. NLW, MS, 9051E, 72.
54. *The Gentleman's Magazine*, LV (1785), p. 32; A. L. Rowse, *The Elizabethan Renaissance: The Life of the Society* (London: Macmillan, 1971), pp. 109–10.
55. J. Simon, *Education and Society in Tudor England* (Cambridge University Press, 1967), pp. 63ff.; K. Charlton, *Education in Renaissance England* (London: Routledge & Kegan Paul, 1965), pp. 82–6; F. Caspari, *Humanism and the Social Order in Tudor England* (University of Chicago Press, 1954), pp. 6ff.; W. P. Griffith, 'Schooling and Society', in Jones (ed.), *Class, Community and Culture in Tudor Wales*, pp. 79–119. See also R. O'Day, *Education and Society, 1500–1800* (London: Longman, 1982).
56. Davies, *Rhagymadroddion*, pp. 55–6.
57. Owen, *The Description of Pembrokeshire*, III, pp. 156–7.
58. H. Llwyd, *The Breuiary of Britayne*, trans. T. Twyne (London: Richard Johnes, 1573), fo. 60b–61a.
59. South Glamorgan County Library: Cardiff MS, 4. 58, 54; G. Parry, 'Hanes Ysgol Botwnnog', *Trans. Cymmr.* (1957), pp. 1–4; J. G. Jones, 'Henry Rowlands, Bishop of Bangor, 1598-1616', *Journal of the Historical Society of the Church in Wales*, XXVI (1977–8), pp. 34–53.
60. UCNW, Mostyn MS, 302; PRO Probate 11/93.
61. NLW, MS, 9052E, 352.
62. Kelso, *The Doctrine of the English Gentleman*, pp. 142–3; Charlton, *Education in Renaissance England*, pp. 215–26.

63. Charlton, *Education in Renaissance England*, p. 217; J. Stradling, *A Direction for Traveilers taken out of Justus Lipsius for the behoof of the right honourable lord the young Earl of Bedford being now ready to travell* (1592).

64. Davies, *Rhagymadroddion*, p. 74.

65. E. Roberts (ed.), *Gwaith Siôn Tudur* (Cardiff: University of Wales Press, 1980), II, pp. 229–31.

66. J. G. Jones, 'Educational Activity among the Wynns of Gwydir', *Trans. Caerns. Hist. Soc.*, XLII (1981), pp. 45–8.

67. Smith, (ed.), *Cal. Salusbury Corr.*, no. 149, p. 76; no. 154, p. 78.

68. J. Ballinger, 'Katheryn of Berain', *Y Cymmrodor*, XL (1929), pp. 1–43; E. Roberts, 'Priodasau Catrin o Ferain', *Trans. Denbs. Hist. Soc.*, XX (1971), pp. 21ff.; J. G. Jones, 'Morus Wynn o Wedir c. 1530–1580', *Trans. Caerns. Hist. Soc.*, XXXVIII (1977), pp. 51–9.

69. NLW, MSS, 9052E, 332, 335; 9055E, 699, 765.

70. UCNW, Penrhos MS, II, 29; G. Williams (ed.), *Glamorgan County History: Early Modern Glamorgan* (Cardiff: Glamorgan County History Trust, 1974), p. 110; W. O. Williams, 'The Survival of the Welsh Language after the Union of England and Wales: the First Phase, 1536–1642', *Welsh History Review*, II (1964), pp. 82–3.

71. G. Williams, *Welsh Reformation Essays* (Cardiff: University of Wales Press, 1967), pp. 201–4.

72. T. Parry, *A History of Welsh Literature* (Oxford: Clarendon Press, 1955), trans. H. I. Bell, p. 211.

73. Bowen, *Gruffudd Hiraethog a'i Oes*, pp. 32–7. For the English background to social reorientation in this period, see L. G. Salingar, 'The Social Setting', in B. Ford (ed.), *The Age of Shakespeare* (Hammondsworth: Penguin, 1955), II, pp. 27–33.

74. G. H. Hughes (ed.), *Rhagymadroddion, 1547–1659* (Cardiff: University of Wales Press, 1951), pp. 87–8.

75. Ibid., pp. 74–5.

76. Cardiff MS, 4. 101, 227.

77. G. Thomas, *Eisteddfodau Caerwys* (Cardiff: University of Wales Press, 1967), pp. 105–9.

78. J. Penry, *Three Treatises Concerning Wales*, ed. D. Williams (Cardiff: University of Wales Press, 1960), pp. 41–2.

79. W. Vaughan, *The Golden Fleece* (London, 1626) (Pt i), p. 30 (Pt iii), p. 12.

80. NLW, MS, 9058E, 1075.

81. Ibid., MS, 1559, 388.

82. T. Parry (ed.), *The Oxford Book of Welsh Verse* (Oxford: Clarendon Press, 1962), CXX, p. 246.
83. Lord Mostyn and T. A. Glenn, *The History of the Family of Mostyn of Mostyn* (London: Harrison, 1925), p. 126.
84. J. Thirsk, 'Younger Sons in the Seventeenth Century', *History*, LIV, no. 182 (1969), pp. 358–77.
85. Ford, (ed.), *The Age of Shakespeare*, p. 31.
86. Vaughan, *The Golden Fleece* (Pt. i), pp. 29–39.
87. J. Howell, *Epistolae Ho-elianae: The Familiar Letters of James Howell*, ed. J. Jacobs (London: D. Nutt, 1892), I, Book I, VII, pp. 105–6.
88. Owen, *The Description of Pembrokeshire*, III, p. 57.
89. Smith, (ed.), *Cal. Salusbury Corr.*, p. 11.
90. Jones, 'History of the Bulkeley Family'.
91. NLW, MS, 9052E, 271.
92. Smith (ed.), *Cal. Salusbury Corr.*, no. 89, pp. 53–4; no. 90, p. 54.
93. Ibid., p. 14.
94. T. C. Mendenhall, *The Shrewsbury Drapers and the Welsh Wool Trade in the Sixteenth and Seventeenth Centuries* (Oxford University Press, 1953). See also R. Colyer, *The Welsh Cattle Drovers* (Cardiff: University of Wales Press, 1976), pp. 30–51.
95. T. Jones Pierce (ed.), *Cal. Clenennau Letters and Papers* (Aberystwyth: National Library of Wales Journal Supplement, Series IV, Pt i, 1947), no. 106, p. 31.
96. I. ab O. Edwards (ed.), *A Catalogue of Star Chamber Proceedings relating to Wales* (Cardiff: University of Wales Press, 1929), p. 152.
97. G. D. Owen, *Wales in the Reign of James* I (London: Royal Historical Society, The Boydell Press, 1988), pp. 124–5.
98. A. H. Dodd, 'The Early Stuarts', in A. J. Roderick (ed.), *Wales Through the Ages*, II (Llandybie: Christopher Davies, 1960), pp. 54–61; idem, 'The Pattern of Politics in Stuart Wales', *Trans. Cymmr.* (1948), pp. 14–15, 20–1; S. T. Bindoff, 'The Stuarts and Their Style', *English Historical Review*, LX, (1945), pp. 204–5; J. G. Jones, 'The Welsh Poets and Their Patrons *c.* 1550–1640', *Welsh History Review*, IX (1979), pp. 250–5.
99. A. H. Dodd, 'A Commendacion of Welshmen', *Bulletin of the Board of Celtic Studies*, XIX (1960–2), pp. 235–49.
100. W. Vaughan, *The arraignment of slander...* (London: 1630), p. 323.

101. Llwyd, *The Breuiary of Britayne*, p. 60.
102. W. Rees (ed.), *A Survey of the Duchy of Lancaster Lordships in Wales, 1609–1613* (Cardiff: University of Wales Press, 1953), pp. xxii–xxiv.
103. NLW, Add. MSS, 466E, 595.

2   THE TUDOR SETTLEMENT, 1534–43

1. G. Williams, *Recovery, Reorientation and Reformation: Wales 1415–1642* (Oxford/Cardiff: Oxford and Wales University Presses, 1987), chapter 11, pp. 253–78; idem, *Wales and the Act of Union* (Bangor: Headstart History Series, 1992); C. S. L. Davies, *Peace, Print and Protestantism 1450–1558* (London: Granada, 1977), pp. 176–242; G. R. Elton, *Reform and Reformation: England 1509–1558* (London: Edward Arnold, 1977), pp. 201–20.
2. G. R. Elton, *England under the Tudors* (London: Methuen, 1957), pp. 176–7, 419–20.
3. St. 27 Henry VIII c. 24 ss 1, 2, 3, 18; I. Bowen (ed.), *Statutes of Wales* (London: T. Fisher Unwin, 1908), pp. 73–5.
4. J. E. Lloyd and R. T. Jenkins (eds), *Dictionary of Welsh Biography* (London: Honourable Society of Cymmrodorion, 1959), s. n. (App.).
5. W. Ll, Williams, 'A Welsh Insurrection', *Y Cymmr.*, XVI (1902), pp. 1–93.
6. R. A. Griffiths, 'Gruffudd ap Nicholas and the Rise of the House of Dinefwr', *National Library of Wales Journal*, XIII (1964), pp. 256–68.
7. See R. B. Pugh, 'The Indenture for the Marches between Henry VII and Edward Stafford (1477–1521), Duke of Buckingham', *English Historical Review*, LXXI (1956), pp. 436–41; C. Rawcliffe, *The Staffords, Earls of Stafford and Dukes of Buckingham* (University of Cambridge Press, 1978); W. R. B. Robinson, 'The Marcher Lords of Wales 1525–31', *Bull. Board of Celtic Studies*, XXVI (1974–6), pp. 342–52.
8. W. R. B. Robinson, 'The Welsh Estates of Charles, Earl of Worcester in 1520', *Bull. Board of Celtic Studies*, XXIV (1971), pp. 384–411; idem, 'Early Tudor Policy towards Wales', ibid., XX–XXI, (1962–4, Pt iv), (1964–6, Pt 1).
9. W. Rees, *The Union of England and Wales* (Cardiff: University of Wales Press, 1947), pp. 14–15.

10. T. B. Pugh (ed.), *The Marcher Lordships of South Wales, 1415–1536* (Cardiff: University of Wales Press, 1963); T. B. Pugh (with W. R. B. Robinson), 'Sessions in Eyre in a Marcher Lordship: a Dispute between the Earl of Worcester and His Tenants of Gower and Kilvey in 1524', *South Wales and Monmouthshire Record Society Publications*, IV, (1957), pp. 113–9; A. C. Reeves, *The Marcher Lords* (Llandybie: Christopher Davies, 1983), pp. 86–7, 96–100; P. R. Roberts, 'A Petition Concerning Sir Richard Herbert', *Bull. Board of Celtic Studies*, XX (1962), pp. 45–9.

11. T. B. Pugh (ed.), *Glamorgan County History: The Middle Ages*, III (Cardiff: Glamorgan County History Trust, 1971), p. 567.

12. Williams, *Wales and the Act of Union*, p. 10.

13. *L & P*, VII, no. 781, p. 298; ibid., V, no. 991, p. 462.

14. W. Rees, *South Wales and the March, 1284–1415* (Oxford University Press, 1924), pp. 229–34; D. Lewis, 'The Court of the President and Council of Wales and the Marches from 1478 to 1575', *Y Cymmr.*, XII (1898), pp. 42–6.

15. *L & P*, VI, no. 386, p. 177; ibid., VII, no. 781, p. 298.

16. Pugh, 'The Indenture for the Marches'.

17. *L & P*, VI, no. 210, p. 95.

18. Ibid., VI, no. 946, p. 411.

19. L. Stephen and S. Lee (eds.), *Dictionary of National Biography* (London: Smith, Elder and Co., 1885–1900), XXXII, s.n.; P. Williams, *The Council in the Marches of Wales under Elizabeth I*, (Cardiff: University of Wales Press, 1958), chapter 1, pp. 13–43.

20. J. G. Evans (ed.), *Report on Manuscripts in the Welsh Language*, I, (London: Historical Manuscripts Commission, 1898), p. x.

21. D. Ll. Thomas, 'Further Notes on the Council in the Marches...', *Y Cymmr.*, XVII (1899), App. F, pp. 159–60; W. Ll. Williams, *The History of the Great Sessions in Wales, 1542–1830* (Brecknock: 1899), pp. 126–7.

22. Roberts, 'A Petition Concerning Sir Richard Herbert'.

23. *L & P*, VII, no. 1571, p. 586.

24. Ibid., VIII, no. 1058, p. 417.

25. Ibid., IX, no. 354, pp. 118–19.

26. Ibid., X, no. 754, p. 316.

27. Ibid., VII, no. 988, p. 379.

28. Ibid., X, no. 204, p. 72. See also XIV (Pt ii), no. 384, pp. 133–4.

Notes

29. *Calendar of State Papers Ireland*, 1601–3 (London, 1860–), pp. 254–5.
30. T. Wright, *The History of Ludlow and its Neighbourhood* (Ludlow/London: Longman/J. R. Smith, 1852), p. 378.
31. *L & P*, VIII, no. 839, pp. 321–2.
32. R. Flenley (ed.), *Calendar of the Register of the Council in the Marches of Wales, 1569–91* (London: Cymmrodorion Record Series, no. 8, 1916), p. 47.
33. *L & P*, XII (Pt i), no. 93, p. 49; VII, no. 1353, p. 514.
34. Thomas, 'Further Notes on the Council in the Marches...', App. B, pp. 128–9; D. Mathew, 'Some Elizabethan Documents', *Bull. Board of Celtic Studies*, VI, (1931), pp. 74–7.
35. St. 26 Henry VIII c. 6, in Bowen, *Statutes of Wales*, p. 54.
36. J. G. Edwards, *The Principality of Wales 1267–1967* (Caernarfon: Caernarfonshire Historical Society, 1969), pp. 5–16, 20–8.
37. Rees, *The Union of England and Wales*, pp. 11–13.
38. J. G. Jones (ed.), *History of the Gwydir Family and Memoirs* (Llandysul: Gomer Press, 1990), p. 49.
39. Wright, *The History of Ludlow*, pp. 383–5.
40. St. 26 Henry VIII c. 4, in Bowen, *Statutes of Wales*, pp. 51–2.
41. H. Ellis (ed.), *Original Letters Illustrative of English History*, III (3rd Ser.), CCLXXII, pp. 47–50.
42. St. 26 Henry VIII c. 5, in Bowen (ed.), *Statutes of Wales*, pp. 52–4.
43. St. 26 Henry VIII c. 6, in ibid., pp. 54–62.
44. Ibid., pp. 56–7.
45. Ibid., p. 62.
46. G. Owen, *The Description of Pembrokeshire*, ed. H. Owen (London: Bedford Press, 1906), III, pp. 92–4; see also Ellis, *Original Letters History Illustrative of English History*, III (2nd Ser., 1827) CC, pp. 41–4; Thomas, 'Further Notes on the Council in the Marches...', App. B, pp. 128–33; J. G. Jones (ed.), *History of the Gwydir Family and Memoirs*, pp. 39–40, 51–2.
47. St. 26 Henry VIII c. 7, in Bowen (ed.), *Statutes of Wales*, p. 63.
48. St. 27 Henry VIII c. 7, in ibid., pp. 69–72.
49. E. Herbert (of Chirbury), *The Life and Reign of King Henry the Eighth* (London: M. Clark, 1682 imp.), p. 436.
50. *L & P*, VII, no. 1456, p. 545.
51. St. 27 Henry VIII c. 5, in Bowen (ed.), *Statutes of Wales*, pp. 67–9.
52. *L & P*, X, no. 453, p. 182.
53. Owen, *The Description of Pembrokeshire*, III, pp. 55–6.

225

54. *L & P*, X, no. 785, p. 331; XI, no. 525, p. 213.

55. W. R. B. Robinson, 'The Tudor Revolution in Welsh Government, 1536–1543; Its Effects on Gentry Participation', *English Historical Review*, CCCCVI (1988), pp. 1–20; T. B. Pugh, 'The Ending of the Middle Ages', *Glamorgan County History*, III, chapter 11, pp. 555–81. For the contribution of gentry and governmental agents in sixteenth and early seventeenth-century Wales, see M. Gray, 'Power, Patronage and Politics: Office-holding and Administration on the Crown's Estates in Wales', in R. W. Hoyle (ed.) *The Estates of the English Crown 1558–1640* (Cambridge University Press, 1992), chapter 5, pp. 137–62.

56. St. 27 Henry VIII c. 26, in Bowen (ed.), *Statutes of Wales*, pp. 75–94.

57. St. 27 Henry VIII c. 24, in ibid., pp. 73–5.

58. Bowen, (ed.), *Statutes of Wales*, pp. 75–6; P. R. Roberts, 'The "Act of Union" in Welsh History', *Trans. Cymmr.* (1972–3), p. 53 ff.; idem, 'The Welsh Language, English Law and Tudor Legislation', *Trans. Cymmr.* (1989), pp. 27–8; W. O. Williams, 'The Survival of the Welsh Language after the Union of England and Wales: The First Phase, 1536–1642', *Welsh History Review*, II (1964), pp. 70–5; idem, *Tudor Gwynedd* (Caernarfon: Caernarfonshire Historical Society, 1958), pp. 14–15; Williams, *Recovery, Reorientation and Reformation*, p. 268; idem, *Wales and the Act of Union*, p. 28.

59. St. 34–35 Henry VIII c. 26, in Bowen (ed.), *Statutes of Wales*, pp. 102–3, 113–7.

60. P. R. Roberts, 'The Union with England and the Identity of "Anglican" Wales', *Transactions of the Royal Historical Society*, XXII (1972), pp. 49–70; idem. 'A Breviat of the Effectes Devised for Wales *c.* 1540–41', *Camden Miscellany*, XXVI (1975), pp. 31–45.

61. *L & P*, XIII (Pt i), no. 1042, pp. 384–5.

62. Ibid., XI, no. 1338, p. 538.

63. Ibid., XIV (Pt i), no. 492, p. 193; Rees, *The Union of England and Wales*, pp. 28–9.

64. Roberts, 'A Breviat of the Effectes', pp. 32, 35, 38, 42; idem, 'The Union with England and the Identity of "Anglican" Wales'.

65. Edwards, *The Principality of Wales*. See also P. R. Roberts, 'Wales and England after the Tudor "Union": Crown, Principality and Parliament 1543–1624', in C. Cross, D. Loades and J. J.

Scarisbrick (eds), *Law and Government under the Tudors; Essays Presented to Sir Geoffrey Elton on His Retirement* (Cambridge University Press, 1988), pp. 111–38.

66. O. M. Edwards, *Wales* (London: Longman, 1901), p. 34; A. F. Pollard, *Henry VIII* (London: Longman, 1905), p. 365.
67. Edwards, *The Principality of Wales*, pp. 35–6.
68. Owen, *The Description of Pembrokeshire*, III, p. 56.
69. Rice Merrick, *Morganiae Archaiographia*, ed. B. Ll. James (Barry: South Wales Record Society, 1983), p. 68.
70. *L & P*, XII (Pt ii), no. 770, p. 274.

3   LAW, ORDER AND GOVERNMENT

1. *Cal. of State Papers Dom., 1547–1580* (London, 1856), CVII(4), p. 514; D. Ll. Thomas, 'Further Notes on the Council of the Marches', *Y Cymmr.*, XVII (1899), App. B, pp. 128–33; D. Mathew, 'Some Elizabethan Documents', *Bull. Board of Celtic Studies*, VI (1931), pp. 74–7. For a comprehensive study of the Welsh gentry and local government in Wales, see G. E. Jones, *The Gentry and the Elizabethan State* (Swansea: Christopher Davies, 1977).
2. G. Owen, *The Description of Pembrokeshire*, ed. H. Owen (London: Bedford Press, 1906), III, p. 24.
3. St. 34–35 Henry VIII c. 26, in I. Bowen (ed.), *Statutes of Wales*, (London: T. Fisher Unwin, 1908), p. 102; P. Williams, *Council in the Marches*, pp. 17–18.
4. Owen, *The Description of Pembrokeshire*, III, p. 23.
5. S. Haynes (ed.), *A Collection of State Papers...at Hatfield House* (London: W. Bowyer, 1740), pp. 193–201.
6. *L & P,* XII (Pt ii), no. 896, p. 312.
7. H. Ellis, *Original Letters Illustrative of English History*, II (3rd Ser.), CCLII, p. 370.
8. *L & P,* XII (Pt i), no. 1148, p. 530.
9. Ibid., XII (Pt ii), no. 1237, p. 434.
10. Ibid., XIII (Pt ii), no. 276, p. 110. See also XIII (Pt i), no. 152, p. 52.
11. Ibid., XII (Pt i), no. 1091, p. 508; XIV (Pt i), no. 492, p. 193.
12. Ibid., XIV (Pt i), no. 492, p. 193.
13. Ibid., X, no. 778, p. 329; XIII (Pt i), no. 66, p. 21; W. J. Smith (ed.), *Calendar of Salusbury Correspondence, 1553–c.1710* (Cardiff: University of Wales Press, 1954), Appendix i, p. 238.

14. *L & P*, XIV (Pt ii), no. 384, p. 133.
15. St. 34–35 Henry VIII c. 26, in Bowen (ed.), *Statutes of Wales*, pp. 114–15.
16. Owen, *The Description of Pembrokeshire*, III, pp. 67, 71.
17. Ibid., p. 54.
18. Ibid., p. 58.
19. W. O. Williams (ed.), *Calendar of the Caernarvonshire Quarter Sessions Records: I, 1541–1558* (Caernarvonshire Historical Society, 1956), pp. 2–29, W. R. B. Robinson, 'The Tudor Revolution in Welsh Government', 1536–1543; Its Effects on Gentry, Participation, *English Historical Review*, CCCCVI (1988).
20. Thomas, 'Further Notes on the Council in the Marches', p. 131; Mathew, 'Some Elizabethan Documents', p. 76.
21. D. R. Thomas, '*The Life and Work of Bishop Davies and William Salesbury* (Oswestry: Caxton Press, 1902), App. C, p. 49; G. Williams, *Welsh Reformation Essays* (Cardiff: University of Wales Press, 1967), pp. 175–80.
22. Ellis, *Original Letters Illustrative of English History*, III (2nd Ser. 1827), CC, p. 42.
23. NLW, MS, 9051E, 170; J. R. Dasent (ed.), *Acts of the Privy Council* (London, 1890), XXV, p. 307; T. Jones Pierce (ed.), *Cal. Clenennau Letters and Papers*, no. 106, p. 31.
24. Ellis, *Original Letters Illustrative of English History*, III (2nd Ser.), CC, pp. 43–4.
25. PRO, SP 12, 159/1; P. Williams, *Council in the Marches under Elizabeth I*, (Cardiff: University of Wales Press, 1958), pp. 259–60.
26. R. Flenley (ed.), *Calendar of the Register of the Council in the Marches of Wales, 1569–91* (London: Cymmrodorion Record Series: no. 8, 1916), p. 124.
27. Owen, *The Description of Pembrokeshire*, III, pp. 24, 91.
28. T. Jones Pierce (ed.), *Cal. Clenennau Letters and Papers*, pp. 31–9.
29. St. 27 Henry VIII c. 26, in Bowen (ed.), *Statutes of Wales*, p. 76.
30. PRO. St. Ch. 5/L2/10; I. ab O. Edwards (ed.), *Catalogue of Star Chamber Proceedings Relating to Wales* (Cardiff: University of Wales Press, 1929), p. 40; J. G. Jones, *Wales and the Tudor State*, 1534–1603 (Cardiff: University of Wales Press, 1989), pp. 194–6.
31. Thomas, 'Further Notes on the Council in the Marches', p. 163.
32. W. Vaughan, *The Golden Fleece* (1626), Pt ii, pp. 31, 35.
33. NLW, MS, 9052E, 271.

34. H. Lewis, *Hen Gyflwyniadau* (Cardiff: University of Wales Press, 1948), p. 52. See W. P. Griffith. 'Schooling and Society', in J. G. Jones (ed.), *Class, Community and Culture in Tudor Wales* (Cardiff: University of Wales Press, 1989), pp. 110, 119.

35. NLW, MS, 9051E, 145.

36. W. O. Williams, *Calendar of the Caernarvonshire Quarter Sessions Records*, pp. 1xxx–1xxxii; J. G. Jones, *Concepts of Order and Gentility in Wales 1540–1640* (Llandysul: Gomer Press, 1992), pp. 33–4.

37. G. E. Jones, 'A Case of Corruption', in S. Williams (ed.), *Glamorgan Historian,* V ((Cowbridge: D. Brown, 1968), pp. 121–32; idem, 'Local Administration and Justice in Sixteenth-century Glamorgan', *Morgannwg,* IX, (1965), pp. 11–37.

38. *Historical Manuscripts Commission. Calendar of the Manuscripts of the Marquis of Salisbury* (Hatfield MSS.), XIII (London: Historical Manuscripts Commission, 1910), pp. 481–2; J. G. Jones, 'Law and Order in Merioneth after the Acts of Union 1536–43', *Journal of the Merioneth Historical Society,* X, (1986), pp. 125–6.

39. T. Jones Pierce (ed.), *Cal. Clenennau Letters and Papers,* no. 48, p. 15.

40. Owen, *The Description of Pembrokeshire,* III, pp. 93–4.

41. *L & P,* X, no. 453, p. 182.

42. J. E. Lloyd and R. T. Jenkins (eds), (London: Honourable Society of Cymmrodorion, 1959), *Dictionary of Welsh Biography* s.n.; J. Y. W. Lloyd, *History of the Princes, the Lords Marches, and the Ancient Nobility of Powys Fadog* (London: T. Richards/ Whiting 1881–7) IV, pp. 254–6; 'Law and Order in Merioneth', pp. 133–5.

43. NLW, MS, 9052E, 351.

44. Flenley (ed.), *Calendar of the Register of the Council...,* pp. 198–9.

45. NLW, MS, 5057E, 970.

46. Ibid., MS, 9052E, 351.

47. *Cal. State Papers Dom.,* 1623–25 (Addenda), p. 560 [CXXXIII, no. 44].

48. Ibid., 1619–23, CXXVII, no. 1, p. 332.

49. Ibid., 1611–18, LXXXIV, p. 337.

50. NLW, MSS, 9056E, 813, 819.

51. J. G. Evans (ed.), *Report on Manuscripts in the Welsh Language* (London: Historical Manuscripts Commission, 1898), I, pp. 271–2. See also N. W. Powell, 'Crime and the Community

in Denbighshire during the 1590s: The Evidence of the Records of the Court of Great Sessions', in Jones (ed.), *Class, Community and Culture in Tudor Wales,* pp. 261–88.

52. Flenley (ed.), *Calendar of the Register of the Council...,* pp. 227–8.

53. J. Penry, *Three Treatises Concerning Wales,* ed. D. Williams (Cardiff: University of Wales Press, 1960), pp. 41–2.

54. NLW, MS, 9051E, 159. See W. O. Williams, 'The County Records', *Trans. Caerns. Hist. Soc.,* X (1949), p. 90. For detailed studies of the evidence provided by Caernarfonshire Quarter Sessions records, see J. G. Jones, 'Caernarvonshire Administration: The Activities of the Justices of the Peace, 1603–1660', *Welsh History Review,* V (1970), pp. 130–63; idem, 'Aspects of Local Government in pre-Restoration Caernarvonshire', *Trans. Caerns. Hist. Soc.,* XXX (1972), pp. 7–32.

55. Gwynedd Archives Service (Caernarfon): XQS 1618.

56. *Cal. State Papers Dom.,* 1619–23, CXXXIII, no. 52, p. 455.

57. Ibid., CXLII, no. 4(i), p. 546; NLW MS, 9058E, 1064.

58. Gwynedd Archives Service (Caernarfon): XQS 1636.

59. Ibid., n.d.

60. Ibid.

61. NLW MS 9060E, 1248.

62. Dasent (ed.), *Acts of the Privy Council,* 1625–26, p. 321.

63. NLW, MS, 1595E.

64. *Cal. State Papers Dom.,* 1637–38, CCCLXXXV, no. 17, pp. 312–13.

65. T. Jones Pierce (ed.), *Cal. Clenennau Letters and Papers,* nos. 162, 166, pp. 47–8; Dasent, *Acts of the Privy Council,* XXX, pp. 59, 65, 92, 142, 152.

66. *Cal. State Papers Dom.,* 1637–8, CCCLXXX, no. 98, p. 220; M. D. Gordon, 'The Collection of Ship Money in the Reign of Charles I', *Trans. Royal Historical Society,* IV (1910), pp. 141–53; A. H. Dodd, 'Wales in the Parliaments of Charles I', *Trans. Cymmr.* (1946–7), pp. 34–5; Jones, 'Caernarvonshire Administration', pp. 152–3.

67. *Cal. State Papers Dom.,* 1639–40, CCCCXLVIII, no. 13, p. 554.

68. Ibid., 1637–8, CCCLXXXV, no. 88, p. 312; CCCXXXI, no. 20, p. 76; 1635–6, CCCXIII, no. 76, p. 221. See also 1636, CCCXII, no. 49, pp. 191–2, CCCXVII, no. 62, p. 335; ibid., no. 71, p. 337.

69. B. E. Howells (ed.) *Pembrokeshire County History: III, Early Modern Pembrokeshire* 1536–1815 (Haverfordwest: Pembrokeshire Historical Society, 1987), p. 155.

70. NLW, Add. MS, 464E, 241.
71. J. G. Jones, 'Sir John Wynn of Gwydir and His Tenants: The Dolwyddelan and Llysfaen Land Disputes', *Welsh History Review*, XI (1982), pp. 1–30; G. D. Owen, *Wales in the Reign of James I* (London: Royal Historical Society, Boydell Press, 1988), pp. 59–63.
72. A. H. Dodd, 'The Pattern of Politics in Stuart Wales, *Trans. Cymmr.* (1948), pp. 9–20; G. Williams, *Religion, Language and Nationality in Wales* (Cardiff: University of Wales Press, 1979), VII, pp. 148–70.
73. NLW, MS, 9056E, 813.
74. Gwynedd Archives Service (Caernarfon): XQS, 1620.
75. Ibid., 1630.
76. NLW, MS, 9053E, 508.
77. Ibid., MS, 537.
78. Ibid., MS, 532.
79. BL, Stowe MS 570, f. 79; H. A. Lloyd, *The Gentry of South-West Wales, 1540–1640* (Cardiff: University of Wales Press, 1968), p. 143.
80. Lloyd, *The Gentry of South-West Wales*, pp. 167–73; idem. 'Wales and the Star Chamber', *Welsh History Review*, V (1971), pp. 157–60; P. Williams, 'Star Chamber and the Council in the Marches of Wales, 1559–1603', *Bull. Board of Celtic Studies*, XVI (1956), pp. 287–97; idem. *Council in the Marches under Elizabeth I*, pp. 213–25; idem, 'The Activity of the Council in the Marches under the Early Stuarts', *Welsh History Review*, I (1961), pp. 133–60.

4   RELIGION AND SOCIETY

1. G. R. Elton, *England under the Tudors* (London: Methuen, 1957), pp. 127–37; idem, *Reform and Reformation: England, 1509–1558* (London: Edward Arnold, 1977), pp. 174–200; J. J. Scarisbrick, *The Reformation and the English People* (Oxford: Clarendon Press,1982), chapter 10, pp. 305–54.
2. J. Caley (ed.), *Valor Ecclesiasticus temp. Henr. VIII...*, (London, 1810–34), IV, pp. 345–78, 379–414, 415–32, 433–56; G. Williams, *The Welsh Church from Conquest to Reformation* (Cardiff: University of Wales Press, 1962), p. 270.
3. H. Ellis, *Original Letters Illustrative of English History*, II (2nd Ser. 1827), CXXX, pp. 82–3; W. G. Evans, 'Derfel Gadarn – a

Celebrated Victim of the Reformation', *Journal of the Merioneth Historical Society*, XI (1991), pp. 137–51.

4. Williams, *The Welsh Church*, pp. 346–50, 412–13.

5. T. Wright (ed.), *Letters Relating to the Suppression of Monasteries* (London: Camden Society, 1843), pp. 77–8.

6. *L & P*, X, no. 393, p. 160.

7. R. W. Hays, *The History of the Abbey of Aberconway* (Cardiff: University of Wales Press, 1963), p. 178.

8. G. Williams, *Recovery, Reorientation and Reformation: Wales, 1415–1642* (Oxford/Cardiff: Oxford and Wales University Presses, 1987), pp. 283–301; idem, *Welsh Reformation Essays* (Cardiff: University of Wales Press, 1967), pp. 14, 19–20, and 'The Dissolution of the Monasteries in Glamorgan', in ibid., pp. 91–110; M. Gray, 'Change and Continuity: The Gentry and the Property of the Church in South-east Wales and the Marches', in J. G. Jones (ed.), *Class, Community and Culture in Tudor Wales* (Cardiff: University of Wales Press, 1989), pp. 1–35.

9. G. Williams, 'The Protestant Experiment in the Diocese of St David's, 1534–55', in *Welsh Reformation Essays*, pp. 111–24; idem, 'Carmarthen and the Reformation', in T. Barnes and N. Yates (eds), *Carmarthenshire Studies: Essays Presented to Major Francis Jones* (Carmarthen: Carmarthenshire County Council, 1974), pp. 136–51; D. Walker, 'Religious Change, 1536–1642', in B. E. Howells (ed.), *Pembrokeshire County History: III, Early Modern Pembrokeshire, 1536–1815* (Haverfordwest: Pembrokeshire Historical Society, 1987), pp. 94–108.

10. G. Williams, 'The Reformation in Sixteenth-century Caernarvonshire', in *Welsh Reformation Essays*, pp. 39–47.

11. G. Williams, 'The Elizabethan Settlement of Religion in Wales and the Marches, 1559–60', in *Welsh Reformation Essays*, pp. 141–53; idem, 'The Royal Visitation of the Diocese of Llandaff, 1559', *National Library of Wales Journal*, IV (1945–6), pp. 189–97; T. J. Prichard, 'The Reformation in the Deanery of Llandaff', *Morgannwg*, XIII (1969), pp. 38–42; J. G. Jones, 'The Reformation Bishops of Llandaff, 1558–1601', *Morgannwg*, XXXII (1988), pp. 38–40.

12. D. McCulloch, *The Later Reformation in England, 1547–1603* (London: Macmillan, 1990), pp. 11–26; P. N. Brooks, *Thomas Cranmer's Doctrine of the Eucharist* (London: Macmillan, 1965); C. Cross, *Church and People, 1450–1660* (London: Fontana/ Brighton: Harvester, 1976), IV, pp. 81–100; C. S. L. Davies.

Peace, Print and Protestantism, 1450–1558 (London: Granada 1977), pp. 263–91.

13. J. G. Jones, *Wales and the Tudor State, 1534–1603* (Cardiff: University of Wales Press, 1989), p. 236.

14. Ibid., pp. 237–8.

15. Wright, *Letters*, pp. 184–5.

16. Ibid., p. 185; G. Williams, 'Carmarthen and the Reformation', in Barnes and Yates, *Carmarthenshire Studies*, pp. 147–9.

17. C. Davies (ed.), *Rhagymadroddion a Chyflwyniadau Lladin 1551–1632* (Cardiff: University of Wales Press, 1980), p. 19; Williams, *Welsh Reformation Essays*, p. 196; I. Thomas, *William Salesbury and His Testament* (Cardiff: University of Wales Press, 1967), pp. 39–43; idem, *Y Testament Newydd Cymraeg, 1551–1620* (Cardiff: University of Wales Press, 1976), pp. 70–99.

18. G. Williams, 'William Salesbury's *Baterie of the Popes Botereulx*', *Bull. Board of Celtic Studies*, XIII (1949), pp. 146–50; idem, *Welsh Reformation Essays*, pp. 195–6; W. A. Mathias, 'William Salesbury – ei Ryddiaith', in G. Bowen (ed.), *Y Traddodiad Rhyddiaith* (Llandysul, Gomer Press, 1970), pp. 54–7.

19. G. Williams, 'The Protestant Experiment in the Diocese of St David's, 1534–55; II. The Episcopate of Robert Ferrar, 1548–55', in *Welsh Reformation Essays*, pp. 124–35; idem, 'Carmarthen and the Reformation', in Barnes and Yates, *Carmarthenshire Studies*, pp. 150–7; idem, 'Wales and the Reign of Queen Mary I', *Welsh History Review*, X (1981), pp. 334–58.

20. J. G. Jones (ed.), *History of the Gwydir Family and Memoirs* (Llandysul: Gomer Press, 1990), p. 62.

21. Williams, *Welsh Reformation Essays*, p. 49.

22. Williams, 'Wales and the Reign of Queen Mary I'. For background, see D. A. Thomas (ed.), *The Welsh Elizabethan Catholic Martyrs* (Cardiff: University of Wales Press, 1971), introduction.

23. E. G. Jones, *Cymru a'r Hen Ffydd* (Cardiff: University of Wales Press, 1951), pp. 18–22; R. G. Gruffydd, *Argraffwyr Cyntaf Cymru: Gwasgau Dirgel y Catholigion adeg Elisabeth* (Cardiff: University of Wales Press, 1972), pp. 1–22.

24. G. Williams, 'Religion and Welsh Literature in the Age of the Reformation', in *The Welsh and Their Religion* (Cardiff: University of Wales Press, 1991), V, pp. 138–72.

25. N. Jones, *Faith by Statute: Parliament and the Settlement of Religion, 1559* (London: Royal Historical Society, 1982); G. Williams, 'The Elizabethan Settlement of Religion in Wales

and the Marches', in *Welsh Reformation Essays*; Cross, *Church and People, 1450–1660*, VI, pp. 124–52.

26. For background, see Williams, 'Religion and Welsh Literature'; idem, 'Religion', in T. Herbert and G. E. Jones (eds), *Tudor Wales: Welsh History and its Sources Series* (Cardiff: University of Wales Press, 1988), pp. 107–16; idem, 'Dadeni, Diwygiad a Diwylliant Cymru', in *Grym Tafodau Tân: Ysgrifau Hanesyddol ar Grefydd a Diwylliant* (Llandysul: Gomer Press, 1984), pp. 63–86; R. G. Gruffydd, 'The Renaissance and Welsh Literature', in G. Williams and R. O. Jones (eds), *The Celts and the Renaissance: Tradition and Innovation* (Cardiff: University of Wales Press, 1990), pp. 17–39.

27. G. Williams (ed.) *Glamorgan County History, IV: Early Modern Glamorgan* (Cardiff: Glamorgan County History Trust, 1974), pp. 232–9, 249–52; F. H. Pugh, 'Glamorgan Recusants, 1577–1611', *South Wales and Monmouthshire Record Society Publications*, III (1954), pp. 49–52; idem, 'Monmouthshire recusants in the Reigns of Elizabeth I and James I', ibid., IV (1957), pp. 59–65; E. G. Jones, 'Catholic Recusancy in the Counties of Denbigh, Flint and Montgomery, 1581–1626', *Trans. Cymmr.* (1945), pp. 114–33.

28. T. H. Parry-Williams (ed.), *Carolau Richard White* (Cardiff: University of Wales Press, 1931), p. 32; Thomas, *The Welsh Elizabethan Catholic Martyrs*, introduction.

29. T. H. Parry-Williams (ed.), *Canu Rhydd Cynnar* (Cardiff: University of Wales Press, 1932), XCV, p. 368.

30. D. R. Thomas, *The History of the Diocese of St Asaph* (Oswestry: Caxton Press, 1908), I, pp. 89–90; J. G. Jones, 'The Reformation Bishops of St Asaph', *Journal of Welsh Eccles. History*, VII (1990), pp. 27–8; idem, 'Thomas Davies and William Hughes: Two Reformation Bishops of St. Asaph', *Bull. Board of Celtic Studies*, XXXIX (1980–2), pp. 320–5.

31. J. W. Evans, 'The Reformation and St David's Cathedral', *Journal of Welsh Eccles. History*, VII (1990), pp. 12–14.

32. St. 5 Elizabeth I c. 28, in I. Bowen (ed.) *Statutes of Wales* (London: T. Fisher Unwin, 1908), pp. 149–51. See G. R. Elton, 'Wales in Parliament, 1542–1581', in R. R. Davies *et al.* (eds), *Welsh Society and Nationhood: Historical Essays Presented to Glanmor Williams* (Cardiff: University of Wales Press, 1984), pp. 119–21.

33. Jones, 'Thomas Davies and William Hughes'.

34. G. H. Hughes (ed.), *Rhagymadroddion, 1547–1659* (Cardiff: University of Wales Press, 1951), p. 101.

35. G. Williams, 'Landlords in Wales; The Church', in J. Thirsk (ed.), *Agrarian History of England and Wales, IV, 1500–1640* (Cambridge University Press, 1967), pp. 381–95; Williams, *Welsh Reformation Essays*, pp. 170–5.

36. Hughes, *Rhagymadroddion*, pp. 91–2, 101.

37. Evans, 'The Reformation and St David's Cathedral', pp. 12–13.

38. A. O. Evans (ed.), *A Memorandum on the Legality of the Welsh Bible and the Welsh Version of the Book of Common Prayer* (Cardiff: W. Lewis, 1925), pp. 84–5; G. Williams, 'Some Protestant Views of Early British Church History', in *Welsh Reformation Essays*, pp. 207–19; idem, *Bywyd ac Amserau'r Esgob Richard Davies* (Cardiff: University of Wales Press, 1953), pp. 82–110; S. Lewis, "Damcaniaeth Eglwysig Brotestannaidd', in R. G. Gruffydd (ed.), *Meistri'r Canrifoedd: Ysgrifau ar Hanes Llenyddiaeth Gymraeg* (Cardiff: University of Wales Press, 1973), pp. 116–39.

39. R. Flower, 'William Salesbury, Richard Davies and Archbishop Parker', *National Library of Wales Journal*, II (1941–2), pp 7–14.

40. Hughes, *Rhagymadroddion*, p. 74.

41. Jones, *Wales and the Tudor State*, pp. 238–9.

42. D. Mathew, 'Some Elizabethan Documents', *Bull. Board of Celtic Studies*, VI (1931), pp. 177–8. For more information on the condition of the diocese of Bangor according to the surveys of 1563 and 1603, see M. Gray, 'The Diocese of Bangor in the Late Sixteenth Century', *Journal of Welsh Eccles. Hist.*, V (1988), pp. 31–72.

43. J. A. Bradney, 'The Speech of William Blethin, Bishop of Llandaff, and the Customs and Ordinances of the Church of Llandaff', *Y Cymmr.*, XXXI (1921), pp. 254–8; Jones, *Wales and the Tudor State*, pp. 231–3.

44. I. ab O. Edwards, 'William Morgan's Quarrel with His Parishioners at Llanrhaeadr-ym Mochnant', *Bull. Board of Celtic Studies*, III (1927), pp. 298–321. Many studies of Morgan have appeared in recent years. See G. Williams 'Bishop William Morgan (1545–1604) and the First Welsh Bible', in *The Welsh and their Religion*, VI, pp. 173–229; I, Thomas, *William Morgan and His Bible* (Cardiff: University of Wales Press, 1988); R. G. Gruffydd, *The Translating of the Bible into the Welsh Tongue* (London: British Broadcasting Corporation,

1988). For Morgan's educational background, see G. Williams, 'William Morgan's Bible and the Cambridge Connection', *Welsh History Review*, XIV (1989), pp. 363–79.

45. J. Strype, *Annals of the Reformation* (London: 1728), III, App, pp. 184–6; Jones, 'Reformation Bishops of St Asaph', pp. 32–4; idem, 'Thomas Davies and William Hughes', pp. 332–5. For his heretical views at Cambridge, see W. P. Griffith, 'William Hughes and the "Descensus" controversy of 1567', *Bull. Board of Celtic Studies*, XXXIV (1987), pp. 185–99; Jones, 'Thomas Davies and Williams Hughes', pp. 329, 333–5.

46. J. G. Jones, 'Bishop William Morgan's dispute with John Wynn of Gwydir in 1603–4', *Journal of the Historical Society of the Church in Wales*, XXII (1972), pp. 49–78, esp. 67–8, 73–6.

47. Evans, *A Memorandum on the Legality of the Welsh Bible*, pp. 107–8.

48. G. Williams, 'Bishop Richard Davies (?1501–1581)', in *Welsh Reformation Essays*, p. 182; Flower, 'William Salesbury, Richard Davies and Archbishop Parker'; idem, 'Richard Davies, William Cecil and Giraldus Cambrensis', *National Library of Wales Journal*, III, (1943–4) pp. 11–14.

49. D. R. Thomas, *The Life and Work of Bishop Davies and William Salesbury*, (Oswestry: Caxton Press, 1892), pp. 49, 57–8.

50. Hughes, *Rhagymadroddion*, p. 100; Jones, *Wales and the Tudor State*, p. 245. See also W. Hughes, *Life and Times of Bishop William Morgan* (London: SPCK, 1891), pp. 123–7.

51. Williams, 'Bishop William Morgan and the First Welsh Bible', pp. 207–9.

52. J. G. Jones (ed.), *History of the Gwydir Family and Memoirs*, p. 63; Edwards, 'William Morgan's Quarrel with His Parishioners'.

53. J. G. Jones (ed.), *History of the Gwydir Family and Memoirs*, p. 62; W. A. Mathias, 'William Salesbury – Ei Fywyd a'i Weithiau', in G. Bowen (ed.), *Y Traddodiad Rhyddiaith*, p. 46.

54. G. Williams, 'John Penry, Marprelate and patriot?', *Welsh History Review*, III (1967), pp. 361–80.

55. Thomas (ed.), *Welsh Elizabethan Catholic Martyrs*, p. 93.

56. J. Penry *Three Treatises Concerning Wales*, ed. D. Williams (Cardiff: University of Wales Press 1960), p. 162.

57. Owen, *The Description of Pembrokeshire*, III, p. 99.

58. R. G. Gruffydd, 'Bishop Francis Godwin's Injunctions for the Diocese of Llandaff, 1603', *Journal Hist. Soc. Church in Wales*, IV (1954), p. 19.

59. Jones, *Cymru a'r Hen Ffydd*, pp. 38–9; Pugh, 'Glamorgan Recusants'. and 'Monmouthshire Recusants'.

60. Jones, 'Catholic Recusancy in the Counties...'.
61. *Cal. State Papers Dom.*, 1625–6, XI, no. 37, p. 172; E. G. Jones, *Cymru a'r Hen Ffydd*, pp. 55–7; idem, 'Hugh Owen of Gwenynog', *Trans. Anglesey Antiq. Soc. and Field Club* (1938), pp. 42–9.
62. *Cal. State Papers Dom.*, 1627–8, LXXXVIII, no. 23, p. 487; Jones, *Cymru a'r Hen Ffydd*, pp. 59–60.
63. J. E. Lloyd and R. T. Jenkins (eds), *Dictionary of Welsh Biography* (London: Honourable Society of Cymmrodorion, 1959), s.n.; A. H. Dodd, 'Wales and the Scottish Succession 1570–1605', *Trans. Cymmr.* (1937), pp. 211–25; M. O'Keeffe, *Four Martyrs of South Wales and the Marches* (Cardiff: Archdiocese of Cardiff, 1970).
64. *Calendar of the Manuscripts of the Marquis of Salisbury (Hatfield MSS)* (London: Historical Manuscripts Commission, 1883–), *Cal. Salisbury MSS.*, XI, p. 460.
65. Ibid., XII, t. 673. See also XV, p. 17.
66. *Cal. State Papers Dom.*, 1611–16, LXI, p. 2; J. G. Jones, 'Richard Parry, Bishop of St Asaph: Some Aspects of His Career', *Bull. Board of Celtic Studies*, XXVI (1975) pp. 177–9, 190.
67. *Cal. Salisbury MSS.*, XI, pp. 498–9.
68. G. Williams, 'Wales and the Reformation', in *Welsh Reformation Essays*, pp. 22–3.
69. G. Williams, 'Edward James a Llyfr yr Homilïau', in *Grym Tafodau Tân*, pp. 180–98.
70. J. H. Davies (ed.), *Hen Gerddi Gwleidyddol, 1588–1660* (Cardiff: Cymdeithas Llên Cymru, 1901), pp. 7–11; Parry-Williams, *Canu Rhydd Cynnar*, CXV, pp. 367–72.
71. Penry, *Three Treatises Concerning Wales*, p. 40.
72. *Cal. State Papers Dom.*, 1629–1631, CLXIV, no. 23, p. 230.
73. NLW, MS, 9061E, 1440.
74. M. Morgan (ed.), *Gweithiau Oliver Thomas ac Evan Roberts: Dau Biwritan Cynnar* (Cardiff: University of Wales Press, 1981), introduction, pp. xii–xxvi; R. G. Gruffydd, '*In that Gentile Country...*': the Beginnings of Puritan Nonconformity in Wales (Bridgend: Evangelical Library of Wales, 1975), pp. 22–4: T. Richards, *The Puritan Movement in Wales, 1639 to 1653* (London: National Eisteddfod Association, 1920), chapters 1 and 2, pp. 1–30. See also G. H. Jenkins, *Protestant Dissenters in Wales, 1639–1689* (Cardiff: University of Wales Press, 1992), pp. 1–16.
75. D. G. Jones, *Y Ficer Prichard a 'Canwyll y Cymry'* (Caernarfon: Cwmni'r Llan a Gwasg yr Eglwys yng Nghymru, 1946);

J. Ballinger, 'Vicar Prichard: A Study in Welsh Bibliography', *Y Cymmr.*, XIII, pp. 1–75.

76. G. Williams, 'The Ecclesiastical History of Glamorgan', in *Glamorgan County History*, IV, pp. 252–6: A. H. Dodd, 'Bishop Lewes Bayly, *c.* 1575–1631', *Trans. Caerns. Hist. Soc.*, XXVIII (1967), pp. 13–36.

77. P. S. Seaver, *The Puritan Lectureships: The Politics of Religious Dissent, 1560–1662* (Stanford University Press, 1970).

78. Gruffydd, 'Bishop Francis Godwin's Injunctions', pp. 28–30.

79. Ibid., pp. 22–8; B. Ll. James, 'The Evolution of a Radical: The Life and Career of William Erbery', *Journal of Welsh Eccles. Hist.*, III (1986), pp. 31–48; G. F. Nuttall, *The Welsh Saints, 1640–1660: Walter Cradock; Vavasor Powell; Morgan Llwyd* (Cardiff: University of Wales Press, 1957), II, pp. 18–36; idem, 'Walter Cradock (1606?–1659): The Man and His Message', in *The Puritan Spirit: Essays and Addresses* (London: Epworth Press, 1967), pp. 118–29; N. Gibbard, *Walter Cradock: 'New Testament Saint'* (Bridgend: Evangelical Library of Wales, 1977), pp. 1–25; Richards, *The Puritan Movement in Wales, passim.*

80. Gruffydd, 'Bishop Francis Godwin's Injunctions', pp. 14–16; James, 'The Evolution of a Radical'.

81. Williams, 'Landlords in Wales: The Church' in J. Thirsk (ed.), *Agrarian History of England and Wales*, pp. 389–95; D. Walker, 'The Reformation in Wales', in D. Walker (ed.), *A History of the Church in Wales* (Penarth: Church in Wales Publications, 1976), pp. 70–7; J. E. C. Hill, *Economic Problems of the Church from Archbishop Whitgift to the Long Parliament* (Oxford: Clarendon Press, 1956).

5 POLITICS AND FACTION

1. St. 27 Henry VIII c. 26, in I. Bowen (ed.), *Statutes of Wales* (London: T. Fisher Unwin, 1908), pp. 89–90.

2. St. 34–35 Henry VII c. 26, in ibid., pp. 130–1.

3. For background, see J. Loach, *Parliament under the Tudors* (Oxford: Clarendon Press, 1991), pp. 78–96; G. Roberts, *Aspects of Welsh History*, ed. A. H. Dodd and J. G. Williams (Cardiff: University of Wales Press, 1969), pp. 1–116; M. Gray, 'Power, Patronage and Politics: Office-holding and Administration on the Crown's Estates in Wales', in R. W. Hoyle (ed.),

The Estates of the English Crown, 1558–1640, (Cambridge University Press, 1992), pp. 137–62; A. H. Dodd, 'The Dawn of Party Politics', in *Studies in Stuart Wales* (Cardiff: University of Wales Press, 1952), pp. 177–89; idem, 'Wales's Parliamentary Apprenticeship (1536–1625)', *Trans. Cymmr.* (1942), pp. 8–72; P. S. Edwards, 'The Parliamentary Representation of the Welsh Boroughs in the Mid-Sixteenth Century', *Bull. Board of Celtic Studies*, XXVII (1977), pp. 425–39.

4. F. J. Fisher, 'The Development of London as a Centre of Conspicuous Consumption in the Sixteenth and Seventeenth Centuries', *Trans. of the Royal Hist. Society*, XXX (1948), pp. 37–50.

5. G. R. Elton, *England under the Tudors* (London: Methuen, 1957), pp. 173–4.

6. A. H. Dodd, 'The Pattern of Politics in Stuart Wales', *Trans. Cymmr.* (1948), pp. 20–2.

7. NLW, MS, 9051E, 4.

8. Ibid., Add. MS, 464E, 19.

9. Ibid.

10. J. Williams, *Ancient and Modern Denbigh* (Denbigh, 1856), p. 98.

11. H. A. Lloyd, *The Gentry of South-West Wales 1540–1640* (Cardiff: University of Wales Press, 1968), pp. 110–12.

12. H. G. Owen, 'Family Politics in Elizabethan Merionethshire', *Bull. Board of Celtic Studies*, XVIII (1959), pp. 185–91.

13. J. E. Neale, *The Elizabethan House of Commons* (London: Jonathan Cape, 1955), chapter 5, pp. 111–28; P. Williams, *The Council in the Marches of Wales under Elizabeth I* (Cardiff: University of Wales Press, 1958), pp. 296–8; Dodd, 'Dawn of Party Politics', in Dodd, *Studies in Stuart Wales*, pp. 182–4, 186–7; idem, 'Wales and the Scottish Succession', *Trans. Cymmr.* (1937), pp. 214–22.

14. P. S. Edwards, 'Cynrychiolaeth a chynnen: agweddau ar hanes seneddol a chymdeithasol Sir Fôn yng nghanol yr unfed ganrif ar bymtheg', *Welsh History Review*, X (1980), pp. 43–61.

15. Owen, 'Family Politics in Elizabethan Merionethshire'.

16. Neale, *The Elizabethan House of Commons*, chapter 4, pp. 99–110.

17. Lloyd, *Gentry of South-West Wales*, pp. 99–100.

18. Ibid., pp. 93–112.

19. Dodd, 'Pattern of Politics in Stuart Wales', p. 23; B. E. Howells (ed.), *Pembrokeshire County History, Early Modern*

Pembrokeshire, 1536–1815 (Haverfordwest: Pembrokeshire Historical Society, 1987), III, pp. 151–4.

20. *Journal of the House of Commons*, I, p. 38.

21. Williams, *Council in the Marches*, pp. 231, 236–7.

22. J. E. Lloyd and R. T. Jenkins (eds), *Dictionary of Welsh Biography* (London: Hon. Soc. Cymmr, 1959), s.n.; G. Williams (ed.), *Glamorgan County History, IV: Early Modern Glamorgan* (Cardiff: Glamorgan County History Trust, 1974), p. 99ff; *History of Pembrokeshire*, III, pp. 147–51; H. A. Lloyd, 'The Essex Inheritance', *Welsh History Review*, VII (1974), pp. 13–39.

23. E. G. Jones, 'The Caernarvonshire Freeholders and the Forest of Snowdon', in 'The Caernarvonshire Squires, 1558–1625' (unpublished University of Wales MA dissertation, 1936), pp. 233–54; T. Pennant, *Tours in Wales*, ed. J. Rhys (Caernarfon: H. Humphreys, 1883), II, p. 332, III, App. XIV, pp. 380–1; C. A. Gresham, 'The Forest of Snowdon in Its Relationship to Eifionydd', *Trans. Caerns, Hist. Soc.* XXI (1960), pp. 53–62; NLW, MSS, 9051E, 57, 58, 59, 63, 70, 103; Add. MSS, 464E, 65, 69, 93; Cardiff MS, 4. 58, 49; BL, Lansdowne MS, 45, 190–2.

24. J. M. Traherne (ed.), *Stradling Correspondence* (London: Longman, 1840), LXVIII, p. 77.

25. NLW, MSS, 9052E, 195, 197.

26. Williams, *Council in the Marches*, p. 238ff. For an examination of the dispute between Council and the border counties, see P. Williams, 'The Attack on the Council in the Marches, 1603–42', *Trans. Cymmr.* (1961) (Pt i), pp. 1–22; idem, 'The Activity of the Council in the Marches under the Early Stuarts', *Welsh History Review*, I (1961), pp. 133–54; R. E. Ham, 'The Four Shire Controversy', *Welsh History Review*, VIII (1977), pp. 381–400; G. D. Owen, *Wales in the Reign of James I* (London: Royal Historical Society, Boydell Press, 1988), chapter 1, pp. 8–63.

27. Williams, *Council in the Marches*, pp. 284–5, 288–9, 296–7; Lloyd, *Gentry of South-West Wales*, pp. 113–18.

28. A. H. Dodd, 'North Wales in the Essex Revolt of 1601', *English Historical Review*, LIX (1944), pp. 348–70; R. Ashton, *Reformation and Revolution 1558–1660* (London: Granada, 1985), pp. 184–91.

29. Williams, *Council in the Marches*, pp. 288, 293–4, 296, 300–3.

30. Ibid., pp. 298–311.

31. E. G. Jones, *Cymru a'r Hen Ffydd* (Cardiff: University of Wales Press, 1951), pp. 2–40; idem, 'Catholic Recusancy in the Counties of Denbigh, Flint and Montgomery, 1581–1625', *Trans. Cymmr.* (1945), pp. 114–33; A. H. Dodd, 'Wales and the Scottish Succession, 1570–1605', ibid. (1937), pp. 201–25.

32. Williams, 'The Attack on the Council in the Marches, 1603–42', pp. 13–22.

33. J. G. Jones, 'Sir John Wynn and His Tenants: The Dolwyddelan and Llysfaen Land Disputes', *Welsh History Review*, XI (1986), pp. 1–30; Owen, *Wales in the Reign of James I*, pp. 60–3;

34. 'The Pattern of Politics in Stuart Wales', pp. 20–7.

35. NLW, MS, 9058E, 1186.

36. T. Jones Pierce, 'Clenennau Estate in J. B. Smith (ed.), *Medieval Welsh Society* (Cardiff: University of Wales Press, 1972), E. N. Williams, 'Sir William Maurice of Clenennau'; J. G. Jones, 'The Welsh Poets and Their Patrons, *c.* 1550–1640', pp. 250–4; S. T. Bindoff, 'The Stuarts and Their Style', pp. 204–5; Owen, *Wales in the Reign of James I*, pp. 46–8.

37. T. Jones Pierce (ed.) *Cal. Clenennau Letters and Papers*, no. 204, p. 61.

38. D. H. Willson (ed.), *The Parliamentary Diary of Robert Bowyer, 1606–1607* (Minneapolis University Press, 1931), p. 1.

39. Ibid., pp. 206–7.

40. Jones, 'Welsh Poets and Their Patrons', p. 252; A. H. Dodd, 'The Early Stuarts', in A. J. Roderick (ed.), *Wales Through the Ages*, II (Llandybie: Christopher Davies, 1960), pp. 54–5.

41. E. G. Jones, 'County Politics and Electioneering, 1558–1625', *Trans. Caerns. Hist. Soc.*, I (1939), pp. 40–6; J. K. Gruenfelder, 'The Wynns of Gwydir and Parliamentary Elections in Wales 1604–40', *Welsh History Review*, IX (1978), pp. 123–41.

42. NLW, MS, 9057E, 921.

43. Ibid., MS 9058E, 1033.

44. T. C. Mendenhall, *The Shrewsbury Drapers and the Welsh Wool Trade in the Sixteenth and Seventeenth Centuries* (Oxford: Oxford University Press, 1953); Dodd, 'The Pattern of Politics in Stuart Wales', pp. 27–9.

45. A. H. Dodd, 'Wales in the Parliaments of Charles I', *Trans. Cymmr.*, I, (1945), 1625–9, pp. 16–49; II, (1946–7), 1640–2, pp. 59–96.

46. Owen, *Wales in the Reign of James I*, pp. 22–55.

47. Williams, 'The Attack on the Council in the Marches', p. 10.

48. Dodd, *Studies in Stuart Wales*, p. 61.
49. A. H. Dodd, 'Wales and the Second Bishops' War (1640)', *Bull. Board of Celtic Studies*, XII (1948), pp. 92–6.
50. Williams, 'The Attack on the Council in the Marches'. p. 19.
51. Dodd, 'Wales in the Parliament of Charles I', *Trans. Cymmr.*, I (1945), 1625–9, pp. 38–43.
52. Dodd, 'Pattern of Politics in Stuart Wales', pp. 47–9.
53. Dodd, 'Wales in the Parliaments of Charles I', *Trans. Cymmr*, II (1946–7), 1640–2, pp. 59–96. See also A. H. Dodd, 'Caernarvonshire Elections to the Long Parliament', *Bull. Board of Celtic Studies*, XII (1946), pp. 44–8.
54. Dodd, 'Pattern of Politics in Stuart Wales', pp. 41–50; G. Williams, *Recovery, Reorientation and Reformation: Wales c.1415–1642* (Oxford/Cardiff: Oxford and Wales University Presses, 1987), pp. 479–89.
55. G. F. Nuttall, *The Welsh Saints, 1640–1660: Walter Cradock; Vavasor Powell; Morgan Llwyd* (Cardiff: University of Wales Press, 1957); T. Richards, *Religious Developments in Wales, 1654 to 1662* (London: National Eisteddfod Association, 1923); R. T. Jones, *Vavasor Powell* (Swansea: John Penry Press, 1971); M. W. Thomas, *Morgan Llwyd* (Cardiff: University of Wales Press, 1984); W. S. K. Thomas, *Stuart Wales* (Llandysul: Gomer Press, 1988), pp. 57–78.
56. Lloyd and Jenkins (ed.), *Dict. Welsh Biog.*, s.n.; N. Tucker, *North Wales in the Civil War* (Denbigh: Gee Press, 1958), pp. 23–4 *passim*; idem, *Royalist Major-General Sir John Owen* (Denbigh: Gee Press, 1963).
57 J. G. Williams, 'Wales and the Civil War', in Roderick, *Wales Through the Ages*, pp. 62–5; Thomas, *Stuart Wales* pp. 309–41.
58. J. G. Williams, 'Sir John Vaughan of Trawscoed, 1603–1674', *National Library of Wales Journal*, VII (1953–4), I, pp. 33–48; II, pp. 121–46; III, pp. 225–41.
59. Lloyd and Jenkins (ed.), *Dict. Welsh Biog.*, s.n.; J. A. Bradney, *A History of Monmouthshire*, III (Pt i) (London: M. Hughes and Clarke, 1921), pp. 96–104.
60. J. H. Davies (ed.), *Hen Gerddi Gwleidyddol*, 1588–1660 pp. 11–38; P. Davies, 'Baledi Gwleidyddol yng Nghyfnod y Chwyldro Piwritanaidd', *Y Cofiadur*, XXV (1955), pp. 3–22; J. Howell, *Epistolae Ho-elianae: The Familiar Letters of James Howell* ed. J. Jacobs (London: D. Nutt, 1892), 11, Book III, XXIV, p. 552.

SELECT BIBLIOGRAPHY

Several manuscript sources have been consulted and the details are contained in the notes for each chapter. Asterisked entries below denote works that contain selections of a variety of official and unofficial printed sources.

PRINTED SOURCES

Ballinger, J. (ed.), *Calendar of Wynn of Gwydir Papers, 1515–1690* (Aberystwyth: National Library of Wales, 1926).

Bowen, D. J. (ed.), *Gwaith Gruffudd Hiraethog* (Cardiff: University of Wales Press, 1990).

Bowen, I. (ed.), *Statutes of Wales* (London: T. Fisher Unwin, 1908).

Calendar of Letters and Papers Foreign and Domestic (London, 1862–).

Calendar of the Manuscripts of the Marquis of Salisbury (Hatfield MSS) (London: Historical Manuscripts Commission, 1883–).

Calendar of State Papers Domestic (London: 1856–).

Calendar of State Papers Ireland (London, 1860–).

Caley, J. (ed.), *Valor Ecclesiasticus temp. Henr. VIII...* (London: Public Records Commission, 1810–34).

Churchyard, T., *The Worthines of Wales* (London, 1587).

Dasent, J. R. (ed.), *Acts of the Privy Council* (London, 1890–).

Davies, C. (ed.), *Rhagymadroddion a Chyflwyniadau Lladin, 1551–1632* (Cardiff; University of Wales Press, 1980).

Davies, J. H. (eds.), *Hen Gerddi Gwleidyddol, 1588–1660* (Cardiff: Cymdeithas Llên Cymru, 1901).

Edwards, I. ab O. (ed.), *Catalogue of Star Chamber Proceedings Relating to Wales* (Cardiff: University of Wales Press, 1929).

Ellis, H. (ed.), *Original Letters Illustrative of English History,* 2nd Series, 4 vols; 3rd Series, 4 vols (London: Harding & Lepard, 1827, 1846).

Evans, J. G., *Reports on Manuscripts in the Welsh Language,* I (London: Historical Manuscripts Commission, 1898).

Flenley, R. (ed.), *Calendar of the Register of the Council in the Marches of Wales, 1569–91* (London: Cymmrodorion Record Series: no. 8, 1916).

Haynes, S. (ed.), *A Collection of State Papers...at Hatfield House* (London: W. Bowyer, 1740).

Herbert, E. (of Chirbury), *The Life and Reign of King Henry the Eighth* (London: M. Clark, 1682 imp.).

Howell, J., *Epistolae Ho-elianae: The Familiar Letters of James Howell,* ed. J. Jacobs (London: D. Nutt, 1892).

Howells, B. E. (ed.), *Calendar of Letters Relating to North Wales* (Cardiff: University of Wales Press, 1967).

Hughes, G. H. (ed.), *Rhagymadroddion, 1547–1659* (Cardiff: University of Wales Press, 1951).

Jones, J. G., (ed.), *History of the Gwydir Family and Memoirs* (Llandysul: Gomer Press, 1990).

Jones Pierce, T., *Calendar of Clenennau Letters and Papers in the Brogyntyn Collection* (Aberystwyth: National Library of Wales Journal Supplement, Series IV, Pt i, 1947).

Journals of the House of Commons (London: 1742–1826).

Leland, J., *Itinerary in Wales,* ed. L. Toulmin Smith (London: George Bell, 1906).

Lewis, H. (ed.), *Hen Gyflwyniadau* (Cardiff: University of Wales Press, 1948).

Llwyd, H., *The Breuiary of Britayne,* trans, T. Twyne (London: Richard Johnes, 1573).

Matthew, D., 'Some Elizabethan Documents', *Bulletin of the Board of Celtic Studies,* VI (1931).

Mathew, D., 'Further Elizabethan Documents', *Bulletin of the Board of Celtic Studies,* VI (1931).

Merrick, R., *Morganiae Archaiographia,* ed. B. Ll. James (Barry: South Wales Record Society, 1983).

Morgan, M. (ed.), *Gweithiau Oliver Thomas ac Evan Roberts: Dau Biwritan Cynnar* (Cardiff: University of Wales Press, 1981).

Morrice, J. C. (ed.), *Barddoniaeth Wiliam Llŷn* (Bangor: University of Wales, 1908).

Owen, G., *The Description of Pembrokeshire,* ed. H. Owen (London: Bedford Press, 1906).

Parry, T. (ed.), *The Oxford Book of Welsh Verse* (Oxford: Clarendon Press, 1962).

Parry-Williams, T. H. (ed.), *Carolau Richard White* (Cardiff: University of Wales Press, 1931).

Parry-Williams, T. H. (ed.), *Canu Rhydd Cynnar* (Cardiff: University of Wales Press, 1932).

Penry, J., *Three Treatises Concerning Wales*, ed. D. Williams (Cardiff: University of Wales Press, 1960).

Pugh, T. B. (ed.), *The Marcher Lordships of South Wales, 1415 1536* (Cardiff: University of Wales Press, 1963).

Rees, W. (ed.), *Survery of the Duchy of Lancaster Lordships in Wales, 1609–1613* (Cardiff: University of Wales Press, 1953).

Roberts, E. (ed.), *Gwaith Siôn Tudur*, 2 vols (Cardiff: University of Wales Press, 1980).

Smith, W. J. (ed.), *Calendar of Salusbury Correspondence, 1553–c.1710* (Cardiff: University of Wales Press, 1954).

Stradling, J., *Direction for Traveilers taken out of Justus Lipsius for the behoof of the right honourable lord the young Earl of Bedford being now ready to travell* (London: 1592).

Thomas D. A., (ed.), *The Welsh Elizabethan Catholic Martyrs* (Cardiff: University of Wales Press, 1971).

Traherne, J. M. (ed.), *Stradling Correspondence* (London: Longman, 1840).

Vaughan, W., *The Golden Fleece* (London, 1626).

Vaughan, W., *The arraignment of slander...*(London: 1630).

Williams, W. O. (ed.), *Calendar of the Caernarvonshire Quarter Sessions Records: I, 1541–1558* (Caernarvon: Caernarvonshire Historical Society, 1956).

Willson, D. H. (ed.), *The Parliamentary Diary of Robert Bowyer, 1606–1607* (Minneapolis University Press, 1931).

Wright, T. (ed.), *Letters Relating to the Suppression of Monasteries* (London: Camden Society, 1843).

SECONDARY WORKS: VOLUMES

Ashton, R., *Reformation and Revolution, 1558–1660* (London: Granada, 1985).

Baker, A. and H., *Plas Mawr* (London: Farmer and Sons, 1898).

Barnes, T. and Yates, N. (eds), *Carmarthenshire Studies: Essays Presented to Major Francis Jones* (Carmarthen: Carmarthenshire County Council, 1974).

Bowen, D. J., *Gruffudd Hiraethog a'i Oes* (Cardiff: University of Wales Press, 1958).

Bowen, G. (ed.), *Y Traddodiad Rhyddiaith* (Llandysul: Gomer Press, 1970).

Bradney, J., *A History of Monmouthshire*, 4 vols (London: M. Hughes and Clarke, 1904–33).

Brooks, P. N., *Thomas Cranmer's Doctrine of Eucharist* (London: Macmillan, 1965).

Burke's Genealogical and Heraldic History of the Landed Gentry (London: 1952).

Caspari, F. *Humanism and the Social Order in Tudor England* (University of Chicago Press, 1954).

Charlton, K., *Education in Renaissance England* (London: Routledge & Kegan Paul, 1965).

Colyer, R., *The Welsh Cattle Drovers* (Cardiff: University of Wales Press, 1976).

Cross, C., *Church and People, 1450–1660* (London: Fontana/Brighton: Harvester, 1976).

Davies, C. S. L., *Peace, Print and Protestantism, 1450–1558* (London: Granada, 1977).

Davies, R. R., Griffiths, R. A., Jones, I. G., and Morgan, K. O. (eds), *Welsh Society and Nationhood: Historical Essays Presented to Glanmor Williams* (Cardiff: University of Wales Press, 1984).

Dodd, A. H., *Studies in Stuart Wales* (Cardiff: University of Wales Press, 1952).

Edwards, J. G., *The Principality of Wales, 1267–1967* (Caernarfon: Caernarfonshire Historical Society, 1969).

Edwards, O. M., *Wales* (London: Longman, 1901).

Elton, G. R., *England under the Tudors* (London: Methuen, 1957).

Elton, G. R., *Reform and Reformation: England, 1509–1558* (London; Edward Arnold, 1977).

Evans, A. O., *A Memorandum on the Legality of the Welsh Bible and the Welsh Version of the Book of Common Prayer* (Cardiff: W. Lewis, 1925).

Everitt, A. M., *Change in the Provinces: The Seventeenth Century* (Leicester University Press, 1969).

Ford, B. (ed.), *The Age of Shakespeare* (Harmondsworth: Penguin, 1955).

Fussner, F. Smith, *The Historical Revolution, 1580–1640* (London: Routledge & Kegan Paul, 1962).

Gibbard, N., *Walter Cradock: 'New Testament Saint'* (Bridgend: Evangelical Library of Wales, 1977).

Griffiths, R. A. (ed.), *Boroughs of Medieval Wales* (Cardiff: University of Wales Press, 1978).

Gruffydd, R. G., *Argraffwyr Cyntaf Cymru: Gwasgau Dirgel y Catholigion adeg Elisabeth* (Cardiff: University of Wales Press, 1972).

Gruffydd, R. G. (ed.), *Meistri'r Canrifoedd: Ysgrifau ar Hanes Llenyddiaeth Gymraeg gan Saunders Lewis* (Cardiff: University of Wales Press, 1973).

Gruffydd, R. G., *'In that Gentile Country...': the Beginnings of Puritan Nonconformity in Wales* (Bridgend: Evangelical Library of Wales, 1975).

Gruffydd, R. G., *The Translating of the Bible into the Welsh Tongue* (London: BBC, 1988).

Hays, R. W., *The History of the Abbey of Aberconway* (Cardiff: University of Wales Press, 1963).

*Herbert, T., and Jones, G. E. (eds), *Tudor Wales: Welsh History and its Sources Series* (Cardiff: University of Wales Press, 1988).

Hill, J. E. C., *Economic Problems of the Church from Archbishop Whitgift to the Long Parliament* (Oxford: Clarendon Press, 1956).

Howells, B. E. (ed.), *Pembrokeshire Country History: III, Early Modern Pembrokeshire, 1536–1815* (Haverfordwest: Pembrokeshire Historical Society, 1987).

Hughes, W., *Life and Times of Bishop William Morgan* (London: SPCK, 1891).

*Jenkins, G. H., *Protestant Dissenters in Wales, 1639–1689* (Cardiff: University of Wales Press, 1992).

Jones, D. G., *Y Ficer Prichard a 'Canwyll y Cymry'* (Caernarfon: Cwmni'r Llan a Gwasg yr Eglwys yng Nghymru, 1946).

Jones, E. G., *Cymru a'r Hen Ffydd* (Cardiff: University of Wales Press, 1951).

Jones, G. E., *The Gentry and the Elizabethan State* (Swansea: Christopher Davies, 1977).

Jones, J. G. (ed.), *Class, Community and Culture in Tudor Wales* (Cardiff: University of Wales Press, 1989).

*Jones, J. G., *Wales and the Tudor State, 1534–1603* (Cardiff: University of Wales Press, 1989).

J. G., Jones, *Concepts of Order and Gentility in Wales, 1540–1640* (Llandysul: Gomer Press, 1992).

Jones, J. G. (ed.), *Agweddau ar Dwf Piwritaniaeth yng Nghymru'r Ail Ganrif ar Bymtheg* (Lewiston: E. Mellen Press, 1992).

Jones, N., *Faith by Statute: Parliament and the Settlement of Religion, 1559* (London: Royal Historical Society, 1982).

Jones, R. T. *Vavasor Powell* (Swansea: John Penry Press, 1971).

Jones Pierce, T., *Medieval Welsh Society*, ed. J. B. Smith (Cardiff: University of Wales Press, 1972).

Kelso, R., *The Doctrine of the English Gentleman in the Sixteenth Century* (Mass.: Peter Smith, 1964).

Lloyd, H. A., *The Gentry of South-West Wales, 1540–1640* (Cardiff: University of Wales Press, 1968).

Lloyd, J. E., and Jenkins, R. T. (eds), *Dictionary of Welsh Biography* (London: Honourable Society of Cymmrodorion, 1959).

Lloyd, J. Y. W., *History of the Princes, the Lords Marcher, and the Ancient Nobility of Powys Fadog*, 5 vols (London: T. Richards/Whiting, 1881–7).

Loach, J., *Parliament under the Tudors* (Oxford: Clarendon Press, 1991).

McCulloch, D., *The Later Reformation in England, 1547–1603* (London: Macmillan, 1990).

Mendenhall, T. C., *The Shrewsbury Drapers and the Welsh Wool Trade in the Sixteenth and Seventeenth Centuries* (Oxford: Oxford University Press, 1953).

Moore, D. (ed.), *Wales in the Eighteenth Century* (Swansea: Christopher Davies, 1976).

Mostyn, Lord, and Glenn, T. A., *The History of the Family of Mostyn of Mostyn* (London: Harrison, 1925).

Neale, J. E., *The Elizabethan House of Commons* (London: Jonathan Cape, 1955).

Nuttall, G. F., *The Welsh Saints, 1640–1660: Walter Cradock; Vavasor Powell; Morgan Llwyd* (Cardiff: University of Wales Press, 1957).

Nuttall, G. F., *The Puritan Spirit: Essays and Addresses* (London: Epworth Press, 1967).

O'Day, R., *Education and Society, 1500–1800* (London: Longman, 1982).

O'Keeffe, M., *Four Martyrs of South Wales and the Marches* (Cardiff: Archdiocese of Cardiff, 1970).

Owen, G. D., *Wales in the Reign of James I* (London: Royal Historical Society, The Boydell Press, 1988).

Parry, T., *A History of Welsh Literature*, trans. H. I. Bell (Oxford: Clarendon Press, 1955).

Pennant, T., *Tours in Wales*, ed. J. Rhys (Caernarfon: H. Humphreys, 1883).

Pollard, A. F., *Henry VIII* (London: Longman, 1905).

Powell, N. W., *Dyffryn Clwyd in the Time of Elizabeth I* (Ruthin: Coelion Trust, 1991).

T. B. Pugh, (ed.), *Glamorgan County History: III: The Middle Ages* (Cardiff; Glamorgan County History Trust, 1971).

Rawcliffe, C., *The Staffords, Earls of Stafford and Dukes of Buckingham* (University of Cambridge Press, 1978).

Rees, W., *South Wales and the March, 1284–1415* (Oxford University Press, 1924).

Rees, W., *The Union of England and Wales* (Cardiff: University of Wales Press, 1947).

Reeves, A. C., *The Marcher Lords* (Llandybie: Christopher Davies, 1983).

Richards, T., *The Puritan Movement in Wales, 1639 to 1653* (London: National Eisteddfod Association, 1920).

Richards, T., *Religious Developments in Wales, 1654 to 1662* (London: National Eisteddfod Association, 1923).

Roberts, G., *Aspects of Welsh History*, ed. A. H. Dodd and J. G. Williams (Cardiff: University of Wales Press, 1969).

Roderick, A. J. (ed.), *Wales Through the Ages*, II (Llandybie: Christopher Davies, 1960).

Rowse, A. L., *The Elizabethan Renaissance; The Life of the Society* (London: Macmillan, 1971).

Royal Commission on Ancient Monuments in Wales and Monmouthshire: Caernarvonshire East (London: Royal Commission on Ancient Monuments, 1956).

Scarisbrick, J. J., *The Reformation and the English People* (Oxford: Clarendon Press, 1982).

Seaver, P. S., *The Puritan Lectureships: The Politics of Religious Dissent, 1560–1662* (Stanford University Press, 1970).

Simon, J., *Education and Society in Tudor England* (Cambridge University Press, 1967).

Smeaton, W. H. O. (ed.), *Francis Bacon's Essays* (London: Dent, 1906).

Smith, P., *Houses of the Welsh Countryside* (London: HMSO, 1975).

Soulsby, I. N., *The Towns of Medieval Wales* (Chichester: Phillimore, 1983).

Stephen, L. and Lee, S. (eds), *Dictionary of National Biography* (London: 1885–1900).

Stephens, R., *Gwynedd, 1528–1547: Economy and Society in Tudor Wales* (Ann Arbor, Michigan: 1979).

Strype, J., *Annals of the Reformation* (London, 1728).

Thirsk, J. (ed.), *Agrarian History of England and Wales, vol. IV, 1500–1640* (Cambridge University Press, 1967).

Thomas, D. R., *The Life and Work of Bishop Davies and William Salesbury* (Oswestry: Caxton Press, 1902).

Thomas, D. R., *The History of the Diocese of St Asaph*, 2 vols (Oswestry: Caxton Press, 1908-13).

Thomas, G., *Eisteddfodau Caerwys* (Cardiff: University of Wales Press, 1967).

Thomas, I., *William Salesbury and His Testament* (Cardiff: University of Wales, 1967).

Thomas, I., *Y Testament Newydd Cymraeg, 1551–1620* (Cardiff: University of Wales Press, 1976).

Thomas, I., *William Morgan and His Bible* (Cardiff: University of Wales Press, 1988).

Thomas, M. W., *Morgan Llwyd* (Cardiff: University of Wales Press, 1984).

Thomas, W. S. K., *Stuart Wales* (Llandysul: Gomer Press, 1988).

Tucker, N., *North Wales in the Civil War* (Denbigh: Gee Press, 1958).

Tucker, N., *Royalist Major-General Sir John Owen of Clenennau* (Denbigh: Gee Press, 1963).

Walker, D. (ed.), *A History of the Church in Wales* (Penarth: Church in Wales Publications, 1976).

Williams, G., *Bywyd ac Amserau'r Esgob Richard Davies* (Cardiff: University of Wales Press, 1953).

Williams, G., *The Welsh Church from Conquest to Reformation* (Cardiff: University of Wales Press, 1962).

Williams, G., *Welsh Reformation Essays* (Cardiff: University of Wales Press, 1967).

Williams, G. (ed. and contrib.), *Glamorgan County History, IV; Early Modern Glamorgan* (Cardiff: Glamorgan County History Trust, 1974).

Williams, G., *Religion, Language and Nationality in Wales* (Cardiff: University of Wales Press, 1979).

Williams, G., *Grym Tafodau Tân: Ysgrifau Hanesddol ar Grefydd a Diwylliant* (Llandysul: Gomer Press, 1982).

Williams, G., *Recovery, Reorientation and Reformation: Wales c.1415–1642* (Oxford/Cardiff: Oxford and Wales University Presses, 1987).

Williams, G., *The Reformation in Wales* (Bangor: Headstart History Series, 1991).

Williams, G., *The Welsh and their Religion* (Cardiff: University of Wales Press, 1991).

Williams, G., *Wales and the Act of Union* (Bangor: Headstart History Series, 1992).

Williams, G., and Jones, R. O. (eds). *The Celts and the Renaissance: Tradition and Innovation* (Cardiff: University of Wales Press, 1990).

*Williams, J., *Ancient and Modern Denbigh* (Denbigh: 1856).

Williams, P., *The Council in the Marches of Wales under Elizabeth I* (Cardiff: University of Wales Press, 1958).

*Williams, R., *The History and Antiquities of the Town of Aberconwy and Its Neighbourhood* (Denbigh: Gee Press, 1835).

Williams, W. O., *Tudor Gwynedd* (Caernarvon: Caernarvonshire Historical Society, 1958).

Williams, W. R., *The History of the Great Sessions in Wales, 1542–1830* (Brecknock, 1899).

*Wright, T., *The History of Ludlow and Its Neighbourhood* (Ludlow/London: Longman/J. R. Smith, 1852).

ARTICLES AND CHAPTERS IN VOLUMES

Ballinger, J., 'Vicar Prichard : A Study in Welsh Bibliography', *Y Cymmrodor*, XIII (1900).

*Ballinger, J., 'Katheryn of Berain', *Y Cymmrodor*, XL (1929).

Bindoff, S. T., 'The Stuarts and Their Style', *English Historical Review*, LX (1945).

*Bradney, J., 'The Speech of William Blethin, Bishop of Llandaff, and the Customs and Ordinances of the Church of Llandaff', *Y Cymmrodor*, XXXI (1921).

Carr, A. D., 'The Making of the Mostyns: The Genesis of a Landed Family', *Transactions of the Honourable Society of Cymmrodorion* (1979).

Carr, A. D., 'The Mostyns of Mostyn, 1540–1642', *Publications of the Flintshire Historical Society Journal*, Pt i, XXVIII (1977–8); Pt ii, XXX (1981–2).

Carr, A. D., 'Gwilym ap Gruffydd and the Rise of the Penrhyn Estate', *Welsh History Review*, XV (1990).

Davies, P., 'Baledi Gwleidyddol yng Nghyfnod y Chwyldro Piwritanaidd', *Y Cofiadur*, XXV (1955).

Dodd, A. H., 'Wales and the Scottish Succession, 1570–1605', *Transactions of the Honourable Society of Cymmrodorion* (1937).

Dodd, A. H., 'Wales's Parliamentary Apprenticeship (1536-1625)', *Transactions of the Honourable Society of Cymmrodorion* (1942).

Dodd, A. H., 'North Wales in the Essex Revolt of 1601', *English Historical Review*, LIX (1944).

Dodd, A. H., 'Caernarvonshire Elections to the Long Parliament', *Bulletin of the Board of Celtic Studies*, XII (1946).

Dodd, A. H., 'Wales in the Parliaments of Charles I': I, 1625–1629, *Transactions of the Honourable Society of Cymmrodorion* (1945); II, 1640–42 (1946–7).

Dodd, A. H., 'The Pattern of Politics in Stuart Wales', *Transactions of the Honourable Society of Cymmrodorion* (1948).

Dodd, A. H., 'Wales and the Second Bishops' War (1640)', *Bulletin of the Board of Celtic Studies*, XII (1948).

Dodd, A. H., 'The Early Stuarts', in A. J. Roderick (ed.), *Wales Through the Ages*, II (Liandybie: Christopher Davies, 1960).

*Dodd, A. H., 'A Commendacion of Welshmen', *Bulletin of the Board of Celtic Studies*, XIX (1960–2).

Dodd, A. H., 'Bishop Lewes Bayly, *c.* 1575–1631', *Transactions of the Caernarvonshire Historical Society*, XXVIII (1967).

*Edwards, I. ab O., 'William Morgan's Quarrel with his Parishioners at Llanrhaeadr-ym-Mochnant', *Bulletin of the Board of Celtic Studies*, III (1927).

Edwards, P. S., 'The Parliamentary Representation of the Welsh Boroughs in the Mid-Sixteenth Century', *Bulletin of the Board of Celtic Studies*, XXVII (1979).

Edwards, P. S., 'Cynrychiolaeth a Chynnen : Agweddau ar Hanes Seneddol a Chymdeithasol Sir Fôn ynghanol yr Unfed Ganrif ar Bymtheg', *Welsh History Review*, X (1980).

Elton, G. R., 'Wales in Parliament, 1542–1581', in R. R. Davies, R. A. Griffiths, I. G. Jones and K. O. Morgan (eds.), in *Welsh Society and Nationhood: Historical Essays Presented to Glanmor Williams* (Cardiff: University of Wales Press, 1984).

Emery, F., 'The Farming Regions of Wales', in J. Thirsk (ed.), *Agrarian History of England and Wales; vol. IV, 1500–1640* (Cambridge University Press, 1967).

Evans, J. W., 'The Reformation and St David's Cathedral', *Journal of Welsh Ecclesiastical History*, VII (1990).

Evans, W. G., 'Derfel Gadarn – a Celebrated Victim of the Reformation', *Journal of the Merioneth Historical Society*, XI (1991).

Fisher, J., 'The Development of London as a Centre of Conspicuous Consumption in the Sixteenth and Seventeenth Centuries', *Transactions of the Royal Historical Society*, XXX (1948).

Flower, R., 'William Salesbury, Richard Davies and Archbishop Parker', *National Library of Wales Journal*, II (1941–2).

Flower, R., 'Richard Davies, William Cecil and Giraldus Cambrensis', *National Library of Wales Journal*, III (1943–4).

Gordon, M. D., 'The Collection of Ship Money in the Reign of Charles I', *Transactions of the Royal Historical Society*, IV (1910).

*Gray, M., 'The Diocese of Bangor in the Late Sixteenth Century', *Journal of Welsh Ecclesiastical History*, V (1988).

Gray M., 'Change and Continuity: the Gentry and the Property of the Church in South-East Wales and the Marches', in J. G. Jones (ed.), *Class, Community and Culture in Tudor Wales* (Cardiff: University of Wales Press, 1989).

*Gray, M., 'Power, Patronage and Politics: Office-Holding and Administration on the Crown's Estates in Wales', in R. W. Hoyle (ed.), *The Estates of the English Crown 1558–1640* (Cambridge University Press, 1992).

Gresham, C. A., 'The Forest of Snowdon in Its Relationship to Eifionydd', *Transactions of the Caernarvonshire Historical Society*, XXI (1960).

Gresham, C. A., 'The Origin of the Clenennau Estate', *National Library of Wales Journal*, XV (1967–8).

*Griffith, W. P., 'William Hughes and the "Descensus" Controversy of 1567', *Bulletin of the Board of Celtic Studies*, XXXIV (1987).

Griffith, W. P., 'Anglicaniaid a Phiwritaniaid : Myfyrwyr a Diwinyddion Prifysgolion Lloegr, 1560–1640', *Llên Cymru*, XVI (1989).

Griffith, W. P., 'Schooling and Society', in J. G. Jones (ed.), *Class, Community and Culture in Tudor Wales* (Cardiff: University of Wales Press, 1989).

Griffiths, M., 'Modern Settlement Patterns, 1450–1700', in D. H. Owen (ed.), *Settlement and Society in Wales* (Cardiff: University of Wales Press, 1989).

Griffiths, M., '"Very Wealthy by Merchandise"? Urban Fortunes', in J. G. Jones (ed.), *Class Community and Culture in Tudor Wales* (Cardiff: University of Wales Press, 1989).

Griffiths, R. A., 'The Rise of the Stradlings of St Donat's', *Morgannwg*, VII (1963).

Griffiths, R. A., 'Gruffudd ap Nicholas and the Rise of the House of Dinefwr', *National Library of Wales Journal*, XIII (1964).

Griffiths, R. A., 'The Twelve Knights of Glamorgan', in S. Williams (ed.), *Glamorgan Historian*, III (Barry: S. Williams, 1966).

Gruenfelder, J. K., 'The Wynns of Gwydir and Parliamentary Elections in Wales, 1604–40', *Welsh History Review*, IX (1978).

*Gruffydd, R. G., 'Bishop Francis Godwin's Injunctions for the Diocese of Llandaff, 1603', *Journal of the Historical Society of the Church, in Wales*, IV (1954).

Gruffydd, R. G., 'The Renaissance and Welsh Literature', in G. Williams and R. O. Jones (eds.), *The Celts and the Renaissance: Tradition and Innovation* (Cardiff: University of Wales Press, 1990).

*Gwyndaf, R., 'Sir Richard Clough of Denbigh c. 1530–1570', *Transactions of the Denbighshire Historical Society*, XIX (1970) (Pt i); XX, (1971) (Pt ii); XXII, (1973) (Pt iii).

*Gwyndaf, R., 'References in Welsh Poetry to Sixteenth and Early Seventeenth Century New and Rebuilt Houses in North-East Wales', *Transactions of the Denbighshire Historical Society*, XXII (1973).

Ham, R. E., 'The Four Shire Controversy', *Welsh History Review*, VIII (1977).

James, B. Ll., 'The Evolution of a Radical: The Life and Career of William Erbery', *Journal of Welsh Ecclesiastical History*, III (1986).

Jones, D. C., 'The Bulkeleys of Beaumaris, 1440–1547', *Transactions of the Anglesey Antiquarian Society and Field Club* (1961).

Jones, E. G., 'The Caernarvonshire Freeholders and the Forest of Snowdon', in 'The Caernarvonshire Squires, 1558–1625' (unpublished University of Wales M A dissertation, 1936).

*Jones, E. G., 'The Lleyn Recusancy Case, 1578–1581', *Transactions of the Honourable Society of Cymmrodorion* (1936).

Jones, E. G., 'Hugh Owen of Gwenynog', *Transactions of the Anglesey Antiquarian Society and Field Club* (1938).

Jones, E. G., 'County Politics and Electioneering, 1558–1625', *Transactions of the Caernarvonshire Historical Society*, I (1939).

Jones, E. G., 'Catholic Recusancy in the Counties of Denbigh, Flint and Montgomery, 1581–1625', *Transactions of the Honourable Society of Cymmrodorion* (1945).

Jones, E. G., 'Some Notes on the Principal County Families of Anglesey in the Sixteenth and Early Seventeenth Centuries', *Transactions of the Anglesey Antiquarian Society and Field Club* (1940).

*Jones, E. G., (ed.), 'History of the Bulkeley Family (NLW MS.9080E)', *Transactions of the Anglesey Antiquarian Society and Field Club* (1948).

Jones, F., 'An Approach to Welsh Genealogy', *Transactions of the Honourable Society of Cymmrodorion* (1948).

Jones, F., 'Welsh Pedigrees', in *Burke's Genealogical and Heraldic History of the Landed Gentry* (London: 1952).

Jones, F., 'The Old Families of Wales', in D. Moore (ed.), *Wales in the Eighteenth Century* (Swansea: Christopher Davies, 1976).

Jones, F., 'The Vaughans of Golden Grove: I: The Earls of Carbery', *Transactions of the Honourable Society of Cymmrodorion* (1963, Pt i).

Jones, G. E., 'Local Administration and Justice in Sixteenth-Century Glamorgan,' *Morgannwg*, IX (1965).

Jones, G. E., 'A Case of Corruption', in S. Williams (ed.), *Glamorgan Historian*, V (Cowbridge, D. Brown, 1968).

Jones, J. G., 'Caernarvonshire Administration: The Activities of the Justices of the Peace, 1603–1660', *Welsh History Review*, V (1970).

Jones, J. G., 'Aspects of Local Government in Pre-Restoration Caernarvonshire', *Transactions of the Caernarvonshire Historical Society*, XXX (1972).

*Jones, J. G., 'Bishop William Morgan's Dispute with John Wynn of Gwydir in 1603–04', *Journal of the Historical Society of the Church in Wales*, XXII (1972).

Jones, J. G., 'Richard Parry, Bishop of St Asaph: Some Aspects of his Career', *Bulletin of the Board of Celtic Studies*, XXVI (1975).

Jones, J. G., 'Changing Concepts of Gentility in Mid-Tudor Wales: Some Reflections', *Brogliaccio I de Lettera*, XIII (1977).

Jones, J. G., 'Morus Wynn o Wedir c.1530–1580', *Transactions of the Caernarvonshire Historical Society*, XXXVIII (1977).

Jones, J. G., 'Henry Rowlands, Bishop of Bangor, 1598–1616', *Journal of the Historical Society of the Church in Wales*, XXVI (1977–8).

Jones, J. G., 'The Welsh Poets and Their Patrons c.1550–1640', *Welsh History Review*, XIV (1979).

Jones, J. G., 'Thomas Davies and William Hughes: Two Reformation Bishops of St Asaph', *Bulletin of the Board of Celtic Studies*, XXIX (1981).

Jones, J. G., 'The Wynn Estate of Gwydir: Aspects of Its Growth and Development', *National Library of Wales Journal*, XXI (1981).

Jones, J. G., 'Educational Activity among the Wynns of Gwydir', *Transactions of the Caernarvonshire Historical Society*, XLII (1981).

Jones, J. G., 'Sir John Wynn of Gwydir and his Tenants: the Dolwyddelan and Llysfaen Land Disputes', *Welsh History Review*, XI (1982).

Jones, J. G., 'Law and Order in Merioneth after the Acts of Union 1536–43', *Journal of the Merioneth Historical Society*, X (1986).

Jones, J. G., 'The Reformation Bishops of Llandaff, 1559–1601', *Morgannwg*, XXXII (1988).

Jones, J. G., 'The Reformation Bishops of St Asaph', *Journal of Welsh Ecclesiastical History*, VII (1990).

Jones Pierce, T., 'Landlords in Wales', in J. Thirsk (ed.), *Agrarian History of England and Wales: Vol. IV, 1500–1640* (Cambridge University Press, 1967).

Jones Pierce, T., 'The Clenennau Estate', in J. B. Smith (ed.), *Medieval Welsh Society*, VIII (Cardiff; University of Wales Press, 1972).

Jones Pierce, T., 'The Gafael in Bangor Manuscript 1939', in J. B. Smith (ed.), *Medieval Welsh Society*, VII (Cardiff: University of Wales Press, 1972).

Jones Pierce, T., 'Agarian Aspects of the Tribal System in Medieval Wales', in J. B. Smith (ed.), *Medieval Welsh Society*, XII (Cardiff: University of Wales Press, 1972).

Lewis, D., 'The Court of the President and Council of Wales and the Marches from 1478 to 1575', *Y Cymmrodor*, XII (1898).

Lewis, S., 'Damcaniaeth Eglwysig Brotestannaidd', in R. G. Gruffydd (ed.), *Meistri'r Canrifoedd* (Cardiff: University of Wales Press, 1973).

Lloyd, H. A., 'Wales and the Star Chamber', *Welsh History Review*, V (1971).

Lloyd, H. A., 'The Essex Inheritance', *Welsh History Review*, VII (1974).

Lloyd, H. A., 'Corruption and Sir John Trevor', *Transactions of the Honourable Society of Cymmrodorion* (1974–5).

Mathew, D., 'Some Elizabethan Documents', *Bulletin of the Board of Celtic Studies*, VI (1931).

Mathias, W. A., 'William Salesbury – ei Ryddiaith', in G. Bowen (ed.), *Y Traddodiad Rhyddiaith* (Llandysul: Gomer Press, 1970).

Mathias, W. A., 'William Salesbury – Ei Fywyd a'i Weithiau', in G. Bowen (ed.), *Y Traddodiad Rhyddiaith* (Llandysul: Gomer Press, 1979).

Mathias, W. A., 'William Salesbury a'r Testament Newydd', *Llên Cymru*, XVI (1989).

Nuttall, G. F., 'Walter Cradock (1606–1659): The Man and His Message', in *The Puritan Spirit: Essays and Addresses* (London: Epworth Press, 1967).

Owen, D. H., 'Tenurial and Economic Developments in North Wales in the Twelfth and Thirteenth Centuries', *Welsh History Review*, VI (1972).

Owen, D. H., 'The Englishry of Denbigh: an English Colony in Medieval Wales', *Transactions of the Honourable Society of Cymmrodorion* (1974–75).

Owen, H. G., 'Family Politics in Elizabethan Merionethshire', *Bulletin of the Board of Celtic Studies*, XVIII (1959).

Owen, l., 'The Population of Wales in the Sixteenth and Seventeenth Centuries', *Transactions of the Honourable Society of Cymmrodorion* (1959).

Parry, B. R., 'Huw Nanney Hen (c.1546–1623), Squire of Nannau', *Journal of the Merioneth Historical and Record Society*, V (1972).

Parry, G., 'Hanes Ysgol Botwnnog', *Transactions of the Honourable Society of Cymmorodion* (1957).

Powell, N. W., 'Crime and the Community in Denbighshire during the 1590s: The Evidence of the Records of the Court of Great Sessions', in J. G. Jones (ed.), *Class Community and Culture in Tudor Wales* (Cardiff: University of Wales Press, 1989).

*Prichard, T. J., 'The Reformation in the Deanery of Llandaff', *Morgannwg*, XIII (1969).

*Pugh, F. H., 'Glamorgan Recusants, 1577–1611', *South Wales and Monmouthshire Record Society Publications*, III (1954).

*Pugh, F. H., 'Monmouthshire Recusants in the Reigns of Elizabeth I and James I', *South Wales and Monmouthshire Record Society Publications*, IV (1957).

*Pugh, T. B., 'The Indenture for the Marches between Henry VII and Edward Stafford (1477–1521), Duke of Buckingham', *English Historical Review*, LXXI (1956).

Pugh, T. B., (with W. R. B. Robinson), 'Sessions in Eyre in a Marcher Lordship: a Dispute between the Earl of Worcester and his Tenants of Gower and Kilvey in 1524', *South Wales and Monmouthshire Record Society Publications*, IV (1957)

Roberts, E., 'Teulu Plas Iolyn', *Transactions of the Denbighshire Historical Society*, XIII (1964).

Roberts, E., 'Priodasau Catrin o Ferain', *Transactions of the Denbighshire Historical Society*, XX (1971).

*Roberts, P. R., 'A Petition Concerning Sir Richard Herbert', *Bulletin of the Board of Celtic Studies*, XX (1962).

Roberts, P. R., 'The Union with England and the Identity of "Anglican" Wales', *Transactions of the Royal Historical Society*, XXII (1972).

Roberts, P. R., 'The "Act of Union" in Welsh History', *Transactions of the Honourable Society of Cymmrodorion* (1972–3).

*Roberts, P. R., 'A Breviat of the Effectes Devised for Wales c. 1540–41', *Camden Miscellany*, XXVI (1975).

Roberts, P. R., 'Wales and England after the Tudor "Union": Crown, Principality and Parliament, 1543–1624', in C. Cross, D. Loades and J. J. Scarisbrick (eds), *Law and Government under the Tudors: Essays Presented to Sir Geoffrey Elton on His Retirement* (University of Cambridge Press, 1988).

Roberts, P. R., 'The Welsh Language, English Law and Tudor Legislation', *Transactions of the Honourable Society of Cymmrodorion* (1989).

*Robinson, W. R. B., 'Sessions in Eyre in a Marcher Lordship', *South Wales and Monmouthshire Record Society*, IV (1957).

*Robinson, W. R. B., 'The Welsh Estates of Charles, Earl of Worcester in 1520', *Bulletin of the Board of Celtic Studies*, XXIV (1971).

*Robinson, W. R. B., 'The Marcher Lords of Wales 1525–31', *Bulletin of the Board of Celtic Studies*, XXVI (1974–6).

*Robinson, W. R. B., 'Early Tudor Policy towards Wales', *Bulletin of the Board of Celtic Studies*, XX–XXI (1976–8).

Robinson, W. R. B., 'The Tudor Revolution in Welsh Government 1536–1543: Its Effects on Gentry Participation', *English Historical Review*, CCCCVI (1988).

Rowse, A. L., 'Alltyrynys and the Cecils', *English Historical Review*, LXXV (1960).

Sil, N. P., 'Sir William Herbert, Earl of Pembroke (c. 1507–70); in Search of a Personality', *Welsh History Review*, XI (1982).

Smith, J. B., 'Crown and Community in the Principality of North Wales in the Reign of Henry Tudor', *Welsh History Review*, III (1966).

*Smith, J. W., 'The Salusburys as Maintainers of Murderers: a Chirk Castle View, 1599', *National Library of Wales Journal*, VII (1952).

Thirsk, J., 'Younger Sons in the Seventeenth Century', *History*, LIV (1969).

Thomas, D. Ll., 'Further Notes on the Council of the Marches', *Y Cymmrodor*, XVII (1899).

Walker, D., 'Religious Change, 1536–1642', in B. E. Howells (ed.), *Pembrokeshire County History: III, Early Modern Pembrokeshire 1536–1815* (Haverfordwest: Pembrokeshire Historical Society, 1987).

Williams, E. N., 'Sir William Maurice of Clenennau', *Transactions of the Caernarvonshire Historical Society*, XXIV (1963).

*Williams, G., 'The Royal Visitation of the Diocese of Llandaff, 1559', *National Library of Wales Journal*, IV (1945–6).

Williams, G., 'William Salesbury's *Baterie of the Popes Botereulx*', *Bulletin of the Board of Celtic Studies*, XIII (1949).

Williams, G., 'The Stradlings of St Donat's', in S. Williams (ed.), *Vale of History* (Barry: S. Williams, 1960).

William, G., 'Landlords in Wales; The Church', in J. Thirsk (ed.), *Agrarian History of England and Wales, IV, 1500–1640* (Cambridge University Press, 1967).

Williams, G., 'Carmarthen and the Reformation', in T. Barnes and N. Yates (eds.), *Carmarthenshire Studies: Essays Presented To Major Francis Jones* (Carmarthen: Carmarthenshire County Council, 1974).

Williams, G., 'Rice Mansel of Oxwich and Margam (1487–1559)', *Morgannwg*, VI (1962).

Williams, G., 'John Penry; Marprelate and Patriot?', *Welsh History Review*, III (1967).

Williams, G., 'Wales and the Reign of Queen Mary I', *Welsh History Review*, X (1981).

Williams, G., 'Religion', in T. Herbert and G. E. Jones (eds.), *Tudor Wales: Welsh History and its Sources Series* (Cardiff: University of Wales Press, 1984).

Williams, G., 'William Morgan's Bible and the Cambridge Connection', *Welsh History Review*, XIV (1989).

Williams, J. G., 'Sir John Vaughan of Trawscoed, 1603–1674', *National Library of Wales Journal*, VIII (1953–4).

Williams, J. G., 'Wales and the Civil War', in A. J. Roderick (ed.), *Wales Through The Ages*, II (Llandybie Christopher Davies, 1960).

Williams, J. G., 'Rhai Agweddau ar y Gymdeithas Gymreig yn yr Ail Ganrif ar Bymtheg', *Efrydiau Athronyddol*, XXX (1968).

Williams, P., 'Star Chamber and the Council in the Marches of Wales, 1559–1603', *Bulletin of the Board of Celtic Studies*, XVI (1956).

Williams, P., 'The Activity of the Council in the Marches under the Early Stuarts', *Welsh History Review*, I (1961).

Williams, P., 'The Attack on the Council in the Marches, 1603–42', *Transactions of the Honourable Society of Cymmrodorion* (1961 Pt i).

Williams, W. Ll., 'A Welsh Insurrection', *Y Cymmrodor*, XVI 1902).

Williams, W. O., 'The County Records', *Transactions of the Caernarvonshire Historical Society*, X (1949).

Williams, W. O., 'The Survival of the Welsh Language after the Union of England and Wales: the First Phase, 1536–1642', *Welsh History Review*, II (1964).

Williams, W. O., 'The Social Order in Tudor Wales', *Transactions of the Honourable Society of Cymmrodorion* (1967 Pt ii).

INDEX

Index

Beddgelert (Caern.), 40
Bersham (Denb.), 161
Bewdley, 62
Bible (1533, 1620, 1630), Welsh,
147, 148–9, 150, 151, 154, 156,
157, 159, 160, 171
Bignon, Philip, 160
Bishops' Bible, 159
Bishop's Castle, 161
Bodeon/Bodowen (Angl.), 19, 184
Bleddyn, William, 157
Blinman, Richard, 174
Blythe, Geoffrey, bishop of Coventry
and Lichfield, 59
Bodfel (Caern.), 22, 165
Bodfel, Sir John I, 124; John II, 202
Bodidris (Denb.), 183
Bolde family, 21
Boleyn, Anne, 48, 51, 58, 132, 143
Boleyn, Sir Thomas, 48,
bond vills, 10
Bonheddig, xii, 3
Bonvilston (Glam.), 32
Book of Common Prayer (1549),
135
Book of Common Prayer (1552),
44, 135, 150
Borras (Denb.), 21
Borromeo, Carlo, 141
Botwnnog (Caern.), 28
Brampton Bryan (Heref.), 161, 173
Brandon, Charles, 50, 56
Brecknock, 8
Brecknock, lordship of, 55
Brecknockshire, 11, 41, 78, 82, 152
Brecon priory, 130
Brereton family, 21
Breuiary of Britayne, The, 43–4
'Breviat of the Effectes Devised for
Wales, A', 84, 98
Bréyr, xii, 3
Bridgwater, earl of, see Egerton, Sir
John
Bristol, 173, 199, 204
Bristol channel, 141
Brittany, 80
Bronheulog (Denb.), 114
Broughton, Richard, 190
Bucer, Martin, 135
Buckingham, duke of, see Villiers,
George

Bulkeley, Arthur, 137
Bulkeley family, 10, 21, 181, 184,
185; Sir Richard I, 75, 79, 133,
137, 179; Sir Richard II, 184; Sir
Richard III, 24, 40, 186, 189,
193, 194
Bulkeley, Mary, 31
Bulkeley, Robert, 32
Bulkeley, William, 184
Burghley, Lord, see Cecil, Sir William

Cae'r Gai (Mer.), 34
Caernarfon, 68, 82, 124
Caernarfon castle, 197
Caernarfonshire, 11, 19, 21, 40, 100,
102, 113, 115, 117, 123, 181,
189, 195, 196
Caeriw (Pemb.), 139
Caerwys (Flint.), 35, 114
Calais, 51, 60
Cambrai, 141
Cambrobrytannicae Cymraecaeve
Linguae Institutiones et
Rudimenta, 155
Cambridge, 27, 155, 160
Cambridgeshire, 28
'Cambriol', 35
Canterbury, archiepiscopate of,
129, 173
Cantref, xii
Carbery, earls of, see Vaughan family
(Golden Grove)
Cardiff (Glam.), 23, 24, 25, 106, 173
Cardiff castle, 204
Cardigan, 185
Cardigan priory, 130
Cardiganshire, 38, 112, 113, 185
Carmarthen, 8, 50, 82, 132, 133,
137, 139
Carmarthenshire, 8, 38, 111, 113,
165
Carne family, 132; Sir Edward, 30,
76; Thomas, 17, 71
Car-wr y Cymru, 171
Cassano, 141
Castellmarch (Caern.), 202
Castiglione, Baldassare, 30
Catherine of Aragon, 47–8, 58
Cecil, Sir Robert, 165, 166, 167, 192
Cecil, Sir William, 15, 102, 143, 156,
163;

261